VICTIM F

VICTIM F

FROM CRIME VICTIMS TO SUSPECTS TO SURVIVORS

Denise Huskins and Aaron Quinn
with Nicole Weisensee Egan

Berkley
New York

BERKLEY
An imprint of Penguin Random House LLC
penguinrandomhouse.com

Library of Congress Cataloging-in-Publication Data

Names: Huskins, Denise, author. | Quinn, Aaron, author. |
Egan, Nicole Weisensee, author.
Title: Victim F : from crime victims to suspects to survivors / Denise
Huskins and Aaron Quinn with Nicole Weisensee Egan.
Description: New York : Berkley, [2021]
Identifiers: LCCN 2021002702 (print) | LCCN 2021002703 (ebook) |
ISBN 9780593099964 (hardcover) | ISBN 9780593099971 (ebook)
Subjects: LCSH: Huskins, Denise. | Quinn, Aaron. | Victims of crimes--
United States--Biography. | Criminal investigation--United States. |
False arrest--United States. | Police misconduct--United States.
Classification: LCC HV6250.3.U5 H87 2021 (print) | LCC HV6250.3.U5 (ebook) |
DDC 362.88/40922794--dc23
LC record available at https://lccn.loc.gov/2021002702
LC ebook record available at https://lccn.loc.gov/2021002703

Printed in the United States of America
ScoutAutomatedPrintCode

Book design by Alison Cnockaert

PUBLISHER'S NOTE
While the author has made every effort to provide accurate telephone numbers,
Internet addresses and other contact information at the time of publication, neither the publisher
nor the author assumes any responsibility for errors, or for changes that occur after publication.
Further, publisher does not have any control over and does not assume any responsibility
for author or third-party Web sites or their content.

Some names and identifying characteristics have been changed to protect the
privacy of the individuals involved.

For our families and friends whose love and support
steadied us during our hardest times

And to baby Olivia, who shows us the joy
in all of life's little wonders

CONTENTS

VICTIM F

Part One

VICTIMS

"Wake up. This is a robbery."

1

DENISE

I ALMOST DIDN'T COME over to Aaron's house that night.

Would it have changed anything if I hadn't? Or would it have just happened a different night? Were we destined to go through what we did? Aaron and I are meant for each other; of that, I have no doubt. But does that mean I had to endure the unimaginable, to experience trauma that no one should have to live through, for us to be together? Are the two so intertwined that one cannot exist without the other? I don't know. What I do know is, I would never take it back, not if it meant I would have to live my life without him.

WE FIRST MET in June 2014 when I moved to Northern California for a nine-month physical therapy residency at the Kaiser hospital in Vallejo. It's a world-renowned program, with physical therapists from across the globe coming to learn a specialized-treatment approach for patients with severe neurological disorders or those with brain or spinal cord injuries. Aaron was a physical therapist working in the same department and taught a couple of classes for the program.

I was initially drawn to his intelligence, the way he made complex topics easy to understand, but he also had this artistic, intuitive, healing way about him when he worked with patients that seemed almost mystical.

I ran into Aaron at some social gatherings in the coming weeks, and we always ended up talking a lot, first about sports, where we grew up, our families, but quickly easing into deeper discussions about our love for our chosen profession, our passion to be the best we can, and our goals for the future. We had an instant connection and chemistry that surprised me. I hadn't felt anything quite like that before. However, I didn't get my hopes up. I knew he was involved with someone we worked with.

In the next couple of weeks, Aaron told me he and this woman, Jennifer Jones*, had been engaged but had broken up months before because she had had an affair. They still lived together, but he'd moved to one of the spare bedrooms while he sorted out his feelings.

We were both hesitant to start dating because of all this and because we all worked together, but Aaron and I couldn't resist each other and quickly fell in love. At the end of August, Jennifer moved out, and for the next seven months of the residency, Aaron and I spent almost every day together. I could see how much pain he was in, and I was often his sounding board, listening as he talked through the complicated situation. We decided to take a break several times so he could process his feelings, but we missed each other so much that it never lasted more than a day or two.

This latest break had been our longest separation. I hadn't seen him since last Monday, nearly a week. I was always scared he would get back with his ex, and my fears had been confirmed at the end of February when I discovered he was still pursuing Jennifer and had been lying to me about it for months. I was absolutely devastated and wasn't sure if he could fully let her go or if I could forgive him. He'd been going to therapy and making changes to show me it was *me* he wanted, and he was over her, but I was still reluctant to go over to his house, the one he'd shared with her for two years. There were too many memories there.

I tried to explain this to him via text when he asked me to come over

---

* Not her real name.

to talk. I told him I missed him and was willing to hear him out, but I didn't want to fall right back into the same old pattern. He needed to court me and be consistent with his actions. I needed time. He said he understood, but he knew this would be a long and difficult conversation and felt it would be better to have it in the privacy of his own home.

We made plans to go out to dinner somewhere on a real date. But at the last minute, I told him I would come over. He was right. I knew it would be an emotional talk and not one we should have in public. I told him I'd pick up a pie from Napoli's, our favorite pizza place.

I PULLED INTO the long driveway of Aaron's beautiful Colonial-style home around 5:30 p.m. on Sunday. I was wearing a long cotton sundress, which was both comfortable and flattering. I wanted to look my best when we talked, but I also knew we would be lounging around at home, so I found something that accentuated my curves without looking like I was trying too hard. These seem like trivial considerations now, but I wanted to feel good about myself going into this crucial talk. I'd brought my work and overnight bags with me in case things went well, though. I still loved him, and I was hoping I could forgive him.

It was a perfect sunny spring day on Mare Island, the temperature in the seventies, so when I got there, the windows in the family room were wide open, letting in the steady ocean breeze that kept the house cool on even the hottest days.

I had my guard up at first, and gave Aaron a halfhearted one-armed hug when I walked into his kitchen. I was still crushed by his betrayal, and I wanted to protect myself. He immediately started sobbing into my neck, apologizing profusely. I started to melt, nuzzling my head against his and wrapping my arms around him.

We grabbed a couple of Lagunitas IPAs and sat down on the couch to talk. He started off by apologizing again, thanking me for coming over and saying how afraid he was that I wouldn't give him a second chance. He talked about how therapy was helping him understand his own behavior.

He said he had cleared out the last of Jennifer's belongings and told her at work that morning they needed to limit their contact to just discussing patients. He was finally ready to commit to me fully and would do whatever it took to show me that.

I told him I wanted to forgive him and move forward, but it might take time. I promised I would never throw it back in his face, but I might need to be honest about my feelings when I was hurting.

As we spoke, we both cried, in relief and in pain, but we understood each other. He grabbed me, kissed me, hugged me like he never wanted to let me go.

Earlier that day I had resolved I wouldn't be intimate with him. But before I knew it, we were wrapped in each other's arms on the couch. There's something so strong and undeniable about our chemistry, and everything about the moment felt right.

As we lay there, he looked at me with those beautiful big green eyes in utter adoration, the same way he had looked at me on our first date, before things got so complicated. Everything in the world seemed a million miles away. It was just him and me, our love, our connection. Nothing else mattered; nothing could touch us.

He offered to make us each an old-fashioned, a whiskey cocktail he'd grown partial to after becoming a fan of *Mad Men*. I watched from the couch as he grabbed what he needed from the cabinets and assembled the drinks on the island. He's a couple of inches shy of six feet, but the confident way he carries himself makes him seem taller. Aaron was shirtless, and the kitchen lighting caught the shadowed definition of his broad shoulders, forearms, pecs, and back perfectly.

Damn, he's gorgeous, I thought.

I must have watched him in admiration like this a hundred times already, as he did his thing in the kitchen and cooked for us. He enjoyed making meals from scratch, creating sauces, stocks, and exotic meals from memory. He told me how he would make every Thanksgiving and holiday meal for his family. It was how he showed his love, through food.

He handed me the cocktail, and we continued talking about my plans

for work after the residency ended next week, and about our future together.

As we got ready to head upstairs around midnight, we heard the sound
of a steady rain falling, yet another thing to be grateful for after a months-
long drought. Mr. Rogers, the stray cat Aaron had adopted, was meowing
to go into the garage, where he slept at night, so Aaron let him out before
making his final rounds downstairs, locking the windows and doors.

We were both emotionally exhausted but in a good way. This time
our reconciliation felt different. Jennifer's presence was gone, banished
from the home they'd once shared. She was no longer haunting us, no
longer haunting him.

As we sank into deep, dreamless sleep, with me snuggled into the crook
of Aaron's left arm, my head on his chest, I suddenly felt his body jerk,
like he had heard a noise outside, near the garage.

It's probably Fat Charlie [the neighborhood raccoon the size of a dog
who liked to knock over the garbage cans], *or maybe it's Mr. Rogers getting
settled in for the night,* I thought. Any other night we might have gone to
check, but we were tired and quickly fell back asleep.

I was glad I'd come over.

We had every reason to look forward to a wonderful future together.
We can only go up from here. Or so I thought.

We would soon find out a pack of wolves had been stalking us from
afar, waiting for the right moment to strike.

What better time than the dead of night, when we were at our most
vulnerable, paralyzed in sleep?

"WAKE UP. THIS is a robbery."

I hear the words through the haze of my sleep-muddled mind, but at
first, I don't know if they are real or part of some terrible nightmare I'm
having. I try desperately to sink deeper into sleep. It's as if my subcon-
scious knows the truth and is trying to shield me from it.

"Wake up. This is a robbery. We are not here to hurt you."

The voice is relentless, repeating the same phrases over and over until I'm forced to open my eyes and see what I somehow knew all along. This is no bad dream.

My eyes open wider as the rest of my body stiffens in fear. I can barely catch my breath.

At first, all I see is a bright white light flashing against the wall from the opposite corner of the room. Two or three red dots dance back and forth past one another on the walls, disappearing as they cross over our bodies.

Are those guns pointed at us?

The flashing stops, illuminating the room in a soft white hue. The air feels heavier, like more people are occupying the space around Aaron's side of the bed, though I can't be sure how many. All I know is we are outnumbered, and they seem to be armed.

Aaron's large master bedroom holds just the king-sized bed, two night-stands, an armchair, and an ottoman, so there was plenty of room for this swarm to silently file in. They were already in place before we woke up. There, in these first few seconds, I don't have to know anything more to realize there is no way this can turn out well for us.

I can feel the adrenaline pumping through my body, causing my pupils to dilate, muscles to tense, heart rate and breathing to quicken. My senses become sharper, clearer. This fight-or-flight response is our body's natu-ral defense against a threatening situation. It prepares us to take action, but I quickly realize the best thing to do is nothing, remain calm, listen, and collect as much information as possible.

"We. Are. Not. Here. To. Hurt. You. Lie. Face. Down," the intruder says. He's clearly trying to make his voice as unidentifiable as possible. There is no accent, no slang. He enunciates each word clearly, sounding almost robotic, which makes it all the more chilling. This voice, the Voice, will be burned into my brain forever.

I turn over onto my stomach, but Aaron lies still.

Shit. He must be in shock. Turn over, baby. Please turn over.

"Aaron," the Voice says, sharper, growing impatient, "you are facing up. Lie facedown."

I feel Aaron's body shift as he finally complies.

Oh, my God, I think, my terror growing. *They know Aaron's name.*

IT'S CLEAR THE Voice will be the sole speaker for the group. He says he's going to place two restraints on the bed: squares created from four zip ties connected together at each end. He tells me to tie Aaron's hands behind his back with one set, then his feet with the other, making sure they're secure.

"Okay," I reply.

He approaches the bed, places the zip ties at the edge between Aaron and me, and swiftly backs away so he can watch me perform the task at a safe distance, out of our reach.

I kneel next to Aaron and reach back with my left hand to find the two restraints. Aaron puts his hands behind his back, takes a deep breath in, and as he exhales, I can hear him whisper, "Oh, my God."

I look down at him as he's lying on his stomach, head turned toward me, away from the intruders. I want so bad to look into his eyes, to tell him, *We'll be okay. We'll get through this together.*

But I can't. I'm afraid of what they'll do if I try. There's an energy between us, an agreement to listen, not to fight back, because not fighting is the best way to protect each other in this situation.

My heart races as I fumble with the zip ties.

You can do this, I tell myself.

Yet it's hard for my eyes to focus; every inch of me is trembling. Such a simple task feels impossible as I think of all the horrific things they could do to us. I wonder whether we have a chance to fight or escape, but we're cornered, defenseless, and I wouldn't be able to live with myself if something happened to Aaron because of how I reacted.

"You. Are. Doing. A. Good. Job," the Voice says.

It's as if he can read my mind.

He continues to encourage me, repeating the phrases, "You are staying calm. You are doing a good job."

At first, his words are reassuring and help me stay focused, but more than anything, this pseudo politeness is disorienting and disturbing. It's a veneer—like he's working from a carefully written script and this is the part where he gives the victim encouragement to keep him or her compliant and show his group means no harm. The obvious level of detailed thought and planning they must have put into this is alarming.

What kind of criminals are these?

It seems like a plot from a movie: an organized group targets the family of a high-ranking government official and breaks into their home in the middle of the night, well-armed and well-prepared.

But we aren't wealthy, powerful, or famous. We are simple people leading simple lives. Why would anyone target us?

I struggle to tighten the restraints around Aaron's wrists because of the angle of his crossed arms, but I do my best and they're left a little loose. I pray they don't notice.

"Good job. Now his feet."

As I scoot backward on the bed toward Aaron's feet, I can sense one of the intruders standing directly to my left, but I dare not turn my head; my eyes stay fixed on Aaron. I'm convinced if I see someone's face, they'll kill us.

"Good job," the Voice says when I finish fastening the zip ties around Aaron's ankles. "Now you are going to walk to the bedroom closet and lie facedown on the floor. Do not look up. Keep your head down."

I do as he says, hanging my head with my hair draped across the sides of my face. As I leave the bed, I see two pairs of legs dressed in all black to the right of me, standing at attention around the corner of the bed. I can only see up to waist level, where they're holding what I assume to be guns. Their weight shifts as I pass and the one closest to the closet follows right behind me.

Before I walk through the dark entryway of the long master bathroom, I'm startled as I nearly trip on Mr. Rogers scurrying across the room.

How did he get in here?

The Voice tells me to lie on the floor in the left corner of the closet, where he then binds my wrists and ankles with the zip ties.

He leaves to get Aaron, and I feel the thuds of Aaron hopping into the closet from the bed. He is now lying down next to me, our heads turned away from each other.

I can feel his warmth, hear his breath, and I wish I could touch him, even just brush my fingers against his. I know better. I don't want to do anything that might provoke a violent response. Who knows what they're willing to do?

I feel vibrations of footsteps leaving the bedroom while the Voice places swim goggles with some kind of dark tape wrapped around the lenses over each of our heads. With mine, he takes his time, carefully trying to make sure he doesn't pull on my hair. These little acts of consideration are eerie and don't match the danger we're in.

The closet is above the living area in the house and I hear someone going through the kitchen cabinets while another uses a drill in the living room. The Voice remains upstairs with us, rummaging through what sounds like a bag of equipment in the master bathroom.

The Voice then places thin headphones over my ears. After he leaves, a recording starts playing. At first, it's wind chime–like music, like something you would hear on a nineties yoga video. The juxtaposition of supposedly soothing music alongside this life-threatening situation is even more frightening. After about thirty seconds, a voice sounding as though it has been digitally altered says:

"Stay calm. . . . We are not here to hurt you. . . . This is not your fault. . . . We are here purely for financial reasons. . . . This will be over soon. . . ."

These phrases cycle through a few times until I hear, "A medical professional will be in shortly to check your vitals. You will be given a mixture of NyQuil and diazepam. If you do not take it orally, it will be injected intravenously. . . ."

I think through my options, wondering if this concoction is something that will kill us. Considering the planning that's clearly gone into this, I know there's no talking our way out of it, and not taking the drug seems pointless since they said they'll inject it if we don't. Every ounce of my energy is spent on trying not to fall apart. I wonder what Aaron will do. I wish I could speak to him. This is all too much to handle.

My thoughts are still racing when the "medical professional," who turns out to just be the Voice, walks back into the closet. He takes our blood pressure, asks us our medical history, if we have any allergies or are on any medications that may be "contraindicated" with the sedative he is about to give us. I hear him tell Aaron to drink it, so I do too when it's my turn. It's better than the alternative.

I am still holding on to the hope that this truly is a robbery. Hearing the noise downstairs makes me believe they are clearing out Aaron's belongings. And now that we are bound and sedated, they can make a clean getaway.

I am so wrong, so terribly wrong.

AFTER SOME TIME, a new recording is played: "We will ask you a series of questions about bank accounts, passwords, and personal information about each other."

Oh, no, I realize, *this isn't just a robbery of Aaron's belongings. They plan to wipe out our bank accounts. I have about twenty-five thousand in mutual funds I can access. Whatever they need, fine. Just don't hurt us. Let us live!*

It feels like an eternity goes by, but no one comes to ask us any questions. The pounding of my heart marks the passing of time, each beat reinforcing the helpless position we're in. We're at their mercy.

Eventually, the Voice reenters and tells me I will be moved to the "router room." Chills run down my spine. This isn't their first time here. They know the location of the router. It's in one of the three spare bedrooms; that bedroom shares a wall with the closet we are in.

He stands behind me, holding both my shoulders to help stabilize me as I hop through the bathroom, turning into the master bedroom. My lips quiver.

Is that the last time I'll be in the same room as Aaron? Was that my last chance to touch him?

These pained thoughts are interrupted by the crackling of a two-way radio. The white light still illuminates Aaron's bedroom, so I'm able to see the outline of a shadowy figure as it brushes past me. A man's voice breaks the static, barking out some kind of military commands that fade behind me. In that same moment, I hear the loud snap of a Taser from the other side of the master bedroom, warning me what will happen if I don't comply.

What is this!?

The Voice tells me to lie on the floor in the middle of this empty room and puts a larger set of headphones over my ears. A different recording begins to play, again saying we'll be asked a series of questions, but this one comes with explicit threats.

"If we believe you are not telling the truth, your partner will be punished by electric shock, then cuts to the face. If you answer our questions honestly, you will be rewarded by staying together in the same room."

I'm horrified. Cuts to the face? This keeps getting worse. And why don't the recordings match what's actually happening? They already separated us even though we haven't done anything wrong. They haven't even asked their questions yet. What is going on?

Time seems to crawl by. The Voice moves in and out of the room, asks where my phone is, then wants to know the pass codes for my iPhone and iTunes accounts.

Before walking away, he pauses and asks if there is anything on my phone that I wouldn't want Aaron to see. "No," I say and think to myself, *What the hell do you care?*

I hear the Voice speak to Aaron through the wall, and I'm somewhat reassured to hear Aaron reciting numbers, still hoping they plan to just take our money, as long as they can spare us from harm. But that possibility quickly fades when the Voice comes back in and says he'll be moving me downstairs to the living room. *Why would he move me downstairs if this is just a robbery?* From the beginning, I wondered if they'd rape me, rape us both and make each other watch, but so far everything they've done seems measured and controlled, not violent. So I don't know what to expect.

I can barely control my panic as he bends down and scoops me up in his arms. It's like watching a tragic accident happen in slow motion, and there's nothing you can do to stop it. He keeps taking me farther and farther away from Aaron, from safety. As he turns the corner of the stairs, he shifts his weight to the left to let someone pass, whispering, "No," as the other person continues up the stairs toward the master bedroom.

He gently places me on the brown leather couch.

Before he leaves, he stops himself and asks, "Are you comfortable?"

This catches me off guard, and I am not sure how to respond.

But I am freezing, and I can feel the throw touching my toes at the other end of the couch.

"Can you please put the blanket on me?" I ask, desperately needing that comfort. "I'm cold."

"Oh, sure, of course," he says, his robotic tone breaking. "There," he says as he drapes it over me, covering my feet.

"Are you comfortable?" he asks again.

He's treating me like I'm his houseguest instead of his hostage, yet I know his concern is not genuine.

When he is back upstairs, I can hear him talking with Aaron above me, though I can't make out the words. While I don't know what's being said, the sound and vibration of Aaron's voice comfort me. My heart aches for him. I long to hold him, kiss him, be back in the protection of his arms.

I hear Aaron breathe a deep, guttural sigh, and my panic grows. The Voice comes back downstairs.

"We have a problem. . . ."

I hold my breath in anticipation, worried about what he's about to say. Did something happen to Aaron? Maybe he couldn't provide them with something. Maybe he couldn't remember a password, couldn't access an account or enough money. But I haven't heard any loud noises or shouting upstairs, no sounds of a struggle.

"This was not meant for you," the Voice says. He pauses as if he regrets what he's about to say. "This was meant for Jennifer Jones. . . . We have to figure out what we are going to do."

I feel the blood drain out of my face as my stomach spasms.

You have got to be kidding me! This is about HER?

—————

I DON'T UNDERSTAND, can't understand, why anyone would be targeted for something like this and why in God's name they chose her. I can hear the intruder whispering to someone at the bottom of the stairs, but I can't hear what's being said. I feel a small flare of hope; maybe they will just leave now that they realize they have the wrong person.

But deep down, with every fiber of my being, I know it isn't over.

I can feel this is just the beginning.

I lie frozen, awaiting my fate.

The intruder slowly walks back through the hallway, into the vast opening of the kitchen and breakfast nook that leads into the living room.

"This is what we are going to do," he says.

Please, please let them tell me they are going to leave. Just leave us be. Please, I silently beg.

"We will take you for forty-eight hours. . . ."

Even though he keeps talking, everything seems to be standing still. I'm in shock as he explains he'll place me in the trunk of Aaron's car, transfer me to another trunk, and drive me for hours to a location where I will be held. I'm terrified that if they take me from here, I'll never return.

But I feel heavy and defeated. There is nothing I can do, so all I manage to respond is "Okay."

What else can I say?

MOVEMENT WHIRLS AROUND me as the intruders prepare for us to leave. I hear footsteps upstairs, some more muffled sounds, movement in the kitchen next to me and in the garage. The outside world seems to have picked up the pace as mine has wound down to a halt.

Someone opens the French doors, starts my Honda CR-V, and quickly backs it out of the driveway to park it on the street.

The Voice finds the overnight bag I brought with me, my work bag, my purse, and my glasses. He says he will bring them with us. He scoops me up into his arms again, and just before he takes me to the car, I muster the courage to ask if I can use the bathroom. I don't know the next time I'll have the chance. I can sense his urgency, but he lets me, closing the door and strangely allowing me "privacy." I awkwardly maneuver my pants down, then back up, inch by inch, with my hands behind my back. I try to hold back tears.

This isn't real. This can't be happening. Please, please let me stay.

"Are you finished?" His creepy voice invades my last moment of freedom, confirming this nightmare.

He then carries me to the garage before he carefully lowers me into the trunk of Aaron's 2000 Toyota Camry. I feel the softness of a comforter and realize he must have taken it off Aaron's bed and lined the trunk with it. I'm shaking—whether from the cold, the fear, or the drugs, I don't know—but I ask him if I can have the blanket from the couch.

His response leaves me dumbfounded.

"Oh, yeah, of course," he says. "We're all wearing wet suits, so I'm not sure how cold it is."

Wet suits? What . . . the . . . fuck?

I don't bother trying to make sense of it. He tells me he has to finish a few more things inside, and I lie curled in a ball, waiting for the trunk to close. I'm hopelessly trying to live second to second, yet I can't stop thinking about what horrible things they have in store for me.

What is it going to be like when the trunk closes? Am I going to be able to breathe? Are they just going to leave the car on the side of the road and burn me alive?

I think that is the worst possible way to die. But then again, I am sure there are more gruesome ways I cannot even begin to imagine.

Before I know it, the Voice returns and shuts the trunk door, sealing me inside like it's my tomb.

2

AARON

I HEAR DENISE HOPPING away from the closet to the "router room." Moments later, a new recording starts that says we will be asked a series of questions. If we tell the truth, we'll be rewarded by being able to stay in the same room together.

I can't decide whether these guys have made a mistake, because Denise and I have already been separated, or if it's just another attempt to toy with me. After the Voice first put the headphones over my ears, I heard someone whisper, "Aaron! Quick, to the window!" The whisper was too clear, too loud, to be authentic. What were they hoping I would do? Hop to the closest window? And do what? We're on the second floor and my hands and feet are tied. I decided it was a trap and they wanted me to attempt an escape so they could assert their dominance over me. I didn't take the bait.

Eventually, this new recording stops, and my headphones are removed. The Voice states, "You grew up at" and names a street address.

No! I scream in my head, but he is right. And my parents still live there.

They have now presented the next serious threat, this time to my family. I am confident this group doesn't know everything, but they know enough that I dare not lie to them. I can't make sense of why this is happening, but now I am starting to realize this group is hell-bent on squeezing the life out of me, like a python does its prey.

He asks me for the passwords to my laptop and Wi-Fi, then for the passwords to my bank and credit card accounts, my email account, my phone, and for my Social Security number. I give it all to him.

Just don't hurt us.

After he finishes gathering all this information, the Voice leaves. I hear him speaking with Denise through the wall. Then I am left in the brutal silence again, searching for any sound, any bump, scratch, footfall, to give me more information.

I finally feel the vibration of footsteps coming toward me across my bathroom tile.

"Do Denise and Jennifer Jones look alike?"

I let out a long, visceral sigh.

"Yes. They both have long blond hair."

"This was intended for Jennifer Jones," he replies. "We got the wrong intel. We need to decide what we are going to do next."

Of all the reasons, all the possibilities why this shit could be happening to us, why does it somehow connect to her?

The Voice leaves the closet and I hear him speaking with Denise, but it's difficult for me to make out what is being said. I can only hope that the misidentification will persuade the invaders to leave us alone. But why were they after my ex? My thoughts immediately jump to the police officer she had an affair with, who was under investigation. I didn't know anyone else in her life who could be associated with something like this.

The minutes tick away silently, and it's becoming increasingly difficult to temper my fantasy that the invaders decided to slip away in the night. But then the Voice returns. He asks me what obligations I have over the next few days and if anyone is supposed to visit.

I briefly think about telling him my brother, Ethan, an FBI special agent in San Francisco, is staying at my house because he's working a case nearby, but I decide against it. They have done their research and must know what my brother does for a living. A lie will just put us in more danger. So I tell him that the only thing I need to do is work.

The deliberate, methodical method of the invaders has sped up to a more urgent pace, and he pops in and out of the closet multiple times. First he asks if I have any bills due soon; then he tells me the pass code to Denise's phone and asks for the password to my router. I'm confused because I thought I already gave it to him, but he says that was for the Wi-Fi and not the router. I apologetically say I can't remember because I set it up years ago.

"Never mind," he replies curtly as he walks out of the bathroom. "We'll figure it out."

There's a unique silence to this terror. It's quiet enough for someone to fall asleep, and not enough sound to wake a neighbor. But there's a hum in the air, as people move swiftly, scurrying throughout my house. It's becoming increasingly clear that this group has something else planned besides a robbery. But then, I had known it since they woke us.

Minutes later, I hear two sets of footsteps walking across the bathroom tile. Someone kneels behind me.

The Voice whispers back over his shoulder, "Are we doing contingency one or contingency two? Contingency one or contingency two?"

I don't hear a response, but I do hear one of them walking away after a brief pause. A person whom I will never see or hear speak but who has helped create multiple contingency plans for my torture glides out of my bedroom to continue one of two plans. The Voice moves to my other side in order to speak directly to my face.

"This is what we are going to do. We are going to take Denise for forty-eight hours."

Take Denise?

"We decided to proceed with the operation because it will allow us to practice our protocols and there is enough financial benefit to us," he says. "It will cost you fifteen thousand dollars to get back Denise. Is that acceptable?"

"Of course."

Is this a fucking negotiation? I'll pay anything to get her back.

He repeats, "We are going to take Denise for forty-eight hours. Pay the money, get her back, and move on with your lives."

I hate myself for bringing this pain upon her. She was going to suffer so much because she loved me, and I had treated her like shit. I'm still berating myself when he places headphones over my ears and another recording begins in the same digitally altered voice:

Aaron, we are going to take Jennifer for a forty-eight-hour period. You will pay the amount provided by your contact to secure Jennifer's return. You may be wondering why this is happening to you. It may help to learn about our organization. We are a black-market group hired to retrieve payments for personal and financial debts. Our group has secured payments across the country. This will be your burden to bear. Do not attempt to go to the police. We will always be watching you and your family. In one instance, a subject moved across the country in the belief we would not find her. Years later, we placed a pie on her doorstep confirming to her that we know her location.

You will be moved to your downstairs living room. A camera has been installed to monitor your movements. The camera's serial number has been filed off and authorities will not be able to trace it. Our cameras are highly sophisticated and work at high temperatures. Foolishly, one subject turned up the heat inside his home in an attempt to short-circuit our cameras. Heh-heh. He was sadly mistaken. Any attempt to change the temperature will result in harm to Jennifer.

The blinds will be shut and there will be markings that you must stay inside. If you do not follow our instructions, we will harm Jennifer. Hidden cameras have been installed throughout the house, except for your down-stairs bathroom. You are allowed to use the bathroom for short periods. If a neighbor or family makes contact, you must make an excuse that does not raise suspicion.

Any attempts to call authorities will result in harm to Jennifer. We will be watching you at the bank. If you attempt to alert the bank teller, we will kill Jennifer.

Waiting will be the hardest part. You should entertain yourself by read-ing. Stay strong for Jennifer and your family.

It's chilling to hear Jennifer's name used throughout the recording. They didn't make a generic message that could be used in multiple situations; these demands were curated for her, and for me.

He quickly leaves the closet. The reality of the situation penetrates deeper into my soul. Through the floor, I hear the Voice telling Denise she'll be placed in the trunk of my car. "Okay," she replies, a slight tremble in her voice. The subtlety of her terror would be missed if you didn't know her. My admiration for her swells as I pray that I will see her again.

Alive.

I HEAR DOORS downstairs opening and closing and I run through my head the possibilities for saving Denise, but every option seems futile. My only choice is to pay the money and hope that this group is truly after financial gain.

Please don't rape her.

My fight-or-flight reaction begins to slow during these painfully long delays, and I begin feeling the effects of being practically naked. I start shivering and my arms grow numb.

The Voice comes back.

"I have a portable phone charger. I will place it on the kitchen counter. You will take it with you when you travel to the bank. Make sure your cell phone battery is fully charged. A dead cell phone is unacceptable. In the morning, you will call in sick to work. You will use Denise's phone to text her manager. State that she has a family emergency and will be gone for the week. We are going to take your laptop. After this is over, we will return it to factory settings and leave it somewhere where you can retrieve it. I am now going to carry you downstairs and place you on the couch. You must stay there until sunrise."

The Voice attempts to pick me up from the floor and immediately realizes that he's incapable of moving me, so he uses a knife to slice through the zip ties around my ankles.

I shift myself onto my knees and stand up for the first time in hours.

The goggles have moved enough that I can see out of the bottom corner of my left eye. The Voice gently holds my arms as he uses a red light to illuminate the ground. The effects of the sedatives begin to display their power. I had easily hopped over to the closet but now my steps are labored, and I have little anticipation of the ground. Upon the first step of the staircase, I almost fall down.

He holds me up like a friend supporting his buddy who has had one too many drinks. I steady myself in order to take the steps one at a time. My feet are now free, and I think I can slip my wrists through the zip ties, but there is not a chance in hell that I can fight back. My nervous system is doing everything it can to keep me upright.

Dung . . . dung . . . dung.

The electronic-bell sound is generated from the corner of my living room as I move toward my couch.

I ask the Voice what's making that sound and he replies it's the camera they installed to watch over me. Without thinking I respond, "Is it going to make that sound the entire time?"

That will surely drive me to madness. In a prison of my own home, Denise kidnapped by monsters, and a repetitive racket intensifying the agony of my torture.

The abruptness of my question throws him off and he almost casually replies they were unable to gain access to my router so they decided to load the camera through the Wi-Fi, and the sound should stop once it's fully operating.

I flop chest-down on my couch, with my head facing the back corner. The Voice states he will duct-tape my ankles.

"I will leave the phones and scissors on the counter. Stay on the couch until the morning. You can then cut yourself free. Your car will be left somewhere on the island. You will be provided the location to retrieve it. Do you have any questions?"

Shamefully I ask, "Can I have a blanket?"

Denise is being kidnapped and I ask for a blanket. But my entire body is shaking. It's probably been two hours since they woke us, and I've been in my underwear the entire time. I need some warmth; I need any small thing to reduce the stress of this situation, because I'm already at my breaking point.

"Oh, yes. I forget how cold it is because we're wearing wet suits."

Wet suits? These guys have thought of everything. What better way not to leave DNA or hairs behind?

"This will be over soon."

He sounds apologetic and encouraging. For a moment I think, *He's not so bad.*

Why am I so willing to give this man the benefit of the doubt? Because he gave me a blanket? As I hear him walk out of the living room to the garage, I know I'll have way too much time to think about this moral dilemma.

Through the door, I hear the Voice tell Denise, "I am going to close the trunk now."

"Okay," she says, her voice carrying in the darkness. It's as if she's still reaching out to me, letting me know she can handle whatever comes next. My soul yearns to hold on to every millisecond, but the trunk abruptly closes, sealing her off, severing our last connection.

She's gone. Stolen. And I can't do a damn thing about it. This can't be the last time I hear her voice.

IT'S HARD TO believe that just a few hours ago, I was sitting on this same couch with Denise, making plans for the future. It feels like a distant memory now. We'd had a rough start to our relationship, not because of our attraction or how we felt about each other but because I was still reeling over my breakup with Jennifer.

When Denise and I first met, I had no intention of starting a romantic relationship. I was barely keeping my head above water. It had been a few months since I found out the full extent of Jennifer's two-year affair with a married police officer from Fairfield, a nearby city. In retrospect, there were warning signs she had trouble being faithful. When we first started dating, she told me about an affair she had with a local FBI agent while still married to her ex-husband. She continued to see the agent after her divorce, but he eventually stopped calling her. We ran into him on our first date and she told me that he began pursuing her again. She said she told him she'd moved on and I believed her. Three months later she was invited to a party she knew he'd be attending—one she didn't want me to go to for that very reason. She told me afterward he'd tried to kiss her, but she'd rebuffed his advances. Although she said she committed herself to our relationship, it was only about a year later when she started cheating on me with the police officer. Clearly, she had a thing for men in positions of authority. But that was the past and there was nothing I could do about that now.

I could hardly get a moment's break from Jennifer. Not only did she still live in my house, but we also saw each other every day at work. Looking back, I wished that I had made her move out sooner. It kept our relationship in limbo. Not together but never apart. I couldn't heal or move forward, like a scab that you can't stop scratching.

One Saturday in July, I invited some physical therapy residents to go to the Lagunitas brewery. Most of them were from outside the area and I enjoyed sharing my favorite local spots. Lagunitas was a great place to hang out on a nice day—good beer, sunshine, music, and tasty food. It also got me out of my house and gave me an excuse to go drown my sorrows. I showed up at the apartment of two of the residents around 3:00 p.m. They had invited Denise to come along as well.

Denise, unlike the boys, who were nursing terrible hangovers, had already gone on a hike that morning. We got to the brewery, grabbed some beers, and sat down on a little hill outside. Denise and I talked while the guys took a nap in the sun. It was an easy and lively conversation, the kind you'd hope for on a first date, even though this wasn't one. I knew I was in trouble. She had beautiful long blond hair, a kind smile, and silver-blue eyes behind her dark-rimmed glasses. Man, I'm a sucker for a girl in glasses. She also had this quiet confidence and passion for physical therapy that was captivating. I still wasn't over my ex, but I could feel myself falling for Denise.

The next week was Denise's birthday and a group of residents was going to San Francisco to celebrate that weekend. I already had plans to visit my friend TJ, who lived in the city, and told the group I might meet up with them. As I was riding the ferry to the city, I got a text from one of the guys asking where I was. I was on the fence about meeting them. I was still fighting my attraction to Denise, and drinking late into the night around her did not seem like a great idea.

I told him that I was on the ferry heading over, expecting they were somewhere else in the city and it would give me an easy excuse not to join them. He replied, Great. We're at a bar in the ferry building grabbing a drink. We'll wait for you.

When I got there, I spotted Denise. I had seen her only at work in our unflattering uniforms or in hiking clothes at the brewery. Tonight, she was stunning in a long, flowing dress with her hair brushed over one shoulder. She flashed me a smile and I felt myself blush a little, obviously excited to see her.

By the end of the night, Denise and I were so engrossed in our conversation it was as if we were the only people in that crowded bar. The next day, I invited her to watch the morning football games at TJ's. My friends had seen me struggling over the last few months, and they had gently told me that the healthiest choice for me was to move on from my ex. So they were encouraged that I invited Denise. She fit right in with her easygoing demeanor, good humor, and surprising familiarity with football, my favorite sport.

What was supposed to be a short day extended into the evening, and we took the last ferry ride back to Vallejo. It was obvious we were attracted to each other, so I confided in her about my situation with Jennifer. I told Denise I wanted to spend more time with her. My feelings for her overwhelmed me, and I couldn't stop myself from kissing her that first time.

I was torn about whether I should try to work it out with my ex or if I should move on. With Jennifer, I had believed we would get married and raise a family together. Yet she cast me aside for another man and blamed me for most of our relationship problems. If I was so wrong about Jennifer, how could I trust these feelings for Denise? What if the same thing happened with her? How many times could someone start over?

About a month later, I caught Jennifer on the phone with the same cop she cheated on me with. Apparently, he called to warn her that she might be contacted by Internal Affairs because he was being investigated.

I couldn't believe it. It was all too much. I needed to separate myself from this mess. I told her she had to move out, which she did that weekend. But we still worked together, making true separation impossible. Every day was a gut punch. Wake up in my large empty house, go to work, see my ex in the hallway . . . pain, see Denise in the therapy gym . . . joy, see my ex in the lunchroom . . . pain, see Denise working with a patient . . . joy, go back to my empty house. Wash, rinse, repeat. But I could never get clean.

Over the next few months, Denise and I kept seeing each other. The rest of my day might have sucked but spending time with Denise was always so easy. Every day, I wished I had not met her until a year or more after learning about my ex because I was deluding myself thinking I was ready to move on. Whenever we'd start getting closer as a couple, I would inadvertently sabotage us moving forward. I was so confused and broken. Our breaks were short-lived because I would instantly miss her. I was fighting the current when I needed to head downstream. She was always so understanding and supportive, and I hated myself for putting her through this.

Our relationship finally came to a head at the end of February. Denise had suspected for a while that I was still communicating with my ex, and she finally checked my phone for proof. Of course, she found it. I was still texting Jennifer and telling her I wanted us to work things out. Rightfully so, this was the final straw for Denise, and she demanded a change.

It was obvious that I needed help. I was lying to myself, thinking I could manage this on my own. So, after months of resisting, I called a therapist first thing the next morning. Those sessions gave me the strength to tell my ex to get the rest of her belongings out of the garage. I even started bringing boxes to work to ensure it happened.

Denise appreciated my efforts, but I knew it would take time to regain her trust. She hadn't come over this past week, and I was afraid she might never forgive me.

That week was terrible. I had a few extra days off work and attempted to keep myself busy by refinishing a rocking chair for my mom. But I still felt alone, isolated, and depressed, and became paranoid that someone was watching me. I kept catching a quick glare of light through my bedroom window, like the one you'd see from the sun reflecting off a watch or a phone. It came from the post on the hill behind my house. In the two years I'd lived there, I'd never seen that before. I thought maybe there was a camera on it, but I convinced myself my mind was turning to dark places because I was sad and lonely. It was probably something less insidious, like a metal bolt or screw.

Now I felt like a fool, and it wasn't the first time I'd felt this way recently. Over the last several months, I'd come home to a house that felt slightly disturbed, as if my stuff had been moved a centimeter. And the front-door sensor kept tripping my alarm for no apparent reason. I'd spent a lot of time on the phone with the security company, trying to figure out what was wrong, but no amount of troubleshooting could fix it.

I will always regret I didn't do more to protect my house. Denise was in the hands of monsters because of me. Because they wanted my ex. I'd already put her through so much and now . . . this.

AFTER I HEAR the sound of my car fading in the distance, I use the armrest of the couch to push the goggles off my face. Across the room, the cable box reads exactly 5:00 a.m. It's at least an hour and a half before sunrise.

I need to stay awake.

I need to think.

I wake up to my phone's alarm going off. I need to call in sick before 7:00 a.m. I'm in such a drugged haze that I have a hard time locating the phone, but I find it on the side table next to the couch. It barely feels like reality. I'm able to wriggle out of the zip ties around my wrists and I wonder if Denise intentionally left them a little loose.

I push myself upright and force my eyes open. I struggle to use my phone, but I manage to follow the sick line protocol.

I don't sound sick. I sound drunk, I think as I hear my slurred voice mail.

I follow the next step of the Voice's instructions and grab Denise's phone to find our manager's contact. I can't call in sick for her, so I write him a text saying there's a family emergency that will occupy her all week. I read his compassionate response. He's a good boss and a good man. If he only knew how much help we really need right now.

I know I need to be awake. I need to be ready, but I'm dragged back down to the couch. Suddenly, it's nine thirty; then eleven; then eleven thirty. Finally, I am able to pull myself out of the deep fog long enough to stay awake. I look around the room. On the kitchen island are a stack of my books, folded piles of my clothes, and my toiletries. All the blinds are shut, striped vertically with lines of red electrical tape, reminding me to keep them down. The same red tape is laid across the tile in front of every door, sealing off my exits. I look across the room to the camera staring down at me, their window into my prison.

Logically, I know that complying with their demands is the best option. You can't win against a group that does this much planning. But I still feel like a coward as I sit on the couch waiting for further instructions.

My hands are free, but I still need to remove the bindings off my ankles. When I stand up, the camera starts making that loud *dung . . . dung . . . dung* sound and continues as I start hopping over to the kitchen counter. I can already tell this noise will haunt me for the rest of my life. I'm like Pavlov's dogs being conditioned to remember this shitty situation.

The sedatives are still having their effects. I can barely clear the ground, but I manage to grab the kitchen shears and bend over to cut free my ankles. Either the stress or the sedative cocktail or a combination of the two has given me diarrhea, so I rush to the half bathroom. There's more red tape just past the door, allowing me access to the bathroom but cutting off the stairs and the hallway to the front door.

As I'm washing my hands afterward, I see my reflection for the first time. The stress is already taking its toll. My skin is lifeless, drained of any color. My hair shoots off in every direction and my eyes are hollow and vacant.

Who is this person?

I make coffee to counteract the sedatives' effects. As the water heats, I get dressed and I return to the bathroom to fix my appearance. I can't go to the bank to take out a large sum of money looking like this.

I take my coffee and a glass of water to the couch. The camera continues to make its maddening sound as I wait for my commands.

For most of last night, I wore my favorite sweatshirt, a gray hoodie from the Mare Island brewery. Fortunately, I left it near my couch, so I put it on. It's the perfect texture, soft and lived in. Denise's perfume still clings to it from when I held her on this same couch less than twelve hours ago. There's comfort in the softness and smell, as if Denise is somehow a little closer.

I pull myself out of those memories. If I stay in them too long, I'll fall apart and become useless.

I scan back over the surreal scene that used to be my living room. I always keep the blinds open because I love the way the natural light warms up the room. With the blinds taped shut, the house seems desolate, which only adds to my despair.

I MOVED TO Vallejo in 2010 and bought my house two years later. It was my first major purchase. I thought I'd found a steal, paying a fraction of its true value because it was in foreclosure.

I brought the house back to life with the help of my family. My father and I share a passion for woodworking, and we built floor-to-ceiling bookcases and a custom entertainment center and installed hardwood floors. At the time, he was battling stage IV melanoma and I didn't know if these would be the last projects that would have both our fingerprints on them. I cherished those pieces. They were physical representations of a great man.

This house was my sanctuary, nestled away from the most dangerous parts of Vallejo, quiet and secluded with the open hillside in the back.

But it's destroyed now.

Forever.

I know I can never live here again.

Everything I loved about it, its remoteness, its privacy, gave them the upper hand and put me in this box.

My home is now a dark and scary place.

MERCIFULLY, ABOUT THIRTY minutes later my phone receives a text message from www.freetext.com. It states, acknowledge that you received this message to the email provided. *Is this a trick?* They told me they would communicate through emails.

Confused, I quickly send a response from my live.com email account to aqjjopkirklandvallejo@hotmail.com, the email address the Voice gave me earlier, asking, Do I need to reply via email as well or should we communicate by text message?

After a few agonizingly long minutes my phone buzzes with a text message from the same free site. Respond ASAP. Panic washes over me. With shaky hands, I text, I did. I sent an email.

I stare at my phone, willing it to produce another message, but the minutes drag on. Those assholes were right. Waiting is the hardest part. Finally, the text arrives: Send email to your Comcast account.

I write from my live.com account to my Comcast account, I replied via text message and I sent an email to aqjjopkirklandvallejo@hotmail.com. I refresh my emails every fifteen seconds. After a few minutes, an email arrives:

We will proceed with this address.

Denise is well. We have a short recorded message so stating that I will format and send at some point.

Are you able to obtain a cash advance from your bank card? If so, cash in the amount of $8500 from one account and cash in the amount of $8500 from the other account would settle this matter. For your own safety, we do not wish to trigger the $10000 reporting limit or other structured transaction regulations. You would be welcome to transfer what money you like back to the credit card.

The drop would happen tomorrow night or early Wednesday morning, with release to follow quickly provided all instructions are followed.

Is this acceptable?

-L

The privilege of my upbringing hits me. I don't know how to get a cash advance from my credit card. My dad is a retired emergency room doctor and my mom is a nurse. I wasn't spoiled as a child. I was required to do chores and have a summer job, but I never worried about money. I reply, The amount is acceptable, but I need instructions on how to get the money necessary.

Six minutes later:

Please contact Chase and find out whether it is possible. If asked, state that the money is for a used ski boat. We will follow up in 30 minutes.

I get up to search for my wallet and find it on the kitchen counter.

There's a rectangular black electronic box with USB ports on the side of it. It must be the portable cell phone charger the Voice told me to carry to the bank to make sure my cell doesn't die. I pull out my Chase credit card and find the phone number on the back. After a couple of rings, I hear, "Thank you for calling Chase. How may I help you?"

Help me! My girlfriend has been kidnapped! Call 911!

"How much can I cash advance on my card? I need to buy a used ski boat," sputters out of my mouth instead.

"Let me see. . . . . You are allowed three thousand five hundred and twenty dollars in a cash advance."

"Thank you," I reply before hanging up.

What am I supposed to do now? That's not enough money to get Denise back.

I write back to report the lesser amount.

Fifteen minutes pass without a response. Thirty minutes. A swell of anxiety begins building inside me as my mind cycles through the possible punishments. Beating her. Cutting her. Raping her. My imagination begins subverting my rational thoughts. I've felt this explosion of fear before when working in the hospital. I was called into a room to perform CPR chest compressions on a patient in cardiac arrest. The life-and-death consequences penetrated every cell of my body, seizing control and causing me to momentarily freeze. I released one good, long exhalation, broke the cycle, and performed my duty. Now I draw strength from that experience and employ the same strategy. Slow down. Breathe. Focus.

Last night, the Voice told me the camera would stop making sounds once it was fully loaded but the sounds haven't stopped. They asked me to respond to an email, but they should have seen me if they were getting a live feed. They must not be able to see me.

This is my first clear opportunity. I can't call 911 because of the monitoring software on my phone. But I can call my brother Ethan.

He'll know what to do. And if the kidnappers see this call, I'll lie that Ethan was supposed to come over and I needed to divert him.

Still, I know it's a risk.

I pause, my heart racing.

I can't trust these assholes to release Denise after I drop off the money. They'll probably take me too and kill us both.

My mind is made up.

I hit the CALL button.

3

AARON

Ethan doesn't pick up.

I'm not surprised. He rarely answers his personal cell phone during work hours. I don't have his work number, so I call his girlfriend, Kathryn. He'll answer her call.

"Hello," she says, sounding slightly concerned.

We've texted before but my calling her at work is clearly not the norm.

"I need you to call Ethan and tell him to call me right now," I whisper. "People broke into my house and kidnapped Denise. They're charging me a ransom and watching me with a camera. They say if I call the police, they're going to kill her. I need Ethan's help."

She's clearly flabbergasted by what I'm saying, but she says she'll call him.

In less than a minute, Ethan's number appears on my cell phone's screen. He's concerned but also composed in a way you'd expect an FBI agent to be. I give him a brief rundown of the previous night's and morning's events.

"Is there any way you can alert other agents or somebody?" I ask him.

"The best thing for you to do is call nine-one-one."

"I can't," I tell him, my voice still barely audible. "They said they would kill her."

"That's what all of them say. We have to get the authorities involved now. I'm coming down. I'll be there as soon as I can."

I hang up the phone and stare at the screen. I know Ethan is right.

I hit 9 and then 1 . . .

I pause.

It's an impossible decision, the hardest one of my life. I would sacrifice myself in a second to save Denise, but making this call will mean I'll be safe, and she might be in more danger. How can I live with myself if this puts her life in jeopardy? But how can I live with myself if I do nothing? I take a deep breath. I've never skydived before, but this must be what it feels like right before you free-fall. There's absolutely no turning back once I do this. I hit the final 1 and tap the CALL button.

It's 1:54 p.m.

"Nine-one-one, what's your emergency?"

"My girlfriend's been kidnapped," I tell the dispatcher, still keeping my voice low. Why, I don't know, because if the kidnappers are monitoring my phone, they'll know I called the police.

I'm ashamed this is the first time I've referred to Denise as my girlfriend. I should have been calling her that months ago. It's all she's wanted from me and I couldn't even give her that.

The dispatcher asks a few questions and tells me officers will be there soon.

Help is on the way.

I BARELY HAVE time to process the enormity of my decision before the police are knocking on my front door. I get up from the couch, walk past my kitchen into the hallway, and hesitate when I see the red tape across the tile. It holds tremendous power for such a basic household item, the final threshold of my outright defiance of the kidnappers. I wonder if I will set off some sort of invisible alarm if I pass it.

These guys are dangerous but they're not omniscient. I cross the tape and open the door to see two Vallejo police officers standing on my front steps.

"I'm Officer Garcia. This is Officer Coelho. What seems to be the problem?"

I repeat what I told the dispatcher.

"Are you on drugs?" Officer Garcia asks.

I'm not offended by the question. I'm sure that I look a mess. "Yes. The kidnappers drugged me."

"Is there anyone upstairs?"

"No."

The two officers head upstairs to clear the house anyway. I know it's protocol but it's pointless. I'm confident no one's there.

Officer Garcia comes down the stairs and I direct him to the family room so they can see all the evidence the intruders left behind.

Dung dung dung.

The sound grabs his attention, and he makes a beeline toward the camera. He looks up at it, traces the cord down the wall to the outlet, and unplugs it. Relief and shock flood my body at the same time—relief I don't have to listen to that torturous sound anymore—but how could he just unplug it?

It might not be sending video but it's at least transmitting some sort of loading signal. Now it won't. He wasn't even wearing gloves. What if there were fingerprints or some other kind of forensic evidence on there?

I want to say all of this to him, but before I can, he starts barking out questions.

He spots about a dozen empty beer bottles neatly placed in boxes next to the garbage can.

"Have you been partying?"

"No."

"What's with the beer?"

"I place them in there so I can take them out to recycling all at once."

"What about these glasses?" He gestures toward the sink at the two lowball glasses I used for old-fashioneds last night. They have clearly been rinsed, waiting to be hand-washed.

"Those are from last night. I need to wash them."

"I see three glasses," he says, his gaze turning toward the glass sitting on the coffee table.

"That's water!"

With each question, I'm getting more and more irritated. *Did they not hear me say she was kidnapped? What does what we had to drink last night have to do with finding her? Why aren't they asking me about what kind of car she was taken in? Or the camera? Or any of the evidence that is strewn around my home?*

My frustration must have been obvious, because the next thing I know, Officer Garcia orders me outside while he continues searching my house. Officer Coelho escorts me and tells me to sit on my front steps. It dawns on me that the air is dry and there's still a layer of dust on the plants.

I thought it rained last night.

"What the hell is his problem?" I ask Officer Coelho.

"He's gotta ask you that," he replies. "He's just doing his job."

I am acutely aware of what this must look like to my neighbors. There's a police car in my driveway and I'm sitting on my front steps being guarded by a cop—there's no way anyone walking or driving by could miss this spectacle.

Thankfully, my brother pulls up but Officer Coelho intercepts him before we can speak. He is only ten feet away, but it might as well be miles. I need Ethan's support, but more important, I need him to take over and use his expertise to help find Denise. I can't keep making these life-and-death decisions by myself.

Officer Garcia returns and asks me to come down to the station to give a statement and provide a blood sample.

He starts calling in to update the station, then pauses, takes a couple of steps back, and lowers his voice as he relays some number. I assume it's the code for kidnapping and he just doesn't want me to overhear and get upset. This small act of kindness gives me a ray of hope that maybe, just maybe, they are taking this seriously now.

When the officers go to their patrol car to grab some paperwork, I quickly fill Ethan in about what's happened since we spoke, and he tells me he'll follow me to the station. Officer Garcia hands me a waiver for a

voluntary search of my property, which I immediately sign. I'll do anything to find Denise.

While Officer Coelho stays at my home, Officer Garcia takes me to
the station. He lets me sit on the passenger side of his car instead of in the
back, which I take as an encouraging sign. On the ten-minute ride to
the station, we cross the bridge that connects Mare Island to the rest of
the city and pass a few of my favorite spots in Vallejo. There's the recre-
ation center where I play basketball with my coworkers every Wednesday
night; Napoli's, where Denise picked up a pizza last night; Mare Island
brewery, our favorite place to watch a Giants game. Despite the sunshine
and the cloudless day, they look dull and dreary to me. These places will
never be the same. I will never be the same. Everything has changed.

Officer Garcia breaks the silence by asking me where I work. I'm in
no mood for small talk but answer politely that I work at Kaiser's rehab
center. He makes some comment about how familiar he is with the place
and then gets to his real question: "Were you and Denise fighting?"

"We've been struggling recently," I reply honestly. "I've had a hard
time getting over my ex, Jennifer. She works at the hospital."

"Are you still in love with Jennifer?" he interrupts.

"No, man. She was cheating on me for two years with some cop from
Fairfield. It's hard because I see her every day at work, but I started seeing
a therapist. She helped me realize that Jennifer was just using me. Denise
is amazing. We had a good night. We were moving forward."

It's a relief to say it out loud. For months, I'd told only a few of my most
trusted friends about Jennifer's infidelity. I was embarrassed and ashamed,
feeling like it was my fault she cheated on me, that I wasn't good enough
for her. But now I know Jennifer's affair wasn't my doing and I don't need
to be ashamed. Yesterday was a new beginning for me, for my relationship with Denise. It was the first time I felt truly content in years. I realize the cops may not see it that way. They might see it as some twisted
love triangle, a motive for me to hurt Denise. But the mountain of evidence at my house should be enough to show them the truth.

I have faith in our justice system.

THE VALLEJO POLICE Department is housed in a nondescript concrete building surrounded by a tall, ominous-looking iron fence. I can't remember if I've ever seen it before but it's not exactly a place I've wanted to visit.

When we arrive, Officer Garcia leads me through the back door and down a short hallway to a small room. It has no clock, no windows, just a table and a few chairs. It is a sterile, depressing room utterly devoid of any warmth, comfort, or personality.

He points me to one of two swivel chairs in the far-left corner of the room. I sit down. When I look up, I see a camera pointing straight at me. *Great. I'm being watched again.*

It's unnerving. These types of cameras are everywhere: restaurants, stores, banks, et cetera. You can't escape them. And I know I'll never see them again without it snapping me back to that *dung dung dung* sound, back to my prison.

Officer Garcia tells me that the detectives will be in soon and asks if I would like some water.

"Yes," I reply.

"I'll have them bring you some," he says, and closes the door. I hear the automatic lock click behind him.

A FEW MINUTES later, two men enter and introduce themselves as Detective Robert Greenberg and Detective Terry Poyser. They say they want to take my blood and my clothing for evidence. I agree even though I told them I was in my underwear during the home invasion and got dressed only in the morning.

A lab tech enters the room and gives me a waiver to sign. It is 3:34 p.m. More than twelve hours since this nightmare started.

The tech takes pictures of my arms, hands, and ankles. She takes DNA samples from my inner cheek. Afterward, they ask me to stand up and move to the other corner of the room so they can photograph my clothing before they take it for evidence.

The procedure goes as follows: 1) Face forward with your arms held out wide, *click*. 2) A quarter turn right, *click*. 3) A quarter turn right, *click*. 4) A quarter turn right, *click*. 5) A final turn, then remove a piece of clothing and place it in a bag.

With each piece of clothing I hand them, a little piece of my identity goes with it. One by one they do this until all I'm wearing is my underwear.

Before I remove it, the female tech hands over the camera to Detective Greenberg and leaves.

"Sorry," he says as he has me take off my last bit of clothing, leaving me completely naked.

He actually sounds like he means it. Stripping me down was degrading and unnecessary, and I think he knows it. But more important, they took my sweatshirt. Even hours later, I could still smell Denise's perfume on it. It's my last tangible reminder of her, and it feels like with each move I make, I drift farther and farther away from her.

After Greenberg takes the final nude photo, he hands me something to wear.

"Sorry. This is all we have."

I expect them to be some old sweats. Instead, he gives me baggy gray linen pants with thick alternating horizontal stripes. SOLANO PRISON is written vertically down the leg. They look like some cartoonist's version of what an inmate wears in prison, like the character on the GET OUT OF JAIL FREE card in Monopoly.

Jesus. It's prison clothes. This is all they have?

The T-shirt is two sizes too big for me and must have been white at some point, but it is so stained it's hard to tell. I sniff it. It smells scorched, like it's been washed one too many times at high temperatures, but it seems to be clean. That's it—no socks, underwear, or shoes.

I can't be naked when they question me, so I put the pants and shirt on as fast as I can. My clothes were my last source of normalcy and comfort, but they were literally stripped away from me. My new outfit feels like I'm being forced into a character I never wanted to play. Well, I'll deal with it for now. It will only be temporary anyway; Ethan should be able to get me some new clothes soon.

Detective Poyser leads the questioning. Over the next hour and a half, we cover every detail from last night. I volunteer my passwords to my phone, email, and bank accounts, with the hope they can use them to track down the kidnappers. If we're lucky, they'll be stupid enough to call my phone.

After we're done, they ask me if I want to go to the bathroom and I agree even though I'm so dehydrated I have no need. Greenberg accompanies me down the hall and around the corner to the men's room, telling me the door needs to stay open. It's a typical men's room with two urinals and a stall. It looks fairly clean, but I find myself wishing I had shoes on, especially when I see the small pool of stagnant gray water underneath one of the urinals. When I go to wash my hands, Greenberg stops me, saying we need to preserve evidence. Doesn't he know they already swabbed me for evidence? He then escorts me back to the same depressing, windowless room and leaves me there alone.

After at least an hour, another officer comes in to offer me some food. Even though my body isn't capable of hunger right now, I haven't eaten since last night and I know I need to put something in my stomach. The officer returns with a bag of chips, which fortunately go down easily. Then I sit there waiting for something to happen, wondering what is going on elsewhere in the station. Detective Greenberg pops in a couple of times to ask a few clarifying questions. During one of those moments, I ask him if Ethan is there.

He hesitates before answering, "Uh, I'm not sure. I'll go check and get back to you."

Finally, a new pair of detectives walks into the room. When they open the door, I see the orange-and-red hues of a setting sun through the windows in the hallway. It must be around seven or eight, which means it's been at least five hours since I called 911. If the kidnappers haven't figured it out already, they must be suspicious that I went to the police. I wonder if the cops have a clever way of handling this, communicating with the kidnappers, pretending to be me, attempting to draw them out. Either way, we're running out of time.

One of the detectives sits down in front of me. He has an air of authority about him like he's the one in charge, so I assume he's here to update me about the investigation. Hopefully, they have some solid leads.

Or could they have found Denise? Rationally, I know they haven't had enough time to do that, but I can't help but wish for a miracle.

"Hi. How ya doing? I'm Mat Mustard."

He sounds confident and competent, like someone who knows exactly how to handle a case like this. I anxiously wait to hear what he has to say.

4

DENISE

AFTER THE VOICE closes the trunk, I begin to panic. I feel like there isn't enough oxygen and I start to hyperventilate, my breaths getting shorter, quicker, making it even harder to get oxygen to my brain.

I'm supposed to be in this trunk for hours? I'm going to suffocate! How do they know if I have enough air back here to breathe?

The driver's-side door closes and the car reverses quickly. The radio is on and turned up.

All of a sudden, just a few turns after leaving Aaron's, the car stops, the trunk opens, and my shoulder is grabbed forcefully.

"DO *NOT* SPEAK. DO *NOT* SCREAM. YOU ARE GOING TO MAKE THIS A *LOT* HARDER ON YOURSELF."

I quietly plead that I didn't say anything, and he slams the trunk, continuing on. The only thing I can think of is that he mistook the woman singing on the radio for me screaming. I can't be sure, but I am now even more terrified.

Breathe . . . breathe . . . in . . . and out, I tell myself, practicing what I teach my patients to help reduce anxiety.

My breathing starts to slow down, starts to normalize.

Eventually, we stop again. As the trunk opens, the dark, the quiet, and the salty breeze make me think we're still close to the water.

His hands shake as he cuts the zip ties off my wrists, to make me "more comfortable" on this longer drive. This knife feels so sharp, and with his hands trembling, I'm afraid it will slice me with even the slightest touch. I'm surprised at how long this is taking, and I picture him, all in black, struggling with a body in front of this open trunk, next to a car with another open trunk. We must be somewhere no one can see us.

He transfers me to the trunk of the other car. The opening of this one is smaller than the one on Aaron's Camry, forcing the Voice to stuff me in.

I hear the rustling of items, the opening and closing of doors. It sounds like he's gathering what he needs from Aaron's car and transferring it to this one. He starts up the car and drives off again.

My head is wedged up against a wheel well. I am cramped and uncomfortable, yet when he closes the trunk, it's much easier to breathe.

Thank God.

But this makes me wonder if the trunk has open access to the rest of the car, allowing him to keep an eye on me during the long drive.

In addition to the smaller trunk, the distinct sound of the exhaust suggests we're now in a sports car. I think of movies I've seen, how a captive would kick out a taillight to get someone's attention. But this isn't a movie and I dare not test him. He just showed me that when he thought I screamed. If he could be that aggressive when I didn't do a thing to warrant it, what would he do if I did?

I feel the car speed up an incline and reach a consistently high speed, as though we're getting on a freeway. I soon hear more cars on the road and figure it is getting light out now, that we are among the many commuters who are sipping their coffees, dreading their workweeks, not realizing there is a woman in desperate need of their help in the trunk of the car that just zoomed by. But how could they know? It's just another Monday morning to them.

BY THE TIME we arrive at our destination, I'm completely disoriented. I can only guess how far we've traveled and where I may be. Thanks to the sedatives, I was unconscious most of the hours-long trip, waking every so often in terror, thinking of all the ways I could die inside this trunk.

I'm anxious to get out, what with the excruciating pain and numbness on the left side of my body, but what new horror will I be met with when I do?

The car creeps slowly over gravel, stops, and the engine quiets. He struggles to pull me out of the trunk, and I can tell by the flood of light through the goggles it must be midmorning. We must be at a secluded house on a lot of land, or one that is accessible only through a long hidden driveway, if he can do this without raising anyone's suspicions.

I am afraid of doing the wrong thing and upsetting him, so I don't help him at first. But I can tell it's impossible for him to do on his own, so I use my now freed hands to help push me out, just enough to expose my head. He is then able to get his arms under me and awkwardly lift me.

He's rushing, panicking. He quickly turns us away from the car, takes a step, and stumbles. His arms and legs give out, and we both go flying to the ground. I land heavily on the left side of my back with him on top of me.

He breathes over me, the first time I can really sense his composure crumbling. He makes one more urgent attempt to lift me from the ground, then grabs my bound feet and drags me across cold concrete into what I assume is a garage.

He drapes the comforter over me and says he will be back shortly; he has to get things ready. Ready for what? I'm afraid to imagine.

I take this moment alone to adjust the plastic piece that lines the goggles that have been digging into the skin of my eye socket.

I lie there for what seems like an eternity. It sounds like he is just on the other side of the wall, scrubbing, scrubbing, scrubbing. The sound taunts my sanity as every horror film I've ever seen flashes before me. I picture him cleaning up the bloody remains of his prior victims, getting ready for his next one—me.

I focus on taking long, deep breaths to quell my growing panic.

I wonder if this is really what these people are in it for: if they take pleasure in torturing victims, watching the blood slowly drain from their body as they scream in agony. Maybe this is what fuels them, excites them.

Right then and there I make a promise to myself: no matter how much they torture me, I won't beg and scream; I won't plead for mercy just so they can shut me up and put me in my place. If that is what they are in this for, I won't give them the satisfaction.

If I am to die, if this is my last day, hour, moment on this earth, I will not live it screaming, panicking, crying in terror. I will not let them win.

I only hope I can keep this promise to myself.

Suddenly, the scrubbing stops.

What now?

I HEAR LIGHT footsteps approaching. I clench every muscle in my body as I curl into a ball, hiding under the comforter as if it will protect me.

It's a false hope.

He pulls the comforter off me. I cower like an abused animal but the violence I expect never comes. Instead, he cuts the zip ties off my feet and tells me the bathroom is ready for me.

The Voice handles me with care as he helps me up and walks me a few steps across the threshold of a door, then straight into a bathroom. I feel the texture of the floor change under my feet. Each small step I take, I take hesitantly, like I am walking a plank, about to drop into an abyss. I feel a shaggy rug between my toes.

He takes my hand and guides it to a toilet to my right, then along the outline of a tub to the left of it; the ripped shower curtains; the faucet and showerhead; the hot and cold knobs; a towel.

I picture myself standing there like a zombie, with my hair disheveled under the tight strap of the goggles.

Showering will remove any particles from my body I may be bringing in from the outside world, he explains. That is also why he had to thoroughly clean before I entered, making sure that no particle, DNA, or other incriminating material that belonged to the house or anyone in it would get on me. This would make my release "clean," make it less likely the police will trace this location.

I'm relieved to hear he still plans to release me, but I can't let myself trust what he's saying. His speech isn't clipped and robotic like it was at Aaron's house, but it is still stiff and formal.

"You will keep your blindfold on during the shower. When you are done, you are to stay in the confines of this rug. Knock three times on the wall so I know you are finished. I will close the door and give you privacy. I do not want to have to dehumanize you any more than we already have."

Dehumanize me? Everything about this is dehumanizing.

He tells me that while I am showering, he will be getting another room ready for me. This will give him more time to finish. He also warns me there's a small window in the shower, which he has covered. I'm not to touch it or attempt to look out of it. I will always be watched. There will be consequences if I defy him.

I hear the door close, and I'm alone. The absolute darkness is terrifying.

Trying to get a feel for my surroundings, I fumble around like someone who has recently lost their sight. I turn on the water and stand folded over, hugging my body in a vain attempt to shield it from whoever may be watching me. I have no doubt they are recording me.

I mechanically rub a bar of soap over my body, not in a way to cleanse, but enough to satisfy his commands. Every drop of water that spills over me and washes down the drain takes a little hope with it.

I finish, stumble out of the shower, carefully feel each piece of clothing as I dress, and knock on the wall.

I can hear noises on the other side, but he doesn't come, so I knock again.

"Wow, that was fast. The room isn't ready yet. Hold on," he says as he rushes in, out of breath.

He wraps the large comforter around me again and walks me out of the bathroom, turning me left, then a short right, then left into the corner of an L-shaped couch.

"You will wait here until I am done. Don't say anything," he warns. After he leaves me, I hear sounds of duct tape, foil, and cardboard in the next room.

Eventually, he gets me up, walking me into a different room around the corner from the couch. I sense it is a smaller, dark room: a bedroom. He guides me to a queen-sized bed just to the left of the door, and I lie down on it.

"This is where you will be staying."

The Voice describes the room—there is a closet on the right wall as we entered the room, and a dresser directly across from the entrance. He tells me that the top drawer has food and water in it if I need it, and my glasses are on top. I can't imagine when I would use them, being blindfolded like this. The fact that he even knows I wear glasses, sought them out in Aaron's home before placing me in the trunk, knew they were mine and not Aaron's, sends chills down my spine. He has seen me wear them before.

"I'm going to be leaving for a little bit," he tells me. "While I'm gone, a man named J is going to be watching over you. If he speaks, don't be alarmed. He sounds like a typical black guy. More than likely, he won't need to talk to you; he'll just check on you occasionally. It is in your best interest to not give him a reason to talk to you."

Not long after that, I hear the loud rumble of a car starting, and it sounds like the same car he used for the drive to this location. The sound moves slowly around the back of the house, then off into the distance. I soon pass out again, still heavily sedated.

HOURS PASS. I have no idea how many. I never heard or saw this man J he referred to. I was unconscious the whole time.

The Voice returns.

In a way, I am relieved it's him. It's as if hearing that familiar voice somehow minimizes the trauma by keeping me from being exposed to all the players. I am being conditioned to feel safe with him.

At first, he apologizes for threatening me in the car when he thought I tried to scream.

"I realized as we kept driving that it wasn't you," he says. "It was the steering wheel of Aaron's car, which squeaks as it turns. I'm sorry to have reacted that way."

Oh, I think to myself, knowing exactly what he's talking about. I remember when Aaron drove me on our first date, he jokingly excused the squeaking, saying his old car had "arthritis." Just a nerdy joke maybe only physical therapists would giggle at, but these little memories give me solace.

He tells me more about their plan.

"Aaron is going to be given instructions on what to do. Once he completes his tasks there will be a drop-off, either late Tuesday night or early Wednesday morning."

I'm afraid to hope this is actually what will happen, so I just listen.

He goes on to explain more about the organization he is a part of.

He says he and his associates developed an underground company that an outside party could hire to fulfill mainly financial and sometimes personal debts. The more he talks, the more I worry. They are clearly organized, intelligent, and cautious. It's impossible to believe they wouldn't assess all the risks of releasing me alive, especially if I know details about their organization.

I timidly ask him to stop, to please not tell me anything more.

"Why?" he asks.

"I don't want you to have any more reason to kill me," I say softly, like a child afraid of being scolded for saying the wrong thing.

He pauses, like he's trying to find the right words to say and the right way to say them.

"The plan is not to kill you. The plan is to release you after forty-eight hours. The things I am telling you are all things I am authorized to say."

He continues, disregarding my concern.

"We are all highly trained. Some of us have a military and technological background. We have intensely studied the psychological effects of victims in situations like this, so we know what to expect. We've even practiced on each other. We have all unexpectedly attacked each other in the middle of the night. It's terrifying, I know."

For him to compare his buddies scaring him in the middle of the night with what they did to us is infuriating. He's obviously trying to connect with me, but his delivery is forced and rehearsed. The more he speaks, the more he reveals about himself, and I get the impression that he is socially awkward in his "normal" life. It's as if he logically knows and understands what social norms and emotions should be—I believe he has studied them extensively so he can try to act them out—but it seems unnatural to him.

He tells me his group gets hired mostly to collect ransom or to scare someone into paying a debt. Or merely just to scare someone—a personal vendetta. They have succeeded in similar missions before and are reliable in their execution and ability to release the victim "unharmed." They watch the victims closely, study their every move before and after the event. They know everything about them: where they work, where they hang out, their family, where they shop. After the release, they continue to watch, for years. The victims are never to go to the police, never to tell anyone what happened. His organization has the technology to monitor their victims' electronics, tap their phones, and see what websites they visit. These victims are to continue on with their lives as if nothing happened, and if the group ever suspects they are going to speak up, there will be consequences.

He even gives an example of one woman who was acting like she was going to speak to authorities about what happened, years after the incident. So, as a threat, his organization sent a pie to the doorstep of her mother, who lived in a different state across the country.

"The threat is not just to the victims, but to their families and loved ones," he says. "We prepare ourselves completely to anticipate all risks, all possibilities that things could go awry, and plan accordingly.

"But with you, we got it wrong," he says. "And it's my fault. It's the first mission I was the lead on, and I was in charge of collecting intel in preparation for it. I'd been in Aaron's home many times in the last few months and I thought you were Jennifer. I knew they were engaged because I found an engagement card in Aaron's desk, where he keeps his mail. I also saw mail addressed to her."

I know the last time Jennifer's mail came to Aaron's house was about six months ago, which tells me how long they have been watching us. It's horrifying yet it also makes sense. So many times I felt like we were being watched. Now I know I was right.

"The last time you stayed over last week, we were there, outside Aaron's bedroom door, ready to proceed. We were going to do it that night but were called off because there were too many police units on the island," he says.

I am stunned and feel sick with fear, wondering how many times they were standing over us in the middle of the night while we slept. Are we safe anywhere?

"If I'd only looked in your purse and checked your identification last night before entering the bedroom, we would have left, and this never would have happened to you."

Really? What am I supposed to do with that particular piece of information?

I don't know how to process any of this. I wonder what parts of this are true. I suspect there are grandiose lies woven in with the truth either to scare me, to make me feel more hopeless, or to manipulate me—whichever ensures I comply.

At the same time, I begin to silently question their omnipotence. They are supposedly so smart, so careful and methodical, yet they somehow mistook me for Jennifer! In the end, I realize that it doesn't matter if what he's saying is true or not. The threats he's making are clear. I am outnumbered by a group of intelligent, trained, armed criminals who will not hesitate, now or in the future, to hurt me or my family if I speak to the police. I understand.

He leaves me again so he can continue to clean. I hear a washing machine going as French pop music plays in the room behind me. Pots, pans, and dishes clank just beyond that. It sounds like the kitchen is just past the living room, in an open format with no walls to divide them.

He comes in again to take me on the first of countless routine bathroom breaks. He takes my right hand in both of his to guide me and I notice his hands feel dry and calloused. I make a mental note of this, not sure if it will be useful information at some point. My left hip slams into the corner of a heavy wooden object halfway there. It happens every single time he takes me, and I picture a large dining room table.

In this first half a day, without really trying, I am getting an image of the layout of the house by what I hear and feel. It's like my brain is trying to put together anything it can to help me try to survive. I am grateful for this. I don't know what little detail might save my life.

I can tell this is a home, unattached from another unit, because there are no sounds of plumbing through the walls, no muffled voices. No other sounds come from outside: no other cars, no city noise, no sounds of others walking nearby. It's quiet, remote. I envision the property being loosely surrounded by trees, like in the woods, or in some kind of farmland or field. I don't even hear the sound of planes overhead. I picture a small town like Penryn, where Aaron's parents live, which is just one stop off Highway 80 on the way to Tahoe from Sacramento.

I do my best to stay alert and listen but I'm still groggy from whatever drugs he gave me this morning, so I drift in and out of sleep.

THE DAY IS fading. Through the goggles I can see the light changing. I have been with him for most of a day, and he hasn't beaten me, so maybe torture isn't their MO. I'm thankful for that—I'm trying to find gratitude in anything I can.

He enters again. Before he even speaks, I sense something is wrong. It's the heaviness of his breath, the weight of each step, the hesitation before he speaks. It reminds me of when he entered Aaron's living room before telling me he would be taking me away, and I know what he's about to say will not be good.

"We have a problem."

Oh, God, what now? Did they hurt Aaron? Please let him be okay.

Instead, it's my second-worst fear.

"One of us is going to have to have sex with you."

5

AARON

MAT MUSTARD APPEARS to be in his late forties, balding with a short buzz cut. He's wearing an untucked blue T-shirt and jeans. He's about my height, with a stocky build. He's not out of shape but his face looks puffy, like maybe he's had too many years of sleep deprivation. He starts by showing me a copy of both Denise's and Jennifer's driver's licenses and asking me to confirm their identities, which seems a little late to do but I guess it's a procedural requirement.

"We're treating you as a victim in relation to this," he says, his tone friendly and reassuring. "You can get up and walk out of here at any point you want. You're not being detained or anything like that. You're sitting here in jail clothes because that's all we got. We had to take your clothes. I want to make sure you understand where we're at."

I take him at his word about the clothes. I'm eager to hear what their investigation has uncovered. Instead, he asks me to recap that morning's events, even though I'd spent nearly two hours telling the other detectives everything I could remember. I'm a little puzzled but think maybe he'll pick up on something they missed.

He doesn't prompt me with a starting point, leaving it strangely open-ended, so I choose when the Voice woke us, which seems the most logical. There were at least three people, I say, and one of them told me they were wearing wet suits. I continue to scour my memory, trying to give him every detail I can think of, scared that I might forget the crucial piece, the key to finding Denise.

I notice that even though he has a pen and a legal pad on the table, he's not taking any notes, which strikes me as odd. Slowly his questions get more and more hostile. He tells me to "back up" to the previous day—seemingly more interested in what happened between Denise and me on Sunday than the home invasion—as if it was stupid for me to start with the actual crime. He says he hasn't been to my house, which I don't understand. It's only ten minutes away. What has he been doing?

Still, I keep my voice calm as I answer each and every question, although none of my answers seems to be good enough because he keeps prying for more detail.

Were you trying to get back with your ex? (Yes.) Did Denise find anything on your phone? (Yes.) Did you cheat on Denise? (No.) Did Denise feel like you cheated on her? (Yes.)

Unlike when I told Officer Garcia about my recent relationship struggles, it's not a relief to open up to Mustard. In fact, it's the opposite. It feels like some warped version of a confessional, only he's not wearing a clerical collar and there's no absolution here.

I guess this is my penance. If this is what it takes to get Denise back, baring my soul in front of all these strangers (because I have no doubt other people are watching this through the camera), I'll do it. The Bible says "The truth will set you free." *Please, God, take my truth in exchange for Denise's freedom.*

After about forty minutes, Mustard rubs the right side of his forehead while his elbow rests on the table.

"Your story is very elaborate and, in some ways, far-fetched," he says.

"Trust me, I know it sounds . . . I'm—I'm telling you, I know it sounds crazy. I've been—"

Mustard cuts me off. Suddenly, my gut tells me I need to be on defense. The room's energy has completely shifted, backing me into a corner. As though I've been thrown back into the room with the Voice, my throat stiffens, and my heart rate kicks up. I can't figure out what I did wrong or what has changed.

"Listen to me for a second. The part of the story you're telling here, I ain't buying at all," he says, waving his hand to keep me from speaking. "Listen to me. There ain't no frogmen came into your house. Nobody dressed in wet suits or . . . It didn't happen. That didn't happen."

Frogmen? What the hell is he talking about?

I'm stunned by Mustard's suddenly aggressive tone, but he doesn't give me any time to process this abrupt shift before he hits me with another question. "Do you have any idea about what goes on out there on that island? Do you know what that place used to be?"

"What do you mean by that?"

"A military base."

"Yeah, I know that."

Less than four square miles in size, Mare Island, which is part of the city of Vallejo, is barely a mile from downtown; they are separated by the Napa River but joined by a short bridge. During World War II, almost forty thousand people worked on Mare Island, building ships for the Pacific Fleet. However, the riverbed could not be dredged deep enough for the newer submarines, making the base expendable; it was finally closed in the nineteen nineties. My house was part of the first phase of a residential development built a couple of years prior to the crash of the housing market in 2008. The Great Recession halted development until just last year, as the economic recovery slowly spread to the island.

"You've been on the island for three years. I'm assuming you drive in and out of there every day, right? And I'm assuming you're familiar with the neighborhood watches and the people and the businesses out there. I'm sure you're familiar with the ways in and out of that place. Not very many, right?"

Mustard brings his hands down to the table as if he's holding a magical orb and he's reading my future.

There are cameras everywhere on Mare Island, he tells me before I can respond.

"We're going to be able to track everybody that came on and off the island. We're going to be able to track *you*."

"Okay," I say.

"I don't think she was kidnapped from your home," he says, shaking his head.

"What do you think?"

It's clearly the question he wants me to ask.

"I think something bad happened in your house and I think something bad happened between you and her."

"Nothing bad happened . . . between the two of us," I say. "I'm here . . . because I don't have anything to hide." I'm struggling to keep control of my body. It feels like my organs are twisting in opposite directions and my bones want to rip through my skin.

"Okay," Mustard says, rubbing the back of his head and neck. "I can tell you . . . there ain't been no other additional communication to you on a ransom demand. Nobody is trying to reach out to you. . . ."

"There's nothing else?" I somehow manage to say, my horror growing at the ramifications of what he is telling me.

If the kidnappers stopped communicating, they must know I went to the police. I feel myself buckling under the weight of my own guilt and anger. I shouldn't have called Ethan. I should have just done what they said. Now they're going to kill Denise because I disobeyed them. How am I going to live with myself? But maybe there's still time to save her. I feel like I would know if she was already gone, and I can still feel her presence. I can't explain it, but that connection hasn't been severed. Yet.

Mustard barrels on, seemingly oblivious to the shattering effect this news has on me.

"Ultimately, you don't know me, and I don't know you, but I know a *lot* of people that sat in that chair that have made horrible decisions and a lot of people who sat in that chair and made good decisions. I can tell you at the end of the day, the people who make better decisions come out of the entire situation better. Lies are not good decisions."

"I'm not lying," I say, almost whispering.

"So, you want me to believe that unknown people broke into your home by unknown means. Come with prerecorded statements . . . and they're wearing— What, did they swim in wearing their wet suits? I mean, come on, man. It doesn't make any fricking sense."

He pauses to drink from his water bottle and waits for me to answer.

"I know it sounds crazy," I say. "It feels like I'm in some sort of movie. Nothing happened. I did not hurt Denise."

Mustard stares at me, leaning on the table with crossed arms, shaking his head in disbelief.

"You can look at my records. I don't . . . ," I say, my voice trailing off.

"I agree with you," he says. "You don't have a record, which makes me believe you reacted to a situation. That you didn't plan this. Something happened and you were trying to figure out what to do."

I can't win. Even my *lack* of a criminal record will be twisted and warped to fit his version of what happened.

But I don't let any of my frustration or anger show and I don't say any of this out loud. I can't. It'll only get him more pissed off at me and I'll end up in handcuffs.

Because it's become clear to me that's where this is headed. Now I'm fighting for Denise's life and my own. I can't do much from behind bars, so all I can do now is try to delay the inevitable.

Mustard glowers at me. "There's blood in the house," he says.

An image of Denise's face with a gash down her cheek penetrates my mind. I try to suppress it, but it's already taken hold. Still, I scramble through the maze of different possibilities. It doesn't make sense. It was so quiet in my house; I would have known if something like that happened. Maybe it's an old stain? I got cut while playing basketball a few weeks ago and the scab broke when I was sleeping. That must be the explanation.

"I don't know if it's hers or not yet but I'm going to presume it's hers," he goes on. "I'm going to presume she wasn't alive and kicking when she left the house."

Presume?! Wait, this isn't a guessing game! Test the damn blood! But by now

I know it's pointless to argue with him, so I stay silent, looking down at the table.

"Let's play this through for a minute," Mustard says. "Sit in this chair for a minute. Think it through. Listen to me. Intruders come in, right? Intruders hurt, kill, damage, defame, whatever Denise. Do you think they take her? No, they leave. And they probably kill you too. Right? Why, then, do I not find Denise in the home? It makes me think. I don't find Denise in the home because the story doesn't fit."

I said it was a kidnapping, not a murder. How would they collect a ransom if Denise and I are both dead?

"There ain't going to be no frogman as the suspect," he says, nodding his head. "There ain't going to be but one guy. It's going to be *you*. If something bad happened, and you overreacted, that's a lot different from being a monster."

"Nothing happened," I whisper, feeling my defenses crumbling.

"I don't believe that."

His voice is firm, no-nonsense. This is the way it happened. Period. End of story.

"Think about it. You sat for hours and hours and hours and hours," he says, repeatedly pounding his fist into his other palm for emphasis, "trying to figure out, 'Oh, my God, what am I going to do?' . . . *Think* about it. Find twelve of your friends and tell this story to them. How many of them are going to believe you?"

"Not that many," I say, even though the exact opposite is true. I have decades-long friendships with a tight-knit group that would unquestionably believe me. But Mustard is winning. He's breaking me down and I'm saying what he wants to hear. I'm ashamed of myself for admitting to something that isn't true—but maybe my friends . . . wouldn't believe me? I just don't know anymore.

And where are my parents? Have they abandoned me? Do *they* think I'm a monster? It doesn't seem possible. My family is more comfortable teasing one another than saying, "I love you," but we're fiercely loyal, and we always have one another's backs. I'm not saying my brothers and I didn't get into our fair share of squabbles when we were growing up but nothing that a few tears and a trip to Mom or Dad wouldn't fix.

My father met my mother in medical school when she was a nursing student. They got married and had my two older brothers; then I came along in November 1984. I was born in Rutland, Vermont, a small city near Killington where I have my earliest memories of skiing down the frigid mountainsides. In the summer of 1990, my parents decided to start a new life for our family in Northern California. My parents, always the outdoors type, took this momentous move as an opportunity for a month-long camping trip across the country. I remember seeing the carved stone faces of Mount Rushmore, the steam from Old Faithful, and majestic views of the Grand Canyon. And I have just as vivid memories of being crammed between my siblings in the backseat as my eldest brother, Matt, entertained us by reenacting every scene from *Ghostbusters*.

We settled into our new home in Penryn, California, a rural town without a single traffic light nestled in the foothills of the Sierra Nevada, only a couple of hours away from great skiing near Lake Tahoe. And there I grew up, son of a doctor and a nurse, but with a life closer to that of a farmhand. My dad is a do-it-yourselfer, and on a two-and-a-half-acre property, there were always fences to mend, sheds to fix, or a few farm animals to feed (though far fewer than we had in Vermont).

Matt used to direct us in homemade movies, usually a *Star Trek* spoof or another adventure of "Super Quinn and Geeky Boy," our long-running series starring Ethan and me as bumbling superheroes. My parents always supported all of our interests, even politely laughing at our immature fart jokes. As we got older, they were at all of our band competitions, cross-country meets, or football games. My mom was the loudest cheerleader in the crowd while my dad quietly filmed us with the camcorder. I cannot understand why they're not here. My mom is a fireball. She would use every ounce of her small frame to break down this door to get to me. But I have no way of knowing what's going on outside this box I'm in. And I need to stay focused on what's happening inside this room right now, because Mustard is like a raging bull with his sights set on me.

I still have this naive hope that the police will believe me. *They have to believe me.* So I keep answering his questions, even as he abruptly shifts to a different tactic.

"I talked with some people that were with her . . . and they totally thought it was heated between the two of you because of [Jennifer]," he says. "She told them, 'My boyfriend is leaving, and he's going back to his ex.' So I know this conversation on Sunday night was heated."

"It wasn't," I insist.

The memory of holding Denise in my arms last night comes rushing back: the way her silky blond hair shone in the pale moonlight; the warmth of her body next to mine. If only Mustard could have seen us together, he would know we were happy. It would be obvious I would never hurt her.

Mustard's voice gets more forceful, almost angry.

"You don't understand the effect in the relationship to the selfish approach you are taking. And you don't understand ultimately how that's going to impact you. . . . People will judge you. How old . . . You're thirty years old?"

"Yeah, I'm thirty years old."

"Did you watch the Laci Peterson or Scott Anderson or whatever the hell his name was? Did you watch that story coming out of Modesto? You're old enough to have watched that. You look at that and you go, 'That dude is a lying son of a bitch.' I don't even know the guy. I don't even know what half the story is about, but there is no way that happened. That's the way people are going to look at you."

Mustard taps his finger against the table as he says, "And then the pieces of the puzzle that do fit start to fall. Then ultimately, here's a guy that went from something that's explainable to a *monster.*

"So, here's what's going to happen," he says. "Denise is going to be found. . . . And when I say she's found, she's *dead.* Understand that, that I've accepted that. She's dead! You want me to go tell her family that she's dead? Because that's what I'm prepared to do. I'm going to tell them I'm not looking for a live Denise. I'm looking for a dead Denise. And it's just a matter now when her body is going to come. . . . She's dead. I've accepted it. Now the question becomes when she's dead, what do I have? Now I got the murder investigation."

He's so sure of himself, so unrelenting, that I'm afraid he knows something he's not telling me. Yet I don't have any time to think as Mustard picks up his pace.

"Okay, what about these frogmen?" he says. "So, I take that approach and I call in the best forensic team I can find, and I send them to your house. . . . I get the results back. Here's the next piece to my puzzle, *bang!*" he says as he smacks the table with his hand. "What's it going to show? It ain't going to show shit. . . . It's going to show that this event is staged."

I welcome that kind of scrutiny because I know the evidence will support what I'm telling him. At the same time, I can't believe they haven't sent a forensics team to my house yet. *What the hell have they been doing for the past several hours?* When I start to speak, he interrupts me, firing off questions one after another.

"Did you vacuum your carpets today?"

"No."

"Did you clean your carpets today?"

"No."

"Did you do any cleanup in relation to chemical cleanup today?"

"No."

And on. And on.

"Did you know the comforter and blanket are missing off your bed?"

"That's what the other officer told me."

"Why do you take a comforter and blanket off a bed? . . . Why do you do that?"

"To take a body," I reply. "I'm assuming that's what you're getting at."

"Well, how's Frogman going to take the body? Frogman is going to take the body and lift it over his shoulder and take it. He don't need to take the evidence of the bedspread and the blanket. You know why the monster does that? Because he sees stuff on it, and he says, 'Holy shit. I need to get rid of it.' . . . It's obvious to me, whatever happened, happened in that bedroom."

Now he's almost yelling.

"Maybe she overdosed? Were you playing with prescription drugs from work? Are you guys experimenting, having fun with prescription drugs? It's okay if you are. If she takes too much and she overdoses, so now you're like, 'Oh, shit, what am I going to do?' I can see that happening too."

We repeat this maddening circle over and over. I deny his accusations; Mustard says I'm lying. We're wasting time and getting no closer to finding Denise. I build up my courage to defend myself. Maybe if I speak forcefully enough, he'll finally believe me and actually start investigating this crime.

"We can keep going back and forth but I'm not admitting to anything," I say. "There's nothing to admit to. I didn't do anything. I'm living a nightmare right now, but I did not hurt her. I did not set this up. I am a victim here. . . . So, what's the next stage here? What do we move forward to? Because I don't have any more information for you besides what I have given you guys multiple times."

Maybe my standing up to him has its intended effect or maybe Mustard realizes he can't break me, because my outburst finally stops his interrogation.

Or perhaps it's something else entirely.

Because the next thing I know Mustard gets a text, looks at it, and after hammering away at me for more than an hour, says, "Give me a minute. Let me think about what's next."

He packs up his stuff, shoves his papers in a binder, and leaves the room. The other detective follows.

I put my head in my hands, my elbows resting on the table. I hear the click of the door locking behind them—driving home a truth I can no longer avoid: I'm a suspect, not a victim.

6

DENISE

THIS IS GOING to happen. Of course it is, I think to myself in despair after the Voice tells me one of them is going to "have sex" with me.

He rambles on, yet it's as if he is speaking to me underwater. I can hardly make out the words as I struggle to come to terms with what's in store. I start to detach, anything to protect myself from what's about to happen.

"This mission was intended for someone else, and since you are not her, we do not have anything on you. So, one of us will have sex with you and it will be recorded. If you do not follow our instructions, and if you attempt to speak about this, it will be released on the Internet."

It's one blow followed by another. They make a mistake and I'm the one who has to pay for it.

The Voice says he isn't sure exactly how they are going to proceed, who or how many of them it will be, and leaves me in the room to wait. *Oh, please, God, don't let it be aggressive and violent; don't let it be one after the other taking their turn with me. Please, God.*

He finally comes in again.

"It has been decided I will have sex with you. It was my fault for not getting the correct intel," he says. "This is more of a punishment for me.

You did nothing wrong. I just proposed to my fiancée two weeks ago and this recording will be used to make sure that I stay on track with the mission. So, it has to look consensual, like we are a couple."

He refers to his "associates" as "T, J, and L" and says he will then send the recording to "T," the person he answers to, who will decide whether it's sufficient.

"I need time to prepare myself," he says as he leaves the room. "This is going to be hard for me."

Talk about gall. Yet a small part of me believes he's sincere. Is it possible he's having a moral dilemma over this? Regardless, it doesn't matter how he's feeling. This is going to happen and there is nothing I can do to change it.

As I lie there, waiting for him to come back, my mind drifts to when I was molested as a child.

It happened at a pivotal moment in my life. I was twelve, about to turn thirteen, moving from childhood into my own as a young woman. I was still innocent, but I thought I was mature for my age, that I had life figured out. I was about to find out the harsh truth of how people in this world can take advantage of such blind trust.

My family went camping at the Colorado River in Southern California, with members of our extended family and some of their friends, many of whom I was meeting for the first time on that trip. One of them was a twenty-nine-year-old man who befriended me and another young girl, spending most of his time with us rather than the other adults. We didn't think anything of it. He was fun to hang out with and he made us laugh. I certainly never felt unsafe with him.

On our last night, he stayed up with a couple of us kids. We were sitting out by the river while the adults slept in the campers and tents nearby. He was drinking beer and let me have some. We wanted to try to stay up to watch the sunrise, so we lay on towels under the stars. When the others were asleep, and I turned drowsily away from him, he crept close behind me, pressing himself against me, and started touching me. I can still feel his hot, beer-soaked breath exhaling heavily into my right ear as he pressed his erection against my back, molesting me through my bathing suit. I couldn't speak, couldn't move away. I was shaking so hard he kept whispering, "Shh. It's okay. Calm down."

He had to know he was traumatizing me, but he wouldn't stop. It went on for hours and hours. I felt like it would never end. I prayed for the sun to come up, knowing he'd have to stop once he lost the cover of darkness and people started to wake up. To my relief, there were some things I could still count on—the sun slowly lit the sky, and he pulled away from me.

Afterward, I felt sick, ashamed, like I'd done something wrong. When we left later that day, I just got in the car and didn't say anything. I threw my bathing suit away as soon as we got home. I felt broken, used, and discarded. Who would love me now?

That was the same summer my parents separated. My mom was working six days a week to provide for us and my father was out of the house. I didn't want to add any more stress to their lives, so I tried to handle these emotions myself.

When I found out that this man attacked another girl a couple of years later, I blamed myself. If I'd spoken out earlier, she might have been spared. I had naively hoped what he did to me was just a onetime mistake he made because he'd had too much to drink. I guess I was still trying to believe that this guy we befriended wasn't really a bad guy.

He violated me at a time when I was just discovering my own sexuality, which led me to believe that my only value was in being treated as an object for men's pleasure. In my head, I knew I had more to offer a man, a partner, the world, but in my heart, I didn't believe it. I didn't know how to respect myself. I certainly didn't know how to demand that respect from others.

Without me realizing it at the time, the experience made me feel that I should expect to be used, like that's just how things work. So instead of living in fear that I would be violated and used again, I figured I might as well "take back control," have fun with it. It was an unhealthy mindset and led me to become promiscuous and deeply depressed.

I wanted to bury it, so I drank and partied to mask those emotions, trying to replace them with "fun," which led to my getting a DUI when

I was twenty. I desperately wanted to be happy, but just didn't know how. Toward the end of college, I started going to therapy. I had learned self-destructive habits and bad coping mechanisms that were hard to break. It was a messy road to healing, but identifying the problem, finding the root cause, was the first step.

I finally told my mom about the molestation when I was twenty-five, after I'd been able to process some of it through counseling. I knew it had been hard for her to see me depressed and drinking too much in my early twenties. I wanted her to know I'd figured out why and to share with her what I'd learned about myself. She was warm and empathetic, just like I knew she'd be.

For so long it had seemed impossible to deal with and heal from being molested. But I did. I survived it. I was still surviving it, and now I know I have the strength to get through this too, whatever shape it takes.

THE WAITING IS excruciating. It seems like hours pass, but it may have just been thirty minutes before the Voice returns.

When he comes back, he asks if he can talk with me a bit before he "has to go through with it." He says he doesn't feel right about it without getting to know me a little better, as if we are on some kind of date. He asks if he can lie on the bed next to me, like it matters what I think, like I have any say whatsoever in what is about to happen to me.

"Okay" is all I reply.

He asks me to tell him about myself.

I'm not sure what I should say, what he wants to hear or how much I should divulge, but I also know I can't lie because they clearly have ways of gathering information about people. So I tell him about my work as a physical therapist, hoping that if he sees I spend my life helping others, he will spare mine.

I tell him about the residency at the hospital, that I have just two weeks left in the program, am excelling in my work, and even have the final written test scheduled the next day.

"Oh, really? I wouldn't worry about that. I am sure they'll let you retake it," he assures me.

I explain I am passionate and determined, that I plan to continue to build my craft and skill so after this residency I can start an orthopedic fellowship. I had spoken to the program directors, written my CV, my résumé, gotten my letters of recommendation, and I planned to print it all out that morning. The deadline is this week.

As a physical therapist with a doctorate degree already having practiced for two years, I had no requirement to pursue residencies or fellowships. In fact, pursuing them meant an investment of time and a significant pay decrease. But I am motivated to do it because I strive to be the best physical therapist I possibly can be. I love to learn, grow, and challenge myself. To me, my education never ends. It is a lifelong journey to seek excellence. The orthopedic fellowship I was about to apply to didn't start until the following January, but the program director told me about a job at Kaiser in Vacaville that would start a few weeks after this residency ended. He and the director in Vacaville basically said the position was mine to help bridge the gap in time before the fellowship started.

I tell the Voice I met Aaron at the hospital, through the residency, and he is a physical therapist too. I explain that we work with patients who are recovering from some of the most challenging injuries and illnesses. How, like me, Aaron is passionate and motivated in his work and how I admire him for that.

"When I spoke to Aaron upstairs, I could tell he's a good guy," he acknowledges. "None of this should be happening to people like you."

Well, then, don't. Don't let this happen.

I still can't tell if he's being genuine, and I don't put any stock in what he says. He tells me a little about himself, saying that he has been in the military, was stationed in the Middle East, and suffers from post-traumatic stress disorder and insomnia.

He says he's tried living a normal life but has been unsuccessful because of these psychological difficulties. Doing this type of work is the only way he can earn a living using the skills he's acquired. He even mentions that a brother he is close to recently underwent surgery that cost a few hundred thousand dollars, and he needs to help him financially. Otherwise he wouldn't be doing this.

It's clear he has something to say and needs someone to talk to. I turn my body slightly toward him, like I'm his therapist here to listen. I'll use that to my advantage, as an opportunity to connect with him. Empathy, compassion, and listening are some of my best skills, and they are the only weapons I have at my disposal. I have always found that killing people with kindness is far better than fighting fire with fire. No matter what the outcome, at least you know you're doing the right thing.

Lying next to him now, I can feel this deeper, darker part of him that thrives on the power he has over me, over a woman. I feel I represent something from his past, maybe some pretty blonde who treated him poorly in high school, and this is how he is getting his revenge. I sense that if I give him any reason at all, he would enjoy forcing me to submit to his will. As hard as it may be, I will show him only kindness and compassion.

I had more than enough practice with this philosophy working in the service industry for nearly nine years as I put myself through school. I learned that no matter how upset, rude, or angry an individual may be, it usually has more to do with them and what they're going through in life than it has to do with me. Often, people look for an excuse to justify this behavior. If I respond negatively, they can tell themselves, "See? She's a bitch. That's why I'm upset." But if I always respond in kindness and warmth, slowly their hard exterior softens. And if I can get them to smile, even the faintest crease in the side of their mouth, we have both won.

This same skill is now helping me connect with that small part inside him that's still human.

I ask if he has been in therapy. He brushes it off, saying it wouldn't work for someone like him, but I get the impression he's never really tried. If he had, if he had been honest with a therapist about his actions, his fears, his trauma, and taken steps to try to do something different, he wouldn't be in this situation.

I confide in him about being molested and how therapy helped me heal.

A part of me hopes that telling him this will change his mind about going through with it. But in the end, I know it will happen. I knew that from the second I heard an unknown man's voice waking Aaron and me from our sleep this morning. And even if he does have a change of heart, it doesn't seem like the decision is up to him.

"I can see you're a strong person" is all he says. "It's admirable how you're handling all of this."

He kind of jokes, saying he's going to have some wine so he can calm his nerves and prepare, chuckling a hideous "Heh-heh."

How evil. Telling me I am going to be raped and recorded, then leaving me alone to think of all the ways it could happen, blindfolded and drugged. It's one thing to be violated unexpectedly. I know what that feels like. But to make me sit here and wait for it to happen, imagining how it will all play out, is psychological torture. And he knows it.

He said they'd studied the psychology of kidnapping victims, but this isn't something you learn from books. This is a skill you fine-tune by practicing it over and over. I will give credit where credit is due. He is a master at his craft. He continues to show me that.

I want to take the goggles off and look around to see if there's any chance I can escape from this room, but I'm still convinced they're monitoring me. I have this image of a computer sitting in the next room displaying the real-time images of the bedroom and bathroom. If they see me trying to look around, the rape could potentially be more brutal as punishment.

"It's time," he says when he walks back into the room. "I have to go through with it. But I promise I will be gentle. I don't want to make this worse for you."

I can feel myself becoming numb, my mind trying to escape what is about to happen. I cannot be mentally present for this.

He tells me he will set up the camera on the dresser facing the bed. He starts to remove my clothes and stands at the foot of the bed. He reassures me he will be gentle, that he will try to help "prepare" me orally, he won't hurt me, and he will use a condom.

In a strange way, this is reassuring. It will be awful, but he's not planning to make it even worse by injuring me or impregnating me or giving me a sexually transmitted disease.

I feel him climb onto the bed, slowly laying his body between my legs, pushing my now frozen lower limbs apart. It feels like the life is being sucked out of me with every touch.

I just lie there, hoping he will get it over with quickly.

After God knows how long, I feel him get off the bed, hear him take his clothes off, put a condom on, and pick up the device from the dresser to begin recording. I feel the weight of his naked body climb on top of me, kissing my neck, my chest, as he forces himself inside me.

I want so badly to hit him, push him off me, bite him, scream, whatever I can do to fight him off, but I know it would be useless. All I'd do is piss him off.

There's this underlying buzz of energy I feel from him, bubbling under his polite surface, ready to explode with the slightest provocation. I'm certain he wants me to fight, that a fight is what he is hoping for: the thrill and excitement of subduing a hysterical woman, to have that level of physical and emotional control and power over her. I remember how angry he got with me when he thought I'd screamed in the trunk of the car.

So I stay limp.

He moves me around the bed a few times, dragging my body into different positions, like playing with a lifeless rag doll. Here I am again, just an object for some sick man's pleasure. He pulls me off the edge of the bed and stands, holding my legs around him as he continues thrusting into me. I feel like I am floating above us, watching. I feel so bad for that woman, blacked-out swim goggles tangled in her hair, naked, head turned to the side as her whole body shakes back and forth from this horrible man violating her. This is not a position he would need to put me in to get the footage they asked for. He is enjoying this.

He flips me over onto my stomach so I'm lying horizontally across the bed. I'm assuming it's to get a better shot of him penetrating me for the camera. I am mortified.

"This is bullshit," he whispers into my right ear as he climaxes on top of me.

As if he was forced to do this against his will, as if he didn't enjoy it, as if he didn't have control over what just happened. This disgusts me, but I do agree with him—this *IS* bullshit. *HE* is bullshit.

And at that moment I know.

There is no way in hell this looked consensual. It's going to happen again.

7

AARON

I GET A GLIMPSE of the outside through the window in the hallway as Mustard leaves the room. It's dark now, though I don't know what time it is.

I put my head in my hands and stare at the table. How could telling the truth go so wrong?

By now I've been sitting for several hours and my back is killing me, so to give it some relief, I pull two of the swivel chairs together and curl up on my side in the fetal position, my arms crossed in front of me like I'm giving myself a hug. I'm in desperate need of some comfort right now.

"What the fuck is going on?" I say, though no one is in the room but me.

SOMEONE KNOCKS ON the door. I cross the small room to open it. It's an officer I haven't seen before, and he asks if I want some pizza. I don't, but I know my body is running on fumes right now and I need to eat something.

A few minutes later, he returns with a slice of cheese pizza. Once

71

again I ask for my brother, but he tells me he's unsure if he's at the station. He practically bolts out of the room to avoid any more of my questions.

Enough time has passed that Ethan has probably called my parents. I wonder if he left to pick them up. It makes sense they would be too upset to drive. I contemplate leaving the room to look for them. If I could just see their faces for a few minutes . . . I just need them to tell me this is all going to be okay. But I know I'll be put in handcuffs if I try to leave the room.

I'm on my own.

The pizza has the taste and texture of an old sponge, like it's been sitting out for hours. I take a bite or two before I push it aside. The last thing I need is food poisoning. I grab the second rolling chair next to me and lie down again, staring at the beige wall.

Mustard said the kidnappers haven't communicated once, yet they were emailing with me earlier. Did that really happen? Have I lost my mind? Did I have a psychotic break?

I can't believe they're making me doubt my own sanity.

I CLOSE MY eyes and images of Denise flash through my mind.

My mind lingers on our first real date. We went to Sonoma for dinner. It was a warm summer evening. The air was dry and dusty from the current drought with the grass already turned to its golden color. I brought Denise to a restaurant in the town square with its own backyard garden. I reached out and held her hand for the first time in public as we passed by the various shops and hotels. She gave mine a little squeeze and smiled.

We didn't want the date to end after dinner, so we walked down the street to one of the local bars with a pool table. I'm not much of a pool player and Denise showed me little mercy, trouncing me quickly. Usually losing frustrates me, but this time I didn't mind. Once the game ended, we took our beers over to a little table to talk. Denise sat with her back to the window with the sun lowering in the sky creating long, wispy shadows. Music was playing, people were laughing, and she was tenderly focusing on me with her silvery blue eyes. It felt like the warmest hug. If I could, I would relive that day forever.

SHARP PAIN IN my lower back jerks me awake as the two chairs roll away from each other. I must have passed out from sheer exhaustion. I woke up from a dream only to be thrust back into a nightmare. The room feels even crueler now. Everything that's happened feels beyond surreal, but I know that I didn't have a psychotic break. I need to convince them the kidnapping is real. She's alive. I can feel it.

I'm losing track of time, but it feels late. I start shivering, whether from the cold or stress, I don't know. Scenes from this morning replay on a constant loop in my head. Part of me wishes I fought back. The cops might believe me if I had cuts or bruises or broken bones. But I know that's stupid. The kidnappers would have hurt Denise if I disobeyed their rules. She would have been the one with cuts and bruises. Fuck, she still might end up with cuts or bruises or something worse.

Please don't rape her.

A FEW AGONIZING hours later I hear keys unlocking the door and Mustard walks into the room. My heart starts thumping and my entire body fills with dread and fear. I have no idea what he has in store for me next, and part of me is not sure if I have it in me to go another round with him.

Instead, he tells me the FBI is now involved because it's an adult kidnapping for ransom. That's what I've been hoping for all along! The FBI has the resources to find Denise and catch these guys! But my excitement is short-lived. His next words rattle me.

"We'd like you to take a lie detector test so we can clear you and move forward," he says.

This doesn't feel right. I thought police stopped using lie detector tests, but apparently I was wrong. I quickly consider the pros and cons. I know lie detectors are unreliable and not admissible in court, but I'm confident I can pass it because I'm telling the truth. And if I do, hopefully they will stop this aggressive interrogation and I can get out of this room. If I don't take it, it'll just confirm to them I'm guilty. In the end, there's really no choice.

"Okay, that's fine," I finally say, resigned.

Mustard leads me out of the room and around a couple of corners, then uses his keys to unlock silver double doors. I hear the automatic lock slide into place as they close. The new room is a mirror image of my previous prison.

There's a man sitting at the table on the far side of the room, dressed in a gray suit, in his mid- to late forties, with a close-shaved head. He looks like a Fed, no-nonsense and routine oriented. He probably goes to the gym at the same time every day. He directs me to sit on the chair at the short end of the table.

"My name is Special Agent Peter French and I work as a polygrapher for the FBI," he tells me as he displays his credentials. "How's it going?"

Why do people keep asking me that? Everyone from the techs who took my blood and fingerprints to the parade of officers and detectives I've been dealing with today has posed that question to me as if this is a normal social interaction we're having when nothing about this is normal.

A memory of my first few months as a physical therapist pops into my head. A patient was the grandfather of a friend from college. My friend told me his grandfather was the leader of the family, still very active up to the day of his stroke. His grandfather's stroke severely affected his physical capabilities but not his cognitive function. The three of us had lunch one day and his grandfather expressed his frustration with his inability to walk or move on his own. "I know what you mean," I said, thinking I was being empathetic.

"No, you don't," he quickly replied. "You have no idea what I'm going through. How could you know?" He was absolutely right, and I vowed from then on to be precise with my words.

You'd think people who work in law enforcement who are used to dealing with people in sensitive situations like this one would be a little more mindful about their word choices.

But "Terrible" is all I respond. It's honest. There's no point in giving them a lecture about the proper way to treat someone going through a trauma.

French passes me a piece of paper with the Miranda rights waiver. He instructs me to read it out loud and then asks me if I want to sign it. I hesitate, knowing there's not a defense attorney alive who would tell me this is a good idea, but at the same time, this is the FBI. They're the best of the best, like Ethan. I trust them. And I already told them I'd take the polygraph. I can't back out now. It'll make me look even worse in their eyes.

I sign it reluctantly, hoping I'm making the right decision. I have to add the date and time and French tells me it's 1:55 a.m. I'm shocked. I can't believe it's almost exactly twelve hours since I called 911. I am so exhausted and beaten down. I just want this to be over.

I'm expecting the whole thing to take about thirty minutes. French will hook me up, ask me a few questions, I'll pass, and then I can leave. Ethan and I will get a hotel room nearby in case the FBI needs my help. Instead, French begins a lengthy lecture about the science involved in a polygraph: how the machine is so sensitive it will pick up the slightest physiological change in heart rate or blood pressure. When we tell the truth, there's no change, but when we lie, we hesitate while we think about what to say, which causes one or the other to fluctuate, and that's what the sensors pick up.

I'm so sleep-deprived I'm not sure I'm even capable of totally grasping, let alone critiquing, what he's telling me. Wouldn't they want me to be in a better headspace to do this? While my internal debate is still raging over whether this is a good idea, he says all of this so confidently, so authoritatively, that he convinces me that polygraphs do work, that everything I've heard about them being unreliable is wrong. They must have improved them over the years, or the FBI wouldn't keep using them. I recall that Ethan even had to pass a polygraph to be accepted into the Bureau.

For some reason, French then asks me a seemingly endless series of questions before we get started with the lie detector. He asks me about every family member, about how my parents raised us and why I decided to become a physical therapist. These questions seem better suited for a job interview than for finding Denise, but I'll do anything they ask.

I was a deathly shy and sensitive child. A nerd who never considered wearing jeans and loved his *Star Trek* T-shirt. I knew the answer to every question asked by my teachers, but I wouldn't dare say them out loud, always whispering them to myself. Any sort of criticism sent me into tears. I don't know where my sensitivity came from; my parents were supportive and involved without being overly strict. It seemed like it was just part of my DNA.

In fourth grade, one of my few friends decided he was going to try Pop Warner football, and for some unknown reason, I joined him. I struggled emotionally my first year, crying multiple times either in practice or after it, but I was a decent player. My next year, I was very good. And the following year, I was dominant. At the same time, I was excelling as a basketball player. My success in sports helped fuel a growth in confidence, which I so badly needed.

In high school, I continued to get straight A's and perform well in football although I stopped playing basketball after my sophomore year, as my lack of height became more difficult to overcome. I became the quarterback and captain of the football team. My girlfriend was smart, pretty, and popular. But at times, I still felt that paralyzing shyness of my younger years and I knew that I was fortunate to mostly be able to overcome it. I also never forgot how my brother Ethan was severely bullied in junior high because he'd preferred playing Dungeons & Dragons rather than kickball. I wanted to use my status to help other people, like my parents did. My mother was the school nurse for the special education kids at the time. Some of her students loved football, so I often spent some of my lunchtime talking with them.

I tell French that for most of my life I wanted to be a doctor like my dad. I majored in genetics because I was always fascinated by the human blueprint, but while I was preparing for the MCATs during my senior year at UC Davis, something didn't feel quite right. The world of a doctor was rapidly changing. My dad talked about having less time with patients, more paperwork, and more liability. A friend was thinking about becoming a physical therapist and told me she thought I would enjoy it. I signed up to volunteer at a PT clinic, and within an hour, I knew that was what I wanted to do. It's part science and part craft, with enough time to hopefully make a positive impact on a patient's life.

After I fill French in on my background for about an hour, he finally goes over the questions he's going to ask me for the polygraph in five separate rounds. In the first round, he tells me to intentionally lie in response to the question "Are the lights on?" so he can get a deception reading.

I'm sitting on a chair with a black pad on top of the seat as French straps a heart rate monitor around my chest and a blood pressure cuff around my right arm; the devices are hooked up to his laptop. He tells me to look straight ahead, keep my feet on the floor, not to shift my weight or contract my leg muscles or even take a deep breath.

French sits on the other side of the table, ninety degrees to my right. He delivers each question slowly and methodically.

"Well, your parents raised you right," he says after we finish the round. "It's obvious when you're lying."

Good, I think. *I'll pass this easily.*

But once we start the official test, I regret my decision. This is torture. Each painfully slow round takes two to three minutes for only seven questions. My arm is throbbing, and my hand is starting to get cold from the lack of blood flow. I desperately want to take a deep breath to calm my nerves but that's against the rules. I feel like a mannequin in a display.

After each of my answers, he pauses to look at the screen. My mind is racing. I know I'm telling the truth, but I have no idea what my responses are showing him, if my body is betraying me. If I'm too calm, will they think I'm a sociopath? If I'm too nervous, does that tell them I'm lying? What is the appropriate response in my body? I have no control over that. This is a nerve-wracking situation and the stakes are high. How can they possibly distinguish between a lie and an increased stress response from fear, fatigue, and anxiety? Heart rate and blood pressure change in a similar way. The science to this seems to be flawed. I'd look at his face to see if I can tell from his expression, but I'm not allowed to move my head.

I reflexively tried to look at him once when he asked me a question, but when I started to turn my head, he barked out, "Look straight ahead."

So I do as he says. Between staying completely still and being unable to tell how I'm doing, I've never felt so much pressure, not to mention that my answers have the power to change the course of my life. The feeling is so awful I find myself wishing I were back in the room with Mustard. At least there I was free to move and breathe.

It's hard to convey how traumatizing the whole experience was. Even today, the slightest reminder, like getting my blood pressure taken for a routine doctor's visit, sends me back into that room. Here's a tool that has helped thousands, if not millions, of people stay healthy, and now it's a trigger, a warning to me that I'm about to enter a dangerous situation, even when I'm not.

At last, it's finally over. French takes off the heart rate monitor and blood pressure cuff, and I rest my head on the table for a moment, relieved to finally be able to move after sitting so still for the past half hour. He tells me to sit in another chair near the far-left corner of the room, then angles another one to my right and sits down. He scoots the chair closer so our knees are only a few inches apart. He leans in and I feel myself recoil. I assume it's going to take him a little while to analyze the results, so I am not prepared at all for what he says next.

"Aaron, there's no question in my mind that you failed this test."

I feel sucker punched, like I'm lying on the ground and all I can do is put my hands up to try to protect myself.

"There's no question in my mind that you know what happened to Denise and where she is."

Why won't anyone believe me?

French puts his hand up in my face.

"I need you to listen to me now," he says. "I think an accident happened; something you didn't intend to happen happened. And you do not know what to do. You've been spiraling out of control ever since this happened and you do not know what to do. And you are scared. Okay?"

I attempt to defend myself, and he waves his hand, dismissing me.

"You've had your chance to talk," he says. "I have a duty and an oath right now. That duty and oath are to convince you to do the right thing because that's how you're wired to do it. You're wired to help people and do the right thing. . . . We wanted to give you the benefit of the doubt because of who you are, what your family is, and give you that elimination test. And you failed it *miserably*."

Barely pausing to take a breath, he goes on a tirade for the next twenty minutes, never changing his position, saying many of the same things Mustard said to me. He never uses the word "frogman," but other than that, there is little difference between their tactics, except French ratchets it up a notch.

The FBI isn't my savior. My faith in them was completely misplaced.

French uses all the information I've given him about my family to try to get me to confess, saying that with a father who's an ER doctor, I have a lot to live up to; that I might have cracked under that pressure and made a mistake; that my family is going to go bankrupt trying to prove my innocence, so it's better I just admit to what I did now before it's too late.

"If you continue with this 'I don't know what happened to Denise. She just disappeared. She just vanished. These three people that I never saw zip-tied me' . . . you are going to dishonor your family, your father, your mother, and your brothers," he says, "and you're going to lose everybody's respect. . . . I believe you sought out this profession because you want to help people. You are in the helping business."

There is altruism throughout my family, he points out, rattling off each of their chosen professions like I don't know it already.

"I'm absolutely convinced that something you did not plan happened," he says. "Something bad happened to Denise and you got scared."

Each time I try to speak, he cuts me off.

"Now listen, the FBI has dealt with kidnapping for ransom—*legitimate* kidnapping for ransom—and this doesn't even pass the smell test. Okay?" he says. ". . . It was an accident, wasn't it? Just acknowledge it was an accident."

"No!" I am finally able to get a word in, but he doesn't miss a beat.

"It's not true. Okay? It's not true. Stop clinging to this because it's making you look *worse*."

How can anyone withstand this type of pressure? I now have the full force of law enforcement—the FBI, the Vallejo police—browbeating me to admit to something I didn't do. You're supposed to be innocent until proven guilty, but it's clear that in their eyes I'm guilty. They are the judge and the jury, and they've already made up their minds.

If I didn't before, I now truly believe there are innocent people in jail. It's no longer something I read about in the news, an abstract idea that will never touch me. I'm going to be one of those people dragged off to jail proclaiming his innocence, and old high school acquaintances will tell their friends how they always knew something was wrong with me. I'm scared of going to jail. I won't be able to handle being caged up. I won't be able to handle having my life ruined.

French, sensing my despair, leans forward in his chair so his face is less than a foot away from mine and puts his hand on my shoulder. It's an almost fatherly gesture but all it makes me want to do is slap his hand away. He's positioned himself so he is sitting between me and the door, though I have no intention of trying to leave. If I do, if I stop cooperating, then I've lost any chance of convincing him I'm telling the truth, especially since he told me that I failed the lie detector test.

But I haven't given him the confession he clearly expects, so he's not done with me yet. He keeps going for another twenty minutes, now trying to use Denise's family to get me to admit I killed her, saying I should confess so they can find her before she decomposes or is "chewed up by animals" and her family can have some closure.

"Have you ever seen a body that's been left, thrown into the ocean? . . . Do you think the mother and father would love to see what happens to it? They would love to have something, something to hold on to, to put into a casket. . . . I know that you cared about her."

As he's saying this, images of the kidnappers leaving Denise's body in the woods to be devoured by animals flash through my head. But I refuse to believe she's dead, that there's no hope. Until I know for sure, I'll keep fighting for her to be found.

"Yeah, I do care about her," I say firmly.

"Okay, you can tell me what happened," French says, clearly annoyed.

"And let's not go down the 'someone abducted her' route! What happened?"

"That's the story I have."

"It's a story—that's exactly right!" French interrupts, pointing his finger at me like I've finally slipped up and he's caught me.

And with that, my frustration boils over, finally outweighing my terror of talking back.

"It's not," I say, my voice firm and strong. "You guys are the ones who keep saying that! This is what happened! Where did the camera come from?"

"You tell me where the camera came from," French replies, a little flustered.

"I don't know where!"

"It came from *you*."

"How?"

"Ah, uh, you tell me how," French stutters, clearly stumped by my question and perhaps a little perturbed by the new way I'm now challenging him.

"I didn't get that camera. I never put that camera up there. I've never seen that camera."

"No one took her except for you."

"I did not take her."

"You know where she is and you know what happened to her," he says.

I try to respond but he puts his hand in my face. "Hold—hold on. . . ."

Finally, I've had it. I realize I could be stuck in here for days, having this same conversation over and over, like some horrific version of *Groundhog Day*. It doesn't matter if it's Mustard or French. They are saying the exact same thing and are refusing to look at the evidence that points elsewhere. I've held off on asking for a lawyer because I had this naive belief that only guilty people need lawyers. But now I know you need one to protect yourself from the police.

There's only one thing I can do, though it's still a difficult decision to make. The police are my only hope of finding Denise. I don't want to alienate them, but I can't take any more of this psychological torture. I have to get an attorney, or this will never stop. I'm pretty even-keeled—if anything I hold in my feelings too much—so I do my best to rein in my emotions when I respond. It takes every ounce of courage I have to say what I say next.

"I guess I need a lawyer," I blurt out, then rush on, the words almost tumbling over one another in my terror over the possible repercussions of what I'm doing.

"I don't know what else to do right now, but I don't know where she is. We can stay here and that's what happened last time, but I don't know where she is. I didn't do anything to her. I did not hurt her. So I guess I need a lawyer because you guys don't believe me. I don't pass this. I don't whatever. But I didn't do anything. I will stick to what . . . happened. Because I did not hurt her. I did not do anything to her. We had a great night. I woke up to guys blinding me and everything I told you guys. I thought they were just going to rob me. I was hoping they were just robbing me. Then they took her. . . . I want you guys to find her. I want you guys to find her! I don't know where she is. I didn't do anything to her. So I guess I need a lawyer."

French's response when I finish is silence. Utter silence. He sits with his hands folded in his lap and stares at me for at least a minute. I know from Ethan this is a strategy designed to get people to talk but I'm not going to say another fucking word to him. Eventually, he stands up and starts packing his equipment. He's moving at a snail's pace, so it takes him a good five minutes.

I put my head in my hands, staring at the dirt on the cheap gray carpet. This is the first time he's stopped talking in the last forty minutes and the silence is a relief.

"Are we done here?" he asks as he heads toward the door.

The question throws me off. I can't understand why he's asking me this. I have had no control over anything that happened since entering the police station.

"Are we?"

"You're answering questions with questions. Are we done here?"

He sounds like an abusive father scolding his child, like I've done something wrong by asking for an attorney.

"Are we done? Yes."

"I'm asking you a question because we are now going to proceed with this, and other conversations are going to be had with other people."

It seems like both an attempt to get me to change my mind and keep talking and a veiled warning that they are going to charge me with Denise's murder now that I've stopped cooperating.

It doesn't work.

"Okay, yes, we're done," I reply as French stares at me. He opens the door to the interrogation room, and before leaving, he points at me to stay, like an owner telling his dog to sit. He heads down the hallway to communicate something I can't make out before coming back into the room to finish packing.

Before he leaves, he grabs a box of tissues and slams them down on the table next to me.

"There you go."

The message is clear: He believes I'm a cold, calculating monster because I haven't cried, that an innocent person would be in tears. But my body is still in fight-or-flight mode and it simply won't let me cry because if I do, there go my defenses and I'm vulnerable to their attacks.

After he leaves, I get off the chair and curl up into a ball on the floor in the corner of the room, my arms wrapped around my chest, a futile attempt to find shelter and comfort in this room, which has neither. I've lost all hope that I will ever see my family again without bars separating us. And I'm having a hard time understanding how I got to this point, how I could be attacked by the very people I went to for help.

"What's going on? What's going on?" I whisper to myself, tears starting to well up now that I'm alone. "I didn't do anything. I didn't do anything."

Whom can I turn to now? Whom *do* you turn to when the heroes turn out to be the villains?

And how in the hell am I going to find an attorney when I'm trapped in this room?

8

JOE QUINN HAD a bad feeling from the moment his son Ethan called to tell him Denise had been kidnapped and Aaron was at the Vallejo police station. A thoughtful, kind man with a comforting air about him that undoubtedly reassured the thousands of patients he'd treated over the years, he knew in his gut Aaron shouldn't talk to the police without an attorney. He'd told Ethan that. He'd dealt with police for most of his career and knew how they thought when a spouse or a girlfriend disappeared: Aaron was going to be their prime suspect.

But Ethan told him that legally Aaron had to be the one to ask for a lawyer, not them, and Ethan was not only an FBI agent, but he had a law degree to boot.

Now here they were, stuck outside the room where God knew what was going on with Aaron. They'd been here since 6:30 p.m. Joe didn't panic easily. He used to say that when the crap hit the fan, he *was* the fan, but right now he was beside himself with worry about his youngest son. There was nothing he could do to help Aaron.

Ethan was a doer, so sitting still for hours on end just wasn't in his nature. He was just over six feet tall, slender and fit from years of training for ultramarathons. He'd joined the Army and served six months in the

Middle East before going to law school, starting out as a lawyer before joining the FBI in 2009. He worked white-collar crimes and corruption and had already handled some high-profile cases, including one that led to a prison sentence for a state senator. He had faith in law enforcement. He *was* law enforcement. It didn't even occur to him his little brother might need protection from the very people he was going to for help.

But as hour after hour passed with no word about Aaron, he was starting to get worried too.

Initially, he'd assumed this was a virtual or fake kidnapping. The Bureau received reports fairly often from victims who got a call or email from someone claiming to have kidnapped a loved one—usually someone who had posted on social media about being on vacation or was otherwise unreachable—and demanding a small ransom. The victims paid before realizing it was a scam and their loved one was safe and sound. These happened so frequently his supervisor had listed it as a threat to look out for when he took his turn as duty agent, the person responsible for answering off-hours calls.

Stranger kidnappings, on the other hand, were rare. Had he thought this was a real stranger kidnapping, he would have called the police instead of telling Aaron to do so, but it just hadn't seemed possible. Yet Aaron had sounded genuinely terrified as he told his brother about the kidnappers breaking in, taking Denise, and demanding the ransom be split into two payments of $8,500. He'd been speaking in this nervous whisper because he said the kidnappers were monitoring his phone. This was what kept going through Ethan's mind on the hour-long drive to his brother's home.

Once he arrived and saw Aaron sitting on his front step, being guarded by a police officer, he knew there was nothing fake about this kidnapping. That had just been wishful thinking, maybe even denial, on his part. If it had been fake, the police would have been interviewing Aaron inside his home, not preparing to search it, as they were clearly starting to do now.

His little brother looked stressed and tense, his shoulders drawn in, a far cry from his usual confident body language. When the police finally let him talk to Aaron, it was clear he was nearly out of his mind with worry about Denise, telling Ethan that the police weren't listening to him, that they'd disconnected the camera the kidnappers had left to watch over him, that the kidnappers might be killing her *right now* while the cops destroyed evidence, that the police seemed to think he'd lost his mind. "*I* don't think you're crazy," Ethan reassured him, both to let him know he didn't need to spend any energy convincing *him* of that and because he was acutely aware of the officer standing right next to them, listening to every word.

A few minutes later, as he watched an officer drive away with Aaron in a patrol car, he was already regretting not telling his brother to get an attorney. It was a regret he would carry with him for years.

Though Ethan arrived at the police station not long after Aaron, and the police let him wait in a side room instead of in the lobby as a professional courtesy, it was an hour before a detective named Mustard came to speak to him. Ethan told him what little he knew. Afterward, he finally called his parents to fill them in. He'd put that call off as long as possible, not wanting to upset them unnecessarily, still hoping this was all some big misunderstanding that would be resolved quickly, but it was clear now that wasn't going to happen. Though it was dinnertime when they spoke and rush hour was in full swing, his mom said they'd leave immediately. He tried to tell her to wait, that this could be a long night, but her only concession was to hold off until after rush hour to make the ninety-minute drive.

Marianne was small in stature but as feisty and outspoken as her husband was quiet and reserved. She was a bundle of energy, still running three miles a day though she was in her sixties. She wasn't sure how they could help Aaron, but at the very least he'd know they were there, or so she thought. Throughout that long night, she repeatedly pressed the police on whether they let Aaron know his parents were at the police station, but she never got an answer.

When it was Joe and Marianne's turn to be questioned, they were escorted back to a conference room where Detective Sean Kenney was waiting for them. He seemed nice, something Marianne would marvel about later when she discovered he'd killed three unarmed men in the space of five months in 2012 and had the highest number of officer-involved shootings in the entire department over a twenty-year period. Not only was he cleared of any wrongdoing in those deaths, but he got a promotion afterward. Thankfully, though, Marianne knew none of that at the time.

She and Joe answered every question Detective Kenney threw at them, all questions painting her son in the worst possible light. When he asked if Aaron had a temper, they told him the truth: no. Desperately trying to convince Kenney her son was not the violent, spoiled rich kid Kenney's questions seemed to indicate the police thought he was, she even told the detective that Aaron got the "Boy of the Year" award his senior year of high school, that it was a big honor, how it was something the faculty voted on, not the students, and was a tribute to his leadership skills. She still had the plaque proudly displayed on the wall of their hallway at home, but Kenney just didn't seem interested in hearing *anything* positive about Aaron.

Joe told him he couldn't recall Aaron ever even having a confrontation with someone, let alone being violent, but Kenney was more interested in the Quinns' net worth. They were comfortable financially, but that was because they had always worked hard, saved their money, made good investments, and lived simple lives. Joe still drove a 1996 Ford pickup truck and used a flip phone, and when Aaron wanted to upgrade to a smartphone after his flip phone died when he was in graduate school, he had to convince Marianne it was worth the extra money. Aaron still drove the 2000 Camry she'd given him when he was in college. Joe and Marianne were always there for their children and always would be, but they did not spoil them and never had.

Aaron had delivered pizzas in high school and cleaned swimming pools in between college and graduate school. He worked with Kaiser's most impaired at their flagship rehab center in Vallejo, which was why he lived on Mare Island. He had taken out and paid his own mortgage. He knew his parents were always there to backstop his life, but he didn't want or need that.

Joe and Marianne told Kenney all of this, but it didn't convince him their son was innocent. In fact, as they were walking out of the interview room, Captain James O'Connell pulled Marianne aside to say the story Aaron was telling them was bizarre, that they believed Denise was dead but hoped she wasn't. She asked him point-blank if Aaron needed a lawyer, but O'Connell insisted Aaron had to be the one to ask for an attorney. Though he didn't come right out and say it, his next words made it clear he thought Aaron had murdered Denise. She nearly passed out, and quickly sat down in a nearby chair to steady herself. She left the room more shaken than ever, fighting the urge to throw up. She didn't have the heart to tell Joe and Ethan about her conversation with O'Connell. It was hard enough for her to absorb all of its awful implications for her youngest son.

So they sat there for hour after hour. They saw women they later found out were Denise's roommates being brought in for questioning. They watched while Lieutenant Kenny Park held a news conference outside the police department and said Aaron's car had been found in the parking lot of the VA clinic on Mare Island, though nobody bothered to tell them that.

With nothing else to do but think, Joe's mind began to work overtime. None of this made any sense, a kidnapping for such an odd amount of money. Maybe Aaron and Denise had gotten into an argument. Maybe Denise had fallen down the stairs. Maybe Joe didn't know his kids as well as he thought. They'd left home, gone to college, lived their own lives. Maybe they were not the people he believed them to be. Maybe. Maybe. Maybe.

Around 2:00 a.m. they heard Aaron's voice through the wall for the first time; he sounded like he was being read his rights. Ethan couldn't help but wonder if the police had moved him to another room closer to his family to put pressure on Aaron, hoping he'd hear his mother cry out or something and it would make him feel bad enough to confess. And Marianne almost did just that. She wanted to jump up and bang on the door and yell for him to ask for an attorney, but she was scared that would only make things worse for her son. Then Ethan spoke up, voicing what everyone was thinking, but too afraid to say.

"He's being arrested."

In his mind, he could actually hear the click of the handcuffs being secured around his brother's wrists.

Marianne collapsed on the floor, sobbing. Joe's chest hurt so badly he thought he might be having a heart attack, so he took the anti-arrhythmic medication he kept in his wallet for emergencies. He had recently undergone treatment for stage IV malignant melanoma, which was now being held at bay by immunotherapy, and he feared the stress was going to bring on a recurrence. He visualized talking to Aaron on a phone while looking at him from the other side of a glass barrier. He saw himself going bankrupt in his son's defense. If that was what it took to prove his son's innocence, so be it. He asked Ethan again if they could get Aaron a lawyer, but Ethan still insisted that Aaron had to be the one to make the request.

When there was still no word by 4:00 a.m. and an army of media began to gather outside, they decided to call it a night and check into a hotel in Vallejo. Ethan was starting to get really worried about his father. He looked exhausted.

After they settled in, Ethan took a shower, collapsed into bed, and fell asleep, only to be woken an hour or so later by a call from Mustard asking him to come back to the station.

When he arrived, Mustard asked him to talk to Aaron, claiming he had failed a polygraph; that he was telling "crazy stories" about "cameras in the walls." Be sure to look at his eyes, Mustard said, because Aaron's pupils looked dilated, which was a sign of schizophrenia.

Maybe I'm wrong. Maybe Aaron really did kill her, Ethan thought. *These are competent professionals. They did their due diligence.*

He agreed to go see what he could find out.

9

DENISE

AFTER HE HAS his way with me, the Voice guides me to the bathroom so I can shower and remove any evidence of his body from mine.

"You can take the goggles off when you are alone in the room now," he says. "I left some toiletries on the counter for you. I know this has been a lot on you. It's the least I can do. Just remember, we will know if you try to remove the covering on the window. When I come back, be sure to put the goggles back on and turn away before I enter."

He is talking softly, his voice tinged with regret and guilt like I imagine an abusive spouse would treat his partner after going on an alcoholic rampage.

I wait for a breath or two after the door is closed to ensure he is truly gone. It's a relief to finally peel off the goggles that have been suctioned to my eye sockets for over half a day. As I bring them over the top of my head, taking a few snarled strands of hair with them, I see myself for the first time since before the kidnapping.

I stare blankly into the eyes of the emotionally and psychologically beaten woman in the mirror in front of me—someone I don't even recognize as myself. I note the dark circles under her eyes, the eyes glazed over with that lost and helpless look. My heart breaks for her, and I want to help her, hold her, tell her everything will be okay. But she is a ghost I cannot touch. I'm still so detached from my emotions I can't even bring myself to cry.

On the counter are travel-sized bottles of shampoo, conditioner, and toothpaste, a toothbrush, and a comb, all brand-new, unused, neatly lined up for me.

They even thought of toiletries?

I take these and this new freedom of sight in his absence as they are intended, rewards for good behavior. I've been a good girl.

I pick up the toothbrush and brush my teeth, comb my knotted hair, and take a shower.

When he takes me back to the bedroom, I ask him what time it is to try to orient myself. I'm able to tell if it's night or day and see shadowy outlines if someone steps in front of the light when I'm wearing the goggles, but I can't see much else. I'm surprised he gives me such a detailed answer about the time.

"It's about six p.m. We left Aaron's house before sunrise, drove about forty five minutes before we transferred cars, and then it took us about three to four hours to get here, arriving around ten a.m."

He then tells me I will have to take another liquid dose of a "benzo," insisting that it's "protocol." The container of liquid feels like it's the size of one of those 5-hour Energy drink vials.

Later that evening, he brings me dinner: pizza and a salad he had delivered. I passed out again after that last dose, and when I wake, the food is neatly arranged on the dresser with a formal place setting and dining chair set up. I eat what I can and gulp down the wine he brought.

All I want is to be unconscious, anything to escape this.

HE COMES IN the next morning to check on me, and I ask if he's heard from Aaron, how he's doing, if anyone's tried to contact me through my phone, and if he thinks I will be released in time for me to return to work the next day.

He pauses, speaking to me in a slow, soft tone like he's talking to a naive child and it's cute that I'm even asking.

"I don't think you realize the severity of the situation and how you will be affected by this," he says. "It is going to be something that will take a long time to recover from. Work is the last thing for you to worry about."

At first, I am irritated that *he* would have the audacity to tell *me* how I will deal with the situation. But then I wonder if it actually bothers him that I'm not showing more fear. If I did, maybe it'd make him feel more powerful, which gives me even more reason not to let him see it.

I ask if he's sent the recording of us from the day before to his associates and if it was what they wanted. He brushes off my concerns, saying he hasn't heard yet.

Not long afterward, he says the "others" are going to stop by in a half hour or so to check on the setup here and make sure everything is in order. Because of that, he will have to zip-tie me to the bike lock linked around the rods at the top of the bed. Again, he warns it's in my best interest to pretend like I am asleep, not to say a word. They may not be as nice as he is.

This news sends a wave of terror through me, so I ask him to sedate me again. Not only do I want to hide from all of this, but I'm also worried panic will consume me when they arrive, to the point where I can't control myself and will say or do something to provoke them, give them a reason to attack me. How can I trust that these people won't come in and force themselves on me? How do I know they won't just decide to kill me and dump my body?

He obliges, giving me the drink, but the effects take some time to kick in.

I HEAR WHAT sounds like a truck engine, higher from the ground than the car from yesterday, slowly approaching the house over a dirt road, stopping directly in front of it. Truck doors open and close; the front door opens.

They're here.

Please, please leave me be.

I hear them open the bedroom door behind me. I am wrapped in the blankets with my back to them, my hands tied over my head, holding my breath as they stand in the entrance.

Thankfully, they leave, closing the door behind them, and I can finally exhale. I hear movement and sounds on the other side of the wall, more than one person could make. There is still music playing, so I am able to decipher only faint whispers, but I can sense heated energy beyond the wall, like a difficult conversation is taking place. It's that energy that makes the hairs on the back of my neck stand up.

What will they decide to do with me?

After about twenty minutes, the front door opens, and I hear the truck start up and slowly back away from the house. As it leaves, the Voice comes in and says, "They're gone. They won't need to come back."

Oh, thank God.

He removes the ties on my hands and leaves me as I pass out again.

An hour or so later, he's back, telling me this time that he needs to record what he calls a "proof of life." I don't know what this entails, so he explains it to me as he coaches me through it. I will need to identify myself, say I've been kidnapped but am fine, prove it's today by relating an event from the news, and prove that it's me by giving some personal detail that only those close to me would know.

I sit at the edge of the bed, barely able to hold myself up; the effect of the drugs is at its peak. We go over each piece of the statement I will record again and again, making sure I repeat everything just right. When he decides I've got it, he gets the recording device ready.

"Okay," he prompts me to begin.

"Okay . . . I am Denise Huskins. I am kidnapped. Otherwise, I'm . . . fine. Umm . . . earlier today there was a plane crash in the Alps. A hundred fifty-eight people . . . died. Umm . . . and . . . one thing that not many people know about me is that my first concert I went to with Bethany and her mom . . . to Blink-One-Eighty-Two and Bad Religion."

I am completely wiped out after I finish recording.

It was so stressful, trying to pay attention and remember all the things he wanted me to say, especially since it took all my effort simply to stay awake, let alone think. I wonder how I will sound to anyone who hears it. I know I don't sound like myself. My voice is dead. Flat. I slur the "s" after "Huskins" and "Alps," the sedatives he gave me making my speech sound thick and drugged. Saying that I was fine was one of the hardest things I had to do. I wasn't fine. Nothing about this was "fine."

When I finish, he says that he got it, that it's good. I immediately plop back into the pillows.

TIME IS GETTING fuzzy as minutes blend into hours. My only orientation to time is the hue of light that breaks through the edges of the cardboard-covered windows, and I assume it's now the afternoon when I wake again. I know I need to eat, so I walk over to the dresser and grab a bottle of water and a breakfast bar, forcing myself to choke them down.

For a while I lie in bed, trying to fall back asleep. Waiting is monotonous, and I just want this day to end. The drugs that have kept me knocked out or numb are wearing off. Without them, I'm not sure I can handle the truth of how this will most likely end, because situations like this rarely turn out well. I believe I'll be killed, and I feel like at any second the horror of all this will sink in and I'll become hysterical. I'm afraid if I cross that line, I'll never return. I know I need to stay lucid if I have a chance in hell to survive.

I close my eyes, and a swirl of emotions and images floods through me. Hope is hard to hold on to, but I'm trying. I picture being stuffed into that trunk, engulfed in darkness, but then a flood of light blinds me as the trunk opens, and a familiar silhouette stands above me. As my eyes adjust, I see it's Aaron, his piercing green eyes looking down at me with sheer gratitude and love. I am finally safe.

I tear up as this fantasy plays over and over again in my mind.

My heart breaks at the loss of our relationship, of what could have been, of the family and memories we could have shared together.

I am overwhelmed with memories of my parents, my brothers, my family, my friends. Now I truly understand what the phrase "your life flashes before your eyes" means.

I think of all the hard work it took to get me to where I am today.

For as long as I can remember, I have known my life's work would one day center around helping others. When I was in second grade, I wrote that I wanted to be a nurse when I grew up so "I can take care of people and be nice." Even then, at age seven, that was what inspired me.

School was my comfort zone. Teachers complimented me on my behavior, on how I worked well with others, and for my diligent learning style. I tried to lead by example, rather than speak up in a group, because I hated, absolutely hated, being the center of attention. My emotions are painfully transparent, and even through graduate school, I would turn bright red answering questions in class. In that same second-grade notebook, I wrote how sharing in front of everyone embarrassed me. It's incredible how certain parts of our personalities are ingrained in us from the beginning, forming and shaping who we become and what we choose for our life's work.

It took me six years to get my undergraduate degree in kinesiology, exercise science, which is similar to premed for physical therapy school. I also minored in business entrepreneurship, hoping to own my own business one day, and graduated from California State University, Long Beach, in May 2009.

Despite the challenges I had in terms of self-worth and how I viewed my place in the world, my education was always my solid foundation, my guiding light. Despite the emotional struggles I had in my twenties, my focus was always on becoming the professional I knew I could be, to help others and lead a meaningful life.

I often visited a friend who lived in New York and I always hoped I could get my graduate degree for physical therapy there. The energy, the culture, the challenge of a new world in New York City hooked me. Its vibe was the complete opposite from the small beach town I grew up in. I worked multiple jobs in restaurants and bars and as an aide and volunteer in PT clinics and hospitals to put myself through college and prepare for grad school. I was overjoyed to be accepted to the doctorate program for physical therapy at Long Island University in Brooklyn, New York. My dream came true.

I was supposed to move to New York at the end of June 2009, but my dad suffered a stroke the day of my graduation in May, and I was torn about whether I should leave. Thankfully, he had a quick recovery, and over the next few weeks, I sat in on his physical therapy sessions at the hospital and watched him regain significant function. Seeing his transformation was yet further confirmation that this was what I was meant to do.

The first six months in Brooklyn were definitely a struggle, and I often called my lifelong friends and family in tears, but it was truly a perfect opportunity to challenge and discover myself in ways that might otherwise have taken half a lifetime. I grew tremendously, and after years of hard, dedicated study, I earned my doctorate degree in physical therapy in May 2012.

I worked for a year as a physical therapist in Boston, but after four years on the East Coast, three thousand miles away from family and friends, and one too many harsh winters, I knew I needed to move back to California. The final push was being mere blocks from the Boston Marathon bombing in 2013. My friends and I made a last-minute decision not to go to the finish line, just minutes before the bombs went off. It made me realize that anything can happen anytime, anywhere. And I wanted to be near the people I valued most.

I decided to go after the residency in Vallejo that had called to me since learning about it in grad school. I'm proud of myself for never giving up, for always challenging myself to improve.

I have so many plans for the future, but waiting to find out what the kidnappers will do, I realize that, at twenty-nine, I have accomplished more in my short life than some do in all of theirs. So if I don't make it to thirty, it will be okay. It *has* to be okay. If this is truly the end, I can go out proud and thankful for the life I have lived so far.

I feel everyone I have loved, alive or dead, with me, lifting me, forming a shell of protection around me. I feel the presence of my deceased grandparents, and the strongest at this moment is my grandmother, my father's mother.

She is the strongest woman I have known, the strongest person. She was a dedicated Catholic who did everything for her children and grandchildren, including putting up with the emotional abuse of my grandfather for most of her life. They had married much too young, when she was eighteen and got pregnant with my dad.

My grandfather was harsh and judgmental toward his children. He never established relationships with them, never pretended to be interested in their activities, never attended one baseball game, and never showed them any love or appreciation. He cheated on my grandmother over and over, but she was faithful to him for her entire life and continued to work for him, keeping the books for his business and investments. He made a fortune in real estate and business but used the money to control his family. Eventually, late in life, he started trying to get to know his grandchildren. When I was about nineteen, he offered to give each of us $10,000 a year as long as we met with him quarterly to prove we were investing—not spending—his money. He even made us sign contracts but would change the terms and requirements routinely so that it was hard to keep up with his demands. In the end, I think my brother Joey and I were the only ones who kept up with it. For most of my cousins, it was too late. He had already caused a lot of damage.

My grandparents never divorced, though they were separated for decades. After he died, we found out he wrote her out of his will, even though legally they were still married, and he went so far as to say that if she or anyone disputed his wishes, no one would get anything. He donated most of his money to charities, allotting each of his children only 1 percent of his estate, and each of his grandchildren 2.5 percent. Anytime he gave me or my brothers any compliment, he always used to say, "Good genes skip a generation," as he continued to criticize and belittle my father and his siblings.

My grandmother was conflicted about challenging his will in court, because of his threats, but we all encouraged her. And she needed the money to support herself, especially with her own health problems. She had an experimental lung surgery in the 1990s and was projected to live only another ten years after that. It seemed my grandpa had always thought he would outlive her. She was in and out of the hospital recovering from pneumonia, and she carried an oxygen tank with her wherever she went. But she wouldn't give up, fighting for her life, for her family. After a couple of years of battling the will, she won, of course. Not long after all that was settled, she passed away, a few days before Thanksgiving in 2013. Although her physical presence is no longer with us, her powerful spirit is within each of us, always.

Thinking about my family gives me comfort. I even sense the presence of people I don't know supporting me. I'm not sure if it's because I am desperately trying to pick up energy from anyone I can, or if it's an answered prayer—God's way of showing me that I am not alone. He may not be able to stop this horrible predator who holds my life in his hands, but He has shown me that I have the strength, spirit, and energy of so many to guide me through this ordeal. Even if death is the next step, I now have the courage to face it, with my powerful grandmother taking my hand to show me the way.

Despite what I may still have to endure, I am at peace. As I fall asleep, I pray that my family knows nothing about what has happened to me. I can't bear to think of them suffering.

10

BUT DENISE'S PARENTS *were* suffering. How could they not be? There is nothing that can prepare you for getting a call like the ones they'd each received from a detective Monday night with the shattering news Denise was missing, and the way the police were handling the situation was only making it worse. They weren't telling them much, just to "hope for the best but expect the worst."

What the hell did that even mean?

Neither of them knew, and if the detective thought those were comforting words, he was sorely mistaken. Jane and Mike Huskins were long divorced but still a united front when it came to their children, so Mike booked the first flight to Vallejo the following morning, hoping the police would be more forthcoming if he spoke to them in person, while Jane stayed behind in Huntington Beach in case Denise was released and somehow made it home.

But when Mike called late Tuesday afternoon to say the police had a proof-of-life recording they thought might be from Denise and wanted her to come listen to it, she and Devin, their youngest child, hopped on the first available flight to Vallejo. It felt good to be doing something proactive. She'd never felt so helpless and lost.

A petite, vibrant woman with softly curled blond hair, a warm smile, and kind eyes, she'd always wanted to be a mom. After several devastating miscarriages, her dreams came true: first, Joey; then, by some miracle, just sixteen months later, Denise; followed by Devin five years after that.

Her children were everything to her. She'd held the family together as a single mom after she and Mike separated in 1998 after nearly twenty years of marriage. The kids learned early to pitch in wherever they could, whether it was making their own dinners or doing their own laundry. There might not have been a lot of luxuries in their lives, but there was always, always a lot of love.

Now her daughter was *missing*? It had taken a while for that to sink in. Jane had even started off to work that morning, then had to pull over to the side of the road after she heard a story about the kidnapping on the radio. She just sat in her car and sobbed, as the reality of what was going on finally hit her.

The detective's words from the night before still rang in her ears.

"Your daughter's boyfriend reported earlier today that she was kidnapped, but we don't believe him, and he is in for questioning now," Poyser, the detective, told her. *The police didn't believe Aaron?* She was dumbfounded. She'd met him for the first time last month when she'd gone to spend some time with Denise in Vallejo. He was so nice, respectful, and courteous, with good old-fashioned manners. He'd taken her luggage out of the car for her and held open doors. He was very hands-on in the kitchen, cooking for them while still very engaged in the conversation. She fumbled for words sometimes, especially when she got emotional, and he assured her he understood what she was trying to say, endearing him to Denise even more.

Jane and Denise were more like best friends than mother and daughter and confided in each other about almost everything. They'd always been close, watching movies and making Toll House cookies together every Friday. One of Jane's favorite photos of her middle child was of Denise licking the cookie dough out of the bowl on one of those Fridays.

Denise was a happy child, always giggling and laughing, always eager to try new things, always wanting to do *something*. She played softball and volleyball, learned how to surf, whatever captured her attention. She was easygoing and creative, warm and thoughtful, and trustworthy enough Jane felt comfortable leaving her home alone when she was at work or at one of her sons' baseball games. Denise would make pillow nests on the couch, where she'd read books and entertain herself while the rest of the family was out. She loved being alone.

She never got in trouble as a child, never even talked back to her mom. She was also very truthful; in her one and only run-in with the law, when she got a DUI at age twenty, Denise immediately confessed. "I was drinking, and I drove," she told the police. "Take me to jail." That was what it said right there in the police report.

She also took it upon herself to pay her mother back for every penny she spent on her legal fees and fines. Her driver's license was suspended for a year and a half, so she'd wake up at 5:30 a.m., ride her bike to the bus stop, and take the bus to class, all without complaining. She rode her bike to and from work as well.

While police would somehow get the impression Denise came from a wealthy family, that wasn't the case. Her grandparents left money for her parents when they died, but for most of her childhood, her mom was scrambling to make ends meet while her father managed an apartment building his father owned in Huntington Beach.

BEING IN VALLEJO hadn't helped Mike get the answers he so desperately needed. He had no idea *how* Denise had even been abducted. *Was she kidnapped walking to the store? Or did somebody see her on the street and just push her into a car?* He still didn't know, though a detective did at least give him his card with a phone number on it and say Mike could call him anytime. Someone would always answer that phone, the detective assured him.

Mike was a tall, burly man with salt-and-pepper hair; despite his imposing physical presence, he was more like a big teddy bear. He wore his heart on his sleeve and hadn't slept a wink all night, worrying about his only daughter.

It didn't take long for the media to find him. A *Good Morning America* producer called him while he was in the process of renting a car at the Oakland airport, and he agreed to do an interview.

They asked about Aaron and Denise's relationship, so Mike told them what he knew, which wasn't much. He and Denise had gone to dinner the week before, and she'd told him she was really falling for Aaron, assuring her father he was a good guy, just like boyfriends she'd had in the past.

The *GMA* interview wasn't his last. Mike quickly became the face of Denise's family on television, his worry and fear evident with every word he spoke, pleading with the kidnappers not to hurt his baby girl.

"It's like a nightmare I can't wake up from," he told reporters, his voice shaking as he fought off tears.

"Please don't hurt her," he begged.

He was soon joined by Denise's uncle Jeff Kane, who arrived mid-afternoon Tuesday and took a ride out to Mare Island to see if he could find out more since the police were saying so little. Kane parked outside the police barricade at Kirkland and Reeves, the closest he could get to Aaron's home, and stayed for about an hour.

It was an absolute circus, with reporters and television crews everywhere. The media quickly got wind of his connection to Denise, and he gave them his name and number, hoping it would ease the burden on Denise's father somewhat. He'd honestly thought the whole matter would be resolved by the time he got there, that maybe Denise had gotten in a fight with her boyfriend and disappeared until they both cooled down. But it wasn't.

Kane went back to the hotel to meet up with Mike, who was feeling a little better after listening to the proof-of-life audio. It was one of the defining moments of Mike's life. He had left the station earlier that day, stopping down the road to finally eat and settle his queasy stomach, when Vallejo police called him to come back in. They didn't tell him why, so he was frantic as he rushed over, his thoughts racing with all the horrible possibilities. *Did they find her dead body??* After listening to the audio and confirming it was Denise, he was elated, which quickly shifted to confusion when the police left the room without saying a word. As Mike walked out, he passed by the investigators, who wouldn't even look at him. It was all deeply unsettling. *Weren't they happy she was alive? Maybe they needed more proof?*

He was still puzzling over their odd response when he got a call from a *San Francisco Chronicle* reporter who wanted a comment about the proof-of-life audio the kidnappers sent the paper. The reporter also told him the kidnappers had said, in the email accompanying the audio, that they planned to release Denise the next day, which the police had *not* told him about:

> As stated, Denise will be returned safely tomorrow. We will send a link to her location after she has been dropped off. She will be in good health and safe while she waits. Any advance on us or our associates will create a dangerous situation for Denise. Wait until she is recovered and then proceed how you will. We will be ready.

Somewhat comforted, though furious with the police for withholding that crucial piece of information from him, Mike fell asleep for a bit, then turned on the television to catch the latest news. He was stunned to see footage of police searching the swamps near Aaron's home with dogs and boats, clearly looking for a body.

Wait a minute. What's going on here? Didn't we just hear proof she was alive?

About a half hour later, a detective called to reassure him.

"You're probably seeing a lot of news out there of us going through the swamp, looking for a body," the detective told him. "We don't believe there is one but we're just looking anyway."

"This is very disturbing," Mike told him. "I heard the proof-of-life audio, and you guys are still looking for her body? What's up with that?"

"We're still investigating," the detective replied.

It was clear he wasn't going to get an answer that made any sense, so Mike just gave up.

That night, he and Kane went for dinner at a restaurant at the marina near his hotel and once again saw Denise's face plastered all over the news. Divers were now searching the bay waters near Vallejo for a body after sonar showed a human-sized mass, though so far they'd found nothing.

"We were just looking at each other going, 'Is this really happening?

This is insane,'" Mike said. "We just waited and waited and waited and heard nothing."

DEVIN WAS A blend of his two older siblings: athletic and competitive like Joey, who got a baseball scholarship to Auburn and played for the minor leagues, but sensitive, passionate, and analytical like his big sister. He and Joey both topped six feet tall and had lean frames, but Devin had Denise's blond hair and light eyes. During the divorce, he had been his mom's best friend, always there to listen and offer support, and he instantly agreed when she asked him to accompany her to Vallejo.

After Jane and Devin arrived at the police department around 9:45 p.m. Tuesday, they were escorted to a small crowded room littered with empty pizza boxes. But instead of asking them to listen to the recording, Poyser peppered them with a litany of insulting and insensitive questions about Denise for more than an hour.

Finally, he asked Jane if anything bad had ever happened to Denise, anything at all. Confused about what exactly he meant, Jane told him Denise had been molested as a child. She didn't know how this would help and wasn't sure if Devin even knew this about his big sister, but the detective was the professional, so he must have had a reason for asking. If he did, he never shared it with them. Instead, he abruptly left the room, leaving Jane and Devin more confused than ever. *Didn't they want us to listen to the recording of her? Isn't this why we rushed here?*

Poyser returned with another detective, Mat Mustard. He had a wad of chewing tobacco wedged between his cheek and gum and every so often spit into a cup he was holding. Mustard was intense and arrogant, but Jane and Devin were completely unprepared for what he said next.

"I just want you to know that in our experience, women who have been sexually assaulted before often pretend that it is happening again to get attention and relive the excitement and thrill of that experience."

Jane was so appalled and angry she could hardly think straight. She just stared at him, then at the spit cup, then back at him, and said, "You know, that's a *really* bad habit."

She wasn't a confrontational person, so it was the best she could come up with to let him know she wasn't happy about the way they'd been treated or the way he talked about her daughter.

Devin hurriedly apologized for his mom. He knew they needed the detectives' help if they were going to find Denise. But Mustard kept going. Every statement he made insinuated that Denise was somehow at fault. Finally, he told them the case was so "bizarre" that it sounded like the movie *Gone Girl* and suggested they watch it to understand what was happening.

They were speechless. It was such a callous, heartless thing to say.

When they were finally allowed to hear the proof-of-life recording, they listened intently, barely able to breathe, not wanting to believe that this could be Denise, that something like this could have actually happened to her. The voice was slow and groggy, the words drawn out, but the way she said "Umm . . ." between each statement convinced both Devin and Jane.

"Oh, my God," Jane whispered, "it's her."

And that was it. There was no reaction from the detectives. Nothing. Not only had they been treated like they were related to some hardened criminal instead of a kidnapping victim, but the detectives didn't seem to care they'd confirmed the voice on the recording was Denise, which was supposedly the reason they'd rushed to Vallejo in the first place.

Afterward, Poyser walked them out to their rental car, chatting all the while. "There's so much going on with this case. It's so bizarre," he told them. "I would like to be able to tell you everything I know about it five years from now."

What in the hell does that mean? Jane thought.

Neither Jane nor Devin knew how to respond to the detective's peculiar statements, and more than five years later, Poyser still hasn't explained himself. As they drove to their hotel in Vallejo, Jane was certain of only two things: Her daughter would never stage her own kidnapping, and Aaron would never do her such harm.

11

AARON

After demanding an attorney, I stay huddled in the corner on the floor for I don't know how long. Time does not exist in this place. Images of Denise's body facedown in the woods and my handcuffed perp walk with the TV camera lights blinding my eyes flash through my mind. Where is my family? Do they believe the police? I am all alone with no sign of help.

My legs begin to fall asleep from sitting on the hard ground. I grab the two nearest chairs to create another makeshift bed. I'm absurdly grateful that these chairs don't swivel, and curl up on my side.

I wake up from pain in my back. Exhaustion must have overtaken me again. I grab the third chair from across the room and put them all in a row so I can lie flat and give my back some more support. Together, they almost feel like a crappy IKEA couch, but in these barren conditions, I'll take what I can get.

I lie facedown on the musty seat cushions. It doesn't matter if they've never been cleaned. I'm numb and nothing seems to matter anymore. I can't be present in this room and I can't be in my thoughts. This is my only option to survive: disconnect from everything. This helps stop my mind long enough so that my body can fall into a fitful sleep. Each time

I wake up, there's a moment when I forget where I am, when I think I'm at home in my bed. The buzzing of the fluorescent lights and the smell of stale air quickly crush that hope. What if I never leave this room?

It's so cold I'm shivering, and I wonder if the police are cranking up the AC.

Suddenly, Mustard opens the door.

Oh, no! Not again!

"Aaron, your brother's here," he says.

Before I can even process that information, Ethan walks into the room. He's hunched down with his hands in the pockets of his windbreaker. His skin is pale, and his eyes are baggy under his glasses, but it's him. Tears flood my eyes. Finally, there's someone here to help me.

I start crying, big shuddering, gasping sobs.

He sits down beside me and puts his left arm around my shoulders. I grab him with both arms, pulling him toward me, and hug him as tightly as I can. I'm close to my family, but we are not huggers. Or criers. Maybe it stems from our New England roots, but we're usually stoic during stressful times. Now, though, every last emotional barrier I have has broken down.

"I don't know what's going on. I don't know what's going on," I repeat over and over through my sobs.

My tears eventually slow down, and I catch my breath. I pull back from him, holding my head in my hands, trying to explain what's happened, but it's all jumbled and disjointed phrases. I finally blurt out, "I'm telling the truth! I know it's the fucking craziest thing!

"I failed the polygraph, the fucking polygraph!" I moan. "I'm terrified. . . . I don't know where she is!"

I ask Ethan what time it is, and he replies it's about six a.m. and that my parents were with him until four. He finally convinced them to get a hotel room so they could try to sleep.

Of course they were here! This must be hell for them. Why didn't the police let them see me, even for a minute?

We go through what the police should be doing to find Denise— searching the area, talking with friends and family, examining the evidence: The camera mounted in my house (Where did I supposedly get that?). The emails sent by the kidnappers (Was I emailing myself back and forth after I killed Denise? Can't they look at the IP address to see where the emails were sent from?). My car (What did I do, drive it somewhere and take a cab back? There must be taxi records. And how did I tie myself up with zip ties?)

"They keep saying, 'You're an amateur making this story up.' I'm not making this up! It's a *stupid* fucking story." I wouldn't lie to them, but if I *wanted* to lie, I could create something more plausible.

"I don't know if they're going to let me back in," Ethan tells me after I finish. "I'm going to get you an attorney. You don't have to speak with them anymore unless there's something you forgot that could help them find Denise."

He's attempting to cover it, but when he repeats, "I don't know if they'll let me back in," I catch the fear in his voice. Then he leaves the room, and the only person who can help me is gone.

WHATEVER DOUBTS ETHAN had about his brother's sanity or guilt were erased as soon as they spoke. Aaron's pupils were normal, not dilated. He looked exhausted, that was all. And his eyes were red from crying, which was understandable. Other than that, nothing.

He'd asked Aaron if he'd told police there were cameras in the walls and he'd said, "No." And that was when it dawned on Ethan that Mustard had lied. When he walked out of the interview room Mustard asked him if he believed Aaron.

"I know I'm his brother, but I believe him," Ethan replied.

"What do you think we should do?" Mustard asked.

"He asked for an attorney and I think we should get one to mediate this," Ethan said.

"In my experience, that doesn't help anything," Mustard said.

"Well, in my experience, it does," Ethan responded.

Mustard shook his head and said, "We'll try something else."

Ethan had gone in there thinking it was remotely possible Aaron could have had some sort of nervous breakdown. Now he knew his little brother was telling the truth—but the police clearly believed Aaron was lying and seemed to be willing to do whatever it took to prove Aaron murdered Denise.

It was clear his brother needed a lawyer. Now.

He walked out to his car and called the public defender's office. It was still early, so he was only able to leave a message. He started googling "criminal defense attorneys" and "homicide" and "Vallejo." Daniel Russo's name popped up. He'd had some prominent cases and gotten good reviews from his clients, so Ethan gave him a call.

Russo was a seasoned defense attorney who'd been representing some of the city's most high-profile defendants for thirty years, from baseball great Tug McGraw's brother to a Superior Court judge accused of attacking his wife. At six feet three inches tall, with his thick New York–accented speech often laced with colorful profanities, he was just the type of scrappy fighter Aaron needed. He came from a working-class background, raised by parents who weren't able to complete high school because they'd had to work to support their families but who had held a deep and abiding respect for higher education and encouraged their son to take his grit, determination, and smarts and go as far as he could in life. Russo had worked his way through both college and night law school, taking whatever job he could find to pay the bills.

His parents had also instilled in him their fierce beliefs about standing up for what you believe in, no matter the cost. His father was a union organizer who sued his own union for racism and anti-Semitism in 1948. His mother had walked in the 1963 Civil Rights March in Washington, DC, and was a member of Women Strike for Peace, a group rallying against nuclear weapons testing in the nineteen sixties. So it was no wonder he wasn't the least bit afraid to take on the Vallejo police or the FBI. Fighting injustice was in his blood.

Though it was barely 6:00 a.m., Russo was already in his office, and he picked up the phone when Ethan called. Ethan quickly explained the situation and Russo told him to come by his office, less than a mile away.

After a brief discussion Russo said he'd head down to the station to talk to Aaron. It was already clear he was going to be a formidable force on Aaron's behalf. As Russo walked out the door, he turned to Ethan and said, "Hey, listen. Let me take this on."

It was such a simple thing to say, maybe something he didn't think twice about, but for Ethan it was a huge relief. He felt like he'd been carrying the weight of his brother's dilemma on his shoulders and it was a heavy burden—one he was glad to hand off to someone else who was a professional.

Ethan went back to the hotel and let his parents know he'd hired Aaron an attorney, who would be in touch after he spoke with Aaron. He walked out in the hall to call his girlfriend, Kathryn. "The cops think he killed her," he told her; then, at last, he broke down sobbing.

"I just had this total feeling of complete, abject helplessness and worry," he later recalled. "It's the most helpless I've ever felt in my life."

He'd been trying to keep it together for his parents. He didn't want them worrying about him too, especially his father.

"Dad said, 'If Aaron killed her, I can't go on,'" Ethan said. "I think he would have killed himself if Aaron had killed Denise. I don't think he could have lived with it. It's one thing to have a kid who screws up. That's life. It's another to have a kid who actually hurts someone."

12

A MEMBER OF THE Vallejo Police Department since 2001, Mat Mustard was one of its most high-profile detectives. His name and number were often the ones next to the "if you have more information" plea for help from the public at the end of crime stories in the local newspaper, and as head of the local police union, he was frequently quoted about contract negotiations or the latest police scandal, of which there had been plenty lately.

Most recently, he himself had come under scrutiny for pressuring the coroner to declare a death a homicide instead of an accidental overdose and convincing the prosecutor to arrest the victim's boyfriend while acknowledging there wasn't enough evidence to prove his guilt. "My opinion is that if we do nothing else, he gets away with murder . . . and another victim of his violence is just a matter of time," Mustard wrote in a September 2013 email to Solano County prosecutor Andrew Ganz. "I think we have done enough cases that have more obstacles than this one, and we need to throw it against the wall and see what sticks."

Even though this strategy ultimately ended with the boyfriend's acquittal and Ganz's law license being suspended for prosecutorial misconduct, Mustard was showing that same bulldog tendency with Aaron and using the same strategy: throw everything against the wall and see what sticks. Only this time, despite his best efforts, it wasn't sticking. He would later offer this rationale for why he didn't believe Aaron:

> *Based on my past experience investigating crime, I found it implausible that unknown persons, wearing scuba gear, would break into the home through unknown means in the middle of the night, with headphones, soothing music, and prerecorded instructions; that they would drug their victims and check their blood pressure; that they would bring Mr. Quinn downstairs with blankets and books for the night; that they would set up a fake camera, fooling a smart and educated man like Mr. Quinn for hours; that they would move Ms. Huskins' car from the driveway so that they could abduct her in Mr. Quinn's car; and that after going to such elaborate lengths, that they would demand such a small ransom.*

Though investigators were careful not to point the finger at Aaron publicly even as they called it an "alleged" kidnapping in their internal communications, reporters were picking up on the nuances, wondering why Aaron waited several hours to call the police even as they were careful to say he was neither a suspect nor a person of interest.

LOCATED JUST ON the outskirts of wine country with its luxurious resorts, Michelin-star restaurants, and boutique hotels, Vallejo was a troubled city. Its financial problems and high unemployment in the wake of the Navy yard closure led to the inevitable surge in crime. It routinely made the list of the most dangerous cities in California.

The city had finally emerged from bankruptcy in 2013 after years of cuts and employee concessions to bridge the budget gap, but its reputation still hadn't recovered. Forbes.com ranked Vallejo one of the ten most miserable cities in the country and it was number two on *Newsweek's* list of dying cities.

Those financial troubles had spilled over into the police department. With just a hundred members, its ranks were at an all-time low and its relationship with the community was in an equally precarious state. A series of scandals and questionable police-involved shootings had tarnished its image and shaken the community's faith in those sworn to protect them.

The new chief was Andrew Bidou, who had less than six months on the job. He'd arrived in Vallejo in October 2014 with nearly twenty-five years in law enforcement under his belt, most recently in nearby Benicia, where he'd successfully implemented community-oriented policing during his eight-year tenure as chief and deputy police chief. Bidou was tall and trim with a full head of brown hair and a youthful face; his friendly demeanor had already earned a vote of confidence from the Vallejo newspaper, which listed his hiring as one of the top ten stories of the year.

He came with an impressive résumé. Not only did he have a master's degree, but he'd completed management training at the FBI National Academy and a series of leadership and executive programs at Cornell University and the Harvard Kennedy School.

He arrived certain he could handle any challenge that came his way, pledging to rebuild the cash-strapped department's depleted ranks—though his $250,000-a-year salary had to rankle the overworked and underpaid cops he supervised, and the department's cushy pension plan was partially responsible for the city's financial woes to begin with.

Bidou was keenly aware of the issues and, just four days prior to Denise's kidnapping, had announced he was launching a new police advisory group made up of Vallejo residents, handpicked by him, who would work hand in hand with the police to address issues in the community.

He'd seen a lot during his career, but he'd never seen a case quite like this one.

Neither had Captain James O'Connell. He was in charge of investigations, reporting directly to Bidou, and oversaw a team of detectives, including Mustard and Kenney. He was just days away from retirement after more than thirty years in law enforcement, some of them in the US Army, twenty-two of them with the Vallejo Police Department. He too was well educated, with a bachelor's and a master's degree in criminal justice. O'Connell had been a member of the city's hostage negotiation team for fourteen years, though kidnappings were a rare occurrence in Vallejo and none he had worked on ever involved a ransom demand. Sexual assault cases crossed his desk more frequently, at least once a month. Throughout his time on the force, he'd attended numerous trainings and conferences to enhance his knowledge of violent crimes and victim behavior, though he would fail to use that knowledge when it came to Denise.

As word spread about her abduction, the department found itself under siege. Frantic residents already alarmed by a rash of recent burglaries and a Peeping Tom on Mare Island were inundating them with calls. Crime had increased since the police had closed a substation on the island a few months earlier, locals told reporters, and this abduction had them terrified.

The heavy police presence on the island only amplified their fears. A long white Winnebago-sized police command vehicle was parked outside Aaron's home while police used search dogs to comb his neighborhood and the marsh behind his house, with TV crews and photographers capturing their every move. About a half mile away, police coordinated search efforts in the parking lot of the local VA clinic, where Aaron's car had been found.

The community's concern was so great that police were forced to hold a meeting at 4:30 p.m. Tuesday. It was standing room only.

"We're not going to give out any information, but we wanted to respond to your concerns," Bidou told the fifty to seventy concerned residents who attended.

He answered general questions during the thirty-minute meeting, doing his best to convince them they were safe.

"It was a very demanding crowd," he would later say. "They were legitimately scared, and they wanted answers. We told them that we didn't believe there was a direct threat to them. . . . We didn't believe it was a random act, that they needed to be fearful."

If only that had been true.

13

DENISE

I WAKE AND NOTICE the room is still lit with a light orange hue. It must still be afternoon on Tuesday. I don't hear much going on in the house, just music playing, and the light hum of the washer and dryer.

I can't lie still anymore. I need to do something.

I can feel my anxiety slowly returning as I worry about what will happen next.

I need a way to escape, to find some peace and shift my focus onto something else. I know movement can help restore and calm the system, so I get down on the floor to do some Pilates exercises, focusing on my breath and slow, meditative movement. Six months before moving to Vallejo, I took a comprehensive Pilates course. I plan to get certified, hoping to blend physical therapy with Pilates and maybe start my own practice one day.

As the light becomes a deeper orange, I hear a knock from my captor. After he takes me for a bathroom break, he tells me they lost contact with Aaron.

Lost contact? Is he hurt? Is he dead?!

The Voice said his group had some "tasks" for Aaron. He never said what they were. Did they ask for an amount of money he didn't have? Did they make him do something dangerous? Or did he just seize an opportunity and escape?

"Either he went to the police or did not want to follow through with what was asked," the Voice says.

I don't believe for a second Aaron would just ignore the danger I'm in. What if he did go to the police? Will I get rescued? Or could that make my situation even worse?

"Even if Aaron went to the police and there is a lot of media coverage, it doesn't worry me," the Voice continues. "It'll be good PR for our group. It will show we can be successful without harming the captive."

Wow, really? They really think they can outsmart the cops? Or maybe he's just trying to convince himself they can.

I'm still not sure how honest the Voice is being, and I'm concerned about Aaron's safety, but also, I tell him, I'm afraid he's going to kill me because of this. The Voice assures me that's not true. "The plan is still to release you," he says. "Even if it came down to that, if that's what the others decide, I won't go through with it. I have an escape plan for me and my family that I would use before it ever came to that."

An escape plan? Oh, good. I'm glad you have some moral compass to limit what you will do! You can put me through everything else you already have, but you'll book it instead of killing me?

It's hard to believe that this is a legitimate possibility. With all that he's told me, with all that he's done, why would he ever risk setting me free? If Aaron is no longer communicating, then how will there be a drop-off? Who will pick me up and where? What incentive does he have to release me?

I have visions of some of the ways this could end: the police knocking down the door and the Voice killing me and himself before they get to me, or a high-speed chase where he drives off a cliff with me in the trunk. I can't trust what he says!

"I don't know who hired us," he goes on. "Another associate is in charge of that end. Different parts of the operation are contained to keep things clean in the event that something gets exposed along the way. Since I'm in charge of watching over the target and having direct communication with her, it is a risk for me to know who hired the group. This ensures my compliance and prevents the identity of the client from being revealed."

He then asks me about Jennifer, what I know about her and if I have any clue as to why someone would hire their group to abduct her, like he is trying to uncover the truth himself, to determine the level of danger we both may be in.

I don't know how to answer this question. I cannot fathom who would want to do this to *anyone*. I tell him I don't know much about her, just the little I know from Aaron.

"Does she come from a wealthy family?"

"I don't think her family has a ton of money," I say. "I think maybe her ex-husband comes from a wealthy family."

The Voice breezes past that, saying, "Mm, no . . . I don't think that's it. Is there anything else?"

"The only other thing I know is that she and Aaron ended their engagement because she cheated on him with some police officer in Fairfield. But I really don't know much else." I almost didn't mention it. I never considered it could be significant.

He pauses for a minute, takes a breath, and says affirmatively, "That sounds right. That must be it."

How could that be it? Is he saying he thinks the cop hired them? But as my mind spins with everything that's happened in the last thirty-six hours, it kind of starts to make sense: the military-like nature of the home invasion; what sounded like a police radio; the information they had on Aaron; the Voice saying they had been in Aaron's home the week before, ready to enter the master bedroom, but were then "called off" because there were too many "police units" on the island; how he demonstrates no fear that he or his group will get caught.

The Voice said they watch their victims closely afterward and know if they go to the police. Is that because someone on "the inside" alerted them if the target came forward? He leaves me alone again to process all of this. It actually makes sense that a police officer might be involved . . . which horrifies me even more.

NOT LONG AFTER, the Voice is back.

I shrink inside myself. I know what's coming.

He says his associates watched the recording of us and it's not good enough.

"You know what? Let me read exactly what they said."

He leaves the room to get his phone, then comes back. Although I'm still blindfolded in his presence, I can tell by the direction his voice is coming from that he is holding his head down to read something in his hand.

"The recording must be believable. You have to look like a legitimate couple who has been having an affair for a while, like this isn't the first time you've been together," he reads. "She can't wear the goggles. You must kiss and say things to indicate that this is an affair. It must seem like you're both enjoying it."

He tells me he isn't sure yet how he would do this without the goggles, without the risk of me seeing his face. He says he needs time to figure it out.

When he comes in again, I tell him I have an idea. I think of the book *Fifty Shades of Grey* and suggest that we use a necktie over my eyes like we are playing some kinky game. I just want to get this over with, so I'll do anything to speed up the inevitable.

He seems almost awestruck as I offer this suggestion. "You are incredible, how strong you are with all of this. But I found some tape that I can put over your eyes. So that way it will just look like you have your eyes closed."

He says he has to prepare and get some things. Before he leaves, I ask him if I can have wine again. He casually replies, "Of course. Red or white?"

"I don't care."

He returns quickly, placing two glasses of wine and a couple of small bottles of booze on the bedside table. He leaves again to get whatever he needs to "prepare." In his absence, I take one of the glasses and chug it, then choke down the bottles of booze. The thought of what is to come is unbearable. Not only will I be violated, and just lie there letting it happen, but this time I can't just detach from it. I have to give the performance of a lifetime to save my own life.

I have already started on the second glass when he knocks, announcing his return. I hurriedly put the goggles on, somewhat ashamed I downed the alcohol.

"Oh, heh-heh, you started without me," he jokes awkwardly. "That's okay."

He hands me clear packaging tape and leaves momentarily while I secure it over my eyes.

"It's time," he says as I hear him position the recording device on the dresser.

I search carefully for the second glass of wine with my hand. I find it and down what's left.

He begins the same way, taking my clothes off. Then he removes his clothes, puts on a condom, and climbs on top of me. My eyes reflexively try to open but the tape allows only enough space to see the top of his head. His hair looks dark, maybe a little wavy, and the light through the cardboard on the window is giving it a brownish red hue.

My eyes shut tight again as he starts to kiss me. The only way I can do this is to pretend like it's Aaron that I'm kissing, it's Aaron I'm holding. But with every kiss, every touch, it is so obviously not him. Instead of Aaron's full, soft lips, these are thin and firm, and I can feel his pronounced chin pushing into mine. This body on top of me is cold, rigid, lean, with that same nervous aggression bubbling below the surface. Like his hands, his back is dry, coarse, like he has back acne or dry, flaky skin. It feels like this body on top of mine has had the warmth of life removed from it.

I try desperately to ignore all of these things, to pretend. I say things to this monster, things I would say to Aaron.

I cringe as I say each word, feeling like I am betraying Aaron, like I am cheating on him, but I can't do this again. I can't let them have any excuse to make me do this again. I won't survive.

I become more vocal as the act continues, repeating phrases that I know men like to hear. I am trying to say things to encourage him to finish quickly, trying to end it as soon as possible. Finally, it's over.

My head is buried in pillows and the comforter, and I feel my eyes well up with tears.

Don't cry. Don't let him see you cry.

I get up quickly, asking him to take me to the bathroom. He has taken everything from me. I just want to be alone.

Once I'm alone in the bathroom, I peel off the tape, which has become gooey and sticky from the tears piling up underneath it. I get a glimpse of the mirror out of the corner of my eye, but I can't even look at myself.

I am so ashamed.

I get in the shower and sit in the tub, knees tucked up into my chest. I squeeze my legs, holding my head in my hands, and I silently sob with the water beating over me.

Please, God, let that be the last time.

14

AARON

A COUPLE OF HOURS after Ethan leaves to find me an attorney, the door opens and a tall, balding man sporting a gray mustache and thick square-rimmed glasses comes into the room.

"Aaron, I'm Dan Russo. Your brother hired me to be your attorney," he says. "We're going to get you out of here, but first, the police want to take a DNA sample. I know you've already given them one, but we'll let them take another.

"If they decide to arrest you, don't fuckin' talk to anyone. If you talk to anyone, they'll use it against you. I got a bail guy. I'll be able to get you out in a couple of hours unless they charge you with murder. Got it? Don't talk to anyone. Okay, let's go."

I have no idea if he's any good, but I have no choice but to trust him. And I'll follow anyone who will get me out of this police station.

As we walk down the hall, I can see the lobby through a small door window on the other side of the room.

Freedom.

Mustard is standing next to a couple of people who look like techs.

He tells me that they are going to take my fingerprints and do a cheek swab for a DNA sample.

I've already done this. Why are we doing this again? Just get me out of here!

It seems to take a long time, much longer than before.

After it's over, Dan hands me a garbage bag full of different articles of clothing. "There are camera crews setting up outside," he explains. "You can't go out in those clothes. Look through this bag and find something to change into."

I find my size and there, in the small room right outside the public lobby, in front of five strangers, I have to strip naked again to put on a pair of khaki pants and a white button-down shirt. Even without socks or underwear, I feel more like myself now that I've shed the jail uniform. I fold the Solano County prison pants and stained white T-shirt, then hand them to Mustard.

He takes the clothes and offers a handshake.

"I wish you the best of luck," he says.

I hold in my rage and shake his hand.

"Yeah" is all I can say.

"No, I mean it," he says, staring into my eyes. "I wish you the best of luck."

On the surface, he sounds like he might be sincere. He almost fools me into saying, "Thanks," but the memories of last night stop me.

"Yeah," I say again.

I turn to Dan, who is standing next to a big guy he introduces as his associate, Mike. He's probably six feet two with muscular shoulders that look like mountain ridges. He reminds me of a gladiator.

"It's a little before nine, so there shouldn't be too many cameras yet," Dan says. "But they want nothing more than to get a shot of you. All these reporters know me, so when I leave, they'll follow me. I'm going to the right and you're going with Mike to his car."

Mike takes over. His voice is a deep baritone you'd expect from a guy his size.

"You will see my SUV across the street on the left. The windows are tinted. Get in the back on the driver's side. Don't look around. Just walk straight to the car. I'll take you to Dan's office."

This is clearly not the first time they've done this.

We head out to the lobby. Through the glass double doors, I see four or five news vans parked on the street. Their large antennae are raised; a couple of reporters are standing next to the camera guys.

This is why the fingerprints and DNA sample took so long. They wanted me plastered across the news, preferably in the prison clothes they'd given me to wear.

But our ruse works, and the photographers and TV cameras don't get a shot of me. The tinted windows in Mike's SUV provide me even more cover as he drives me the short distance to Dan's law office. He asks me when the last time I ate was and if he can get me some food. He says he can't go to my house because it's a crime scene, so he'll go to Target to buy me some clothes. There's genuine concern in his voice. He's treating me like a person and not a cold, calculating monster. I will forever be grateful for that kindness.

We arrive at the law firm and Mike leads me to Dan's office. We pass a signed E-40 album in the hallway. I almost laugh.

Of course Dan represents E-40. Why wouldn't he represent the most famous rapper from Vallejo?

My friends and I have listened to E-40 for years, dancing to his music in college, pretending that we're cooler than our terrible dance moves. I wonder if these funny moments help me keep my sanity during the worst time of my life or if I've already lost my mind.

I sit down in a chair across from Dan's desk and he quickly arrives after us. He tells me that he and his partner, Amy Morton, will be representing me, but because of his current workload, Amy will be the lead attorney on my case. She walks into the office and introduces herself. She's a small woman with dark shoulder-length hair and a raspy voice; she has a calm, quiet way about her, the polar opposite of Dan's frenetic in-your-face energy.

Amy informs me that my family is coming to the office, but we need to go through the last few days' events before I can see them.

We go over the days leading up to the home invasion, the home invasion itself, and the day at the police station. After we finish with my statement, Amy leaves to find my parents and brothers. My brother Matt had arrived earlier that morning, rushing down to Vallejo to bring my father his heart medication.

As soon as my mother sees me, her tears begin, and we embrace, sobbing. Then I turn to hug my dad, who begins crying with long, heavy heaves. I've never seen my father cry before.

He's the epitome of a stoic New Englander. My dad was adopted, left on the doorstep of the Quinns, who took him in despite having nine children of their own. His adopted father died when Dad was only nine years old. He grew up poor, but he excelled at school and went to college on a scholarship, then worked his way through the University of Vermont medical school. As an ER doctor, he was always dealing with life-and-death situations. I've seen him exhausted; I've seen him stressed; I've seen him angry; but I've never seen him break down. I can never forgive the police for that.

I hug both of my brothers.

"I didn't do anything," I say to everyone. I'm not sure what the police have said to them, but I can tell that hearing me deny these accusations reassures them.

Dan returns to the room and asks everyone to gather around.

"The Vallejo police are the most incompetent, corrupt police force around here, and they will do everything they can to railroad this kid," he said. "Be prepared for that."

15

DENISE

AFTER THAT SECOND act, my spirit is depleted. I am barely able to hold on to any hope—hope that depends on trusting this man and his continued promises to release me.

If the forty-eight hours come and go, and he makes up some reason, any reason at all, not to let me go, I will be forced to drastically change my strategy. If he doesn't release me then, he never will. So I'll have to avoid swallowing the drugs to keep my wits and my strength. Any resistance will be a fight, a fight to the death. And I intend to win. I have a lot to live for. But for now I just listen as he comes in again to discuss the drop-off.

"Aaron has gone to the police," he tells me. "He will not be able to pick you up. People are looking for you. It is on the news. I will not be able to drop you in the Bay Area. It's too hot right now with people searching. Do you have any family in Northern California, friends, anyone close to you?"

I tell him that everyone's in Southern California and apprehensively disclose where my parents live. He could find out from my driver's license anyway, and the thought of reaching family is too tempting to ignore. My mom lives a mile from my dad, so I could try to get to either one of them. He asks what I'd do if my parents aren't home, if they're both up in Vallejo.

Why would my family be in Vallejo? I guess I've been in denial until now, naively hoping that they don't know, that I am dealing with this all myself, sparing them the worry. I don't have the emotional capacity to think about the pain they must be in.

"Well, if they're not home, I have many friends and family who live in that area. I will be able to find someone."

I think of one of my aunts who lives a few blocks from my dad, and my childhood friends whose parents live blocks from mine, or even my next-door neighbors I have known my whole life. I will be able to find someone.

I don't care. Just let me go.

"Okay," he says, and we decide on a cross street that's less than a mile from my mom's house.

He then asks me if my family has any money, and I immediately regret everything I just told him.

Oh, no, what have I done? What is he going to ask of them?

"I am not asking you because we plan to get a ransom from them," he says, sensing my hesitation. "I am asking if your family has money because you will need to hire an attorney."

I'm so confused by that last statement I start to stutter. "W-what? W-why?"

"To protect yourself," he says. "Because Aaron went to the police, you will have to speak to them, and they will ask you a lot of questions. You can answer them, but you will want an attorney with you to protect your rights. The average attorney costs about five thousand dollars. Do you think your family can afford that?"

"I, uh, I . . . Yes, I believe so," I respond, dumbfounded.

He says he'll discuss the drop-off plan with the others and asks if I want a TV in here so I can watch a DVD.

"You deserve it."

THE NEXT TIME he knocks, it has been dark out for about an hour. He takes me on another bathroom break and tells me, "I have to give you another benzo. It is protocol."

I welcome the drug, knowing that it will be a long, hard night of worrying if I don't.

He comes in shortly after, telling me that he has something to show me, a news report he wants me to see. With the goggles on, I sit up in bed. Standing over me, he hands me an iPad, saying I can lift the goggles to read it.

The thought of trying to look up at him is fleeting. I don't *want* to see him. It's easier to go through this picturing him as a blurred figure.

The article begins by stating that twenty-nine-year-old physical therapist Denise Huskins has been missing since early Monday morning, and that Aaron Quinn called police Monday afternoon, reporting that his girlfriend had been kidnapped.

Girlfriend?

This is the first time I ever heard Aaron refer to me this way. The irony doesn't escape me. I'd wanted him to claim me publicly as his girlfriend for months. He finally does, quite literally, and these are the circumstances.

I keep reading.

My father is quoted, urging me to stay strong. "If she sees this, I want her to know that the family is there, we love her, and we're not giving up."

Before I finish reading the sentence, I choke out a loud sob. Those heartfelt words from my father shatter my composure, breaking through the numbness that has been protecting me throughout this whole horrible ordeal.

I fold into a ball and cry. My body crumples to one side, away from this creature who is causing me insufferable pain. I feel him put his hand on my back, consoling me as my body convulses with each gasping sob.

"I am sure this finally feels real now, seeing it in writing," he says.

"No," I say between sobs, "that's not it."

I am barely able to speak. The words come out in a whisper.

"I just . . . I just can't imagine what my family is going through right now."

He stands over me as I continue to cry. I am so lost, so desperately in need of comfort from another human being that I shamefully ask, "Can you hold me?"

He climbs onto the bed and stiffly wraps his awkward limbs around me. I sob into his chest as he attempts to console me. I'm immediately embarrassed and ashamed of my actions.

I feel completely and hopelessly weak, shattered. I timidly turn away, trying not to insult him.

"Thank you. I just need to be alone right now. Please."

He gets off the bed and leaves.

That piece of shit.

He broke me.

LATER, HE FEEDS me dinner, gives me more wine, and discusses the plan for the morning. He says we should leave by 2:00 a.m. and that it'll take about eight or nine hours to get there because he'll be taking "back roads."

As promised, he brings in a TV. He puts on a French movie with English subtitles, which I can't follow as my eyes blur and my lids get heavy from the sedatives. I quickly pass out. The next time I wake will either be the first day of the rest of my life . . . or the end of it.

16

AARON

DAN AND AMY think it's best that I go to my parents' house after our meeting.

"You've already given the police plenty of statements," Dan says. "Every news reporter will be looking for you. If the police need you, they know how to contact us."

I don't want to leave. To run and hide while Denise is still out there. I need to stay and help. But what can I actually do? I told the police everything I know, and it didn't matter. I can't get into my house. I can't access any of my accounts; my parents and brother had to use their credit cards to pay the $15,000 retainer for my attorneys. French's remark about my family going bankrupt defending me runs through my head. What that asshole doesn't know is that my family would rather be broke than have me admit to a crime I didn't commit. But I still feel like an anchor that's weighing everyone down.

The drive eastbound on I-80 takes about an hour and a half. Fortunately, I'm able to sleep most of the trip in the backseat of my parents' car. I walk into my childhood home and instantly feel protected by its familiarity.

We're at the house for about fifteen minutes—we haven't even unloaded the bags—before Amy calls me. A surge of energy pumps through me as she says the police received a proof-of-life recording from the kidnappers, and they believe it's Denise. The police want me to come back to the station to listen to it. I reply that I will be there as soon as possible.

I refocus myself; I need to rush back to Vallejo because this could be time sensitive. I run out to tell my parents, who are ecstatic but also exhausted. I see in their faces there's no way they can drive. I'll do it. I don't have an ID and my nerves are shot, but I don't care about the risks. I need to get Denise back.

As I drive, my head is whirling with possibilities.

Maybe the police are contacting the kidnappers? Maybe they'll be able to trace the recording back to her? The kidnappers must want to speak with me. They need my voice. Otherwise, if it's emails, the police would respond back to them. They have my passwords.

I fight the urge to drive a hundred miles per hour, and I safely get us to my attorneys' office.

My father is adamant that I don't go back to the police station. He believes this is another trick by law enforcement. They're looking for any slipup to arrest me. He may be right, but what if he's wrong? I'm not going to take that chance. And this time I will have protection from Amy and her paralegal, Samantha.

It's about 6:30 p.m. by the time we get there. Mustard called to let us know we can come in through the back to avoid the congregated media presence. The media population has exploded since I left at 9:00 a.m. We make a right turn into the station's back parking lot, and I see a variety of police vehicles, cars, vans, and one armored Humvee that's painted black and looks military grade.

Why does Vallejo need that? It's a war machine.

Mustard is there to open the door. He greets me with a look of familiarity, as if we're friends. This time he leads us away from the interrogation rooms toward the opposite side of the building. I feel the gaze of every officer burning through me as we pass among the cubicles. I look straight ahead. They are not going to intimidate me again.

We continue down the hallway and I see a group photo hanging on the wall. It shows twenty or thirty officers posing around the Humvee, all of them in tactical gear, wearing sunglasses and holding shotguns or other heavy firearms. Everyone is displaying their best tough-guy look.

They believe they're at war.

We walk into a large conference room already full of people sitting around a rectangular table.

A man at the head of the table, probably in his mid-forties, with a disarming smile and a warm voice, introduces himself. He's Special Agent Arvinder Ginda, or Agent Vinny as he tells me to call him. He's a hostage negotiator.

Finally!

Also in the room is Special Agent Jason Walter, Solano County deputy district attorney Karen Jensen, Captain James O'Connell, and a few other people whose names I immediately forget. It's clear that Agent Vinny will be in charge.

"I know you were here for a while yesterday answering questions [*understatement of the year*], but I'm catching up on this case, so I'd like to ask you a few more questions."

If you're just catching up, then get out of the room! Denise has been kidnapped. Catch up on your own goddamn time! What have you been doing?

I politely respond that I'll answer any questions.

So I go back through the entire home invasion for the fourth time in two days. However, this time the FBI agents' questions, particularly Walter's, are focused on the kidnappers and not my recent relationship struggles. Walter speculates the kidnappers have a military or police background based on the language and tactics they used during the home invasion. I've held this belief as well and maybe I'm being naive, or hopelessly optimistic, but I feel Walter believes me. Yet I don't understand why they're not playing me the proof-of-life tape. Isn't that the reason I'm here? After about an hour, Vinny decides we should take a dinner break. He feels that I'm losing my strength.

After twenty or thirty minutes, an officer returns with food from McDonald's. People make awkward small talk while they eat their burgers and fries. I eat a few bites, struggling to stop myself from screaming at everyone to pick up the pace, because there's not an ounce of urgency in the room.

Agent Vinny finally directs me to a laptop and says they're going to play the proof of life for me. I lean in toward the computer's speakers as if being next to the recording will somehow bring me closer to Denise.

The same composed but strained voice that I heard during the home invasion comes through the speakers.

I picture Denise blindfolded, robotically repeating the lines fed to her. I need to find her, scoop her up, and carry her back to her family. Her voice is next to my ear, but she's lost, and I have no way to find her. Only the devil would play these games.

I confirm that it's Denise's voice. Agent Vinny asks me what I think about the message. *Why would my opinion matter?* I reply that she sounds scared. *How else would she be?*

They bring in my phone for me to examine it. I'm slightly confused about why I'm going through my phone when the FBI has expert analysts.

I see concerned messages from friends; missed calls from my best friend, Brandon; and countless others, many from numbers I don't recognize.

The pain they must be going through, the pain of being in the dark.

I hear Samantha speaking over my shoulder as I scroll through the messages.

"It's on airplane mode. Aaron, your phone is on airplane mode," she tells me.

I look at the upper-right corner of the screen and sure enough, the little airplane symbol is there.

Airplane mode?! Why would the police put my phone on airplane mode? What if the kidnappers are trying to call? This doesn't make sense.

They instruct me to take it off airplane mode. As soon as I do, a flood of new messages explodes through my phone. My voice mail reaches its maximum limit as text messages keep pumping through. My eyes can't keep up with the storm.

Once they stop, I scroll through the new messages. Again, most are from friends or from the media. We listen to the voice mails from unknown numbers. Most of those are from the media, but a few contain silence and I dread that it was Denise waiting on the other end of the line.

Then I'm asked to log into my email on the laptop. I log into my Live
.com account. I already see there are dozens of new emails. Some contain
the typical business emails alerting you about a sale. Others are from the
media. Then I come upon one that has already been opened.

It's from AARON, the way the kidnappers had been communicating
with me the previous morning.

The email was time-stamped Monday, March 23, at 7:46 p.m.:

> We will call you at about 9 pm on your mobile phone. Your liaison will
> be the same contact as during the acquisition phase. Please verify that
> you have received this message.

There was a follow-up email at 8:13 p.m.:

> We are waiting on your acknowledgment

It's now Tuesday, March 24, after 11:00 p.m., and there's not a response
to either message.

Nothing, fucking NOTHING! And I can see someone opened it.

Yesterday Mustard told me nobody had tried to reach me.

My vision violently shakes, a haze of red on the periphery. If people
are talking, I can't hear them. I've never felt this unbridled rage before.
I've kept my composure for hours and hours, but now I feel like a wild
animal wanting to lash out. I'm losing control.

What's wrong with you people? Are you trying to get Denise killed?

"You . . . There was . . . My phone—" is all I can sputter out as my
rage short-circuits my thought process. I keep trying to speak but I can't
form sentences. The pain and anger are all-consuming, eating me alive.

Then I picture Denise, blindfolded, cold, scared, and alone. She's my
beacon guiding me back to what's important: finding her. So I exercise a
Herculean level of self-control; the red recedes, my vision steadies, and I
settle back into my body. I point my finger directly at Agent Vinny and
firmly say, "We're going to talk about this more later, but what do you
need me to do now? What do we need to do to get Denise back?"

The room is taken aback. In a way, I even surprise myself. Then again, I've always been able to maintain my composure and focus during stressful situations. This trait helped me to play quarterback in football and to cope in code blue situations at the hospital, though I could never have imagined I'd need that skill for something like this. But I know if I get angry, it will only alienate the police and FBI agents, and right now I need their help. Letting my emotions take over is the most selfish thing I could do right now. It's not about me or how I feel.

Agent Vinny, slightly annoyed, responds, "We need to reestablish communication, so we'd like you to write back."

Who cut it off in the first place?

"Okay, what do you want me to write?" I ask.

"What would you like to write?" Agent Vinny replies.

"I don't know! You're the expert. You tell me."

I can't believe this guy. He's the hostage negotiator, not me.

Agent Vinny starts dictating an email. I make a few changes to better reflect my word choices:

This situation has been going on longer than what I had expected. I was hoping by now we would have come to a resolution. However, I am very concerned about Denise. Please provide me with some evidence that Denise is well and that you [are] caring for her. I expect you to be providing the care that you promised. I will also be sending a text message please respond quickly so we can end this.

We write a similar text message.

What a joke, I think. Denise's photo is all over the news. I'm replying at 11:40 p.m., more than twenty-four hours after the kidnappers' last email. Only a fool would respond.

Agent Vinny tells me that they will let me know if the kidnappers answer, but nevertheless, they would like me to come back the next day. They decide I should come back at noon so I can get some sleep, as if sleep is even a possibility.

Before we leave, Agent Vinny says to me, "If the kidnappers ask for a ransom, we cannot legally provide that money. It's against our policies. Would you be willing to provide the required amount?"

Bullshit!

I can't believe they would leave someone in the hands of kidnappers because of money, but I immediately reply, "Of course. It's never been about the money. I'll pay it, or if they ask for more, I'm sure my parents will help. I can't trust these guys, but I don't care about the money."

It's clear that Agent Vinny doesn't like that answer. He was expecting me to balk at the thought of giving up my personal funds. It leaves a bitter taste in my mouth from an already disgusting night, but at the very least, I feel that Agent Walter believes me.

Samantha, Amy, and I drive back to Amy's office around midnight; then I head to the hotel, where my parents are staying. I fill them in on what happened, then try to sleep.

It's the first time in nearly forty-eight hours that I'm in a bed, and I pass out.

A FAR-OFF ALARM starts in my head, but rapidly becomes louder and louder, like the siren of an ambulance barreling down the street. . . . Wake up, wake up, wake UP! My eyes pop open; my heart jumps into hyperdrive. I'm ready to fight or ready to run. Yet there's no floodlight, no red laser sights. It's dark, quiet except for the soft breathing of my sleeping parents. I turn to see the clock.

It's 3:00 a.m., the same time the Voice woke us.

I focus on slowing my breath, attempting to quench the internal wildfire raging inside of me. *You are safe. Denise is alive,* I repeat to myself, which gives me a brief respite until my fears come roaring back. *They're going to kill Denise and your family. They're going to make you suffer because you called the police. You should have paid the money.* I battle this losing war until the sun mercifully rises.

I'll wake up at 3:00 a.m. almost every night for the next year. To this day, it's a blessing to sleep through that hour of the night.

17

DENISE

The next thing I know, the Voice is waking me.

"It's time."

He guides me to the bathroom for one last chance to relieve myself. Before we go out to the car, he says, "Wait. I have shoes for you to wear."

He comes back and puts the shoes on my feet, one at a time, while I stand, holding myself up against the wall for balance.

"Where did these come from?" I ask as he puts on the first shoe.

"We have them here for this reason. They should fit."

They even thought of shoes? Of course they did! When you take someone from their bed in the middle of the night, they aren't going to be wearing shoes.

He tells me that during the first part of the drive I'll be wearing the goggles, but when it starts to get light out, he'll tape my eyes shut and have me wear sunglasses in order not to look suspicious to anyone passing by.

He guides me outside through the back door, and into the passenger seat of a car. He tells me I get to ride up front this time. The comforter is lining the seat, which is tilted back. He tells me he has all my belongings, and the car starts up with a loud purr. We're off.

A glimmer of hope is quickly followed by fear. He could be taking me somewhere to kill me and dump my body where no one can find it. In fact, it's probably the most likely scenario. But for some reason, I do trust him.

Despite all that he has put me through, I believe him when he says he doesn't want to kill me. As fucked-up as this whole thing is, I feel we have developed an understanding, a trust. I have shown him that he can trust me not to scream, not to give him any trouble, that I can comply and be a good captive. He told me he would release me after forty-eight hours, and he's stayed true to his word. So, although fear and hope fluctuate back and forth, I decide the best thing I can do is not give him a reason to change his mind.

Just before we get on a freeway, we stop at a gas station. He tells me he'll get some water and snacks and asks if I want anything. "Parliament Lights," I reply. I've smoked off and on for years, but I never smoked around Aaron. I knew he didn't like it. Quite frankly, I don't like it. It's a stupid, horrible habit, and I'll eventually stop. But right now I don't care about any of that. A cigarette will relieve my stress and smoking is something to do to take my mind off the danger I'm in.

He climbs back in the car and, before heading off again, has me do the "benzo" routine. He says that because of the long drive, he needs to give me a double dose. I take the large bottle of water he hands me, and he suggests I drink as much as possible because I'll likely have a bad hangover tomorrow.

His concern is absurd, given the circumstances.

After that, he lights my cigarette, and I take a few puffs, then stop. "I'm worried I'll smell like an ashtray when I see my parents for the first time."

He laughs.

"I really don't think you have anything to worry about. Are you kidding me? They are going to be so relieved to see you, it won't matter what you smell like."

We both chuckle a little, which disturbs me on some primal level. I know I'm playing along with him to protect myself, but our relationship feels too cozy. I can sense how comfortable he is with me, as if we are friends, accomplices, Bonnie and Clyde.

I shiver in disgust, repulsed by what I have to do to save my life.

He tells me he's double-checked with his associates as to what I can and cannot say to the police.

"You can tell them everything I have told you, everything about our group, what we do and why we do it. You can even tell them about Jennifer. Everything. But there are two things that you cannot tell them under any circumstances. I want you to pay attention. This is very important. If we find out that you ever speak of it to the police, or to anyone, we will come back for you and your family. We now know where your family lives. For their sake, you must be sure to not say these two things."

"Okay," I answer fearfully. The drugs are kicking in, and I am trying to stay alert.

"You cannot mention that any one of us is part of the military. And you cannot mention anything about us having sex."

He repeats this several times throughout the trip. I assure him I understand.

"When you're released, just go straight to your family. Do not bring attention to yourself. If you cannot find them, ask to use someone's phone to call them so they can get to you," he says. "You will eventually have to talk to the police, but it is in your best interest to try to reach your family first. We will be watching."

He recites an email address that should be easy for me to remember, something with my name in it, in case I want to contact him or the group in the future. The drugs are completely taking over, and every time he tells me the address, it goes in one ear and out the other. I am fading.

"Okay," I say, knowing there is no way in hell I will want anything to do with him or his associates ever again.

A FEW HOURS later he wakes me, saying he's found a rest stop, so I can go to the bathroom before it gets light out.

Not until he's opening the car door and I have to stand up in the pitch-black darkness of the early-morning hours does it hit me.

Oh, God, we are in the middle of nowhere.

It is deathly quiet, and I can sense that there's not another living soul for miles and miles. If I scream, only the animals will hear.

This is it. Oh, my God, this is it. He's not taking me to my family. He just said that to keep me compliant. He's going to kill me!

I take step after step over dirt and rocks as he leads me. I get an image of a cliff, and picture him walking me to the edge and quickly pushing me off.

What an easy way to get rid of me.

And then I get a flash of him holding a gun to my head, ending my life with one loud gunshot, the last sound I will hear before it's all over for me. Or a swift cut to the throat, and then I could slowly bleed out in the darkness, choking out blood as I gasp my last breath.

Suddenly, I hear the echo of a door creaking and slamming shut behind me. The noise vibrates against concrete walls and my heart skips a beat in excitement. I lift the goggles, and sure enough, I am in a bathroom. I can't believe it.

It's a bathroom like you would see at a campsite, with concrete walls, a plastic toilet that dumps into a pit underneath, and a dinky metal sink hanging out of the wall.

I have never felt so grateful for such a simple thing.

I take a deep breath of relief. This is his last chance to get rid of me before the sun comes up.

My God. He IS going to release me!

I AM SO sedated I have only momentary bouts of consciousness during the rest of the drive. At one point he wakes me and hands me two small rectangular pieces of tape. I place them over my eyelids, under the goggles. He then hands me a pair of sunglasses to replace the goggles. I obey and pass out again.

THE STOP-AND-GO JOLT of the car wakes me. He tells me we're stuck in LA traffic.

LA? Really? Thank God! Are we really that close?

I notice it's daylight. It must be morning rush hour. I have never been so happy to be stuck in traffic. It's a comfort to know I am so close to home. I start to nod off again, my body slumped against the passenger door.

SUDDENLY, THE BRAKES slam. My body jerks forward against the seat belt.

What? Wait. Did we hit a car?!

"Shit! I bumped a car. Damn it! I'm going to pull over. I think it's just a little fender bender." The Voice is agitated as he pulls off to the side of the road. "I'll be right back," he says as he slams the door shut.

I am afraid, terribly afraid. What might happen if the other driver starts asking questions about me? My eyes try to open against the tape, and I see the black leather interior and white line of the exterior around the window through just a small sliver of my eyelids. Before I have a chance to react, he is back in the car, excited, out of breath.

"It wasn't anything. No damage was done, so we can keep going."

And just like that, the weight of my head drops again. I am out.

"WE ARE HERE," he says, waking me again. "I just need to find a safe, secluded spot for the release."

I feel the car speed up and quickly slow down as it makes turn after turn.

"I found it," he says proudly. "There's a little driveway out of view of the street."

I can hardly breathe.

Do I really get to live? Do I really get to be free and see my family?

Everything I had experienced in the past forty-eight hours flashes before me. Every heightened emotion, every horror, every threat, every hope. It's so overwhelming I can barely hang on to my sanity.

The car stops, then reverses a short distance before it stops again, and the engine becomes quiet.

"This is it," he says with a twinge of sadness as if he is saying good-bye to a dear friend. "Your strength through all of this has been admirable. Doing this, seeing what it does to someone, this isn't what I got into this for."

"You, you've said that before. Are . . . are you going to do it again?"

"No. No, I am done. I am done with all of this. And I have you to thank for that."

I naively believe him. It's uplifting to think that I may have potentially saved lives, spared others from this unspeakable horror, just by treating this guy with respect and understanding.

"I wish we would have met under different circumstances," he says. "You are an incredible person."

I hear him open and close the trunk. He opens the passenger door, takes my hands, and helps me out of the car.

"Count to ten slowly. Do not remove the tape until you know I am gone. We will be recording you as I drive off and will see if you do not obey."

I hear him walk away from me and around the front of the car. The driver's door opens and closes, the engine turns on, and he drives off, turning right out of the driveway.

One . . . two . . . three . . .

I wait for a few breaths after I hear his car fade in the distance.

Can it be true? Is this real? Is he really gone?

I slowly reach my hands up to my eyes and peel off the sticky strips, but I leave the sunglasses on. My eyes are fragile after not being exposed to sunlight for a couple of days.

I turn around and see my bags on the ground: my overnight bag, workbag, and purse. I look around and see that I am in a long alleyway between two apartment buildings. Directly behind me, there is a gate that looks like it leads to a parking lot for the apartments. There are a couple of windows and balconies overlooking the alleyway, but all is silent.

People are likely at work. The alleyway is black pavement with a white concrete gutter in the middle leading out to the street. Bright purple morning glories in full bloom line the fence on one side, their beauty almost ominous in light of what I've just been through.

I pick up all of my bags, wondering where exactly I am. I could be in a completely different town from the one he promised, hours from anyone I know.

I slowly move toward the street.

I look left, then right, and close my eyes, sighing in desperate relief. There, less than a quarter of a block from me, I see a street sign that reads UTICA, the street my mom lives on.

Oh, thank you, God. Thank you! I am home! It's over!

Part Two

SUSPECTS

MARCH 25 THROUGH JUNE 2015

Today there is no evidence to support the claims that this was a stranger abduction, or an abduction at all. Given the facts that have been presented thus far, this appears to be an orchestrated event and not a kidnapping.

—VALLEJO POLICE DEPARTMENT PRESS RELEASE,

MARCH 25, 2015

18

DENISE

My initial feeling of relief doesn't last long. Doubt and trepidation quickly replace it as reality sinks in. I may be almost home, but I am not free. Far from it.

I feel more like a bird with clipped wings just released from its cage. The bars that confined me are gone; the restraints that bound me are cut. But my freedom is an illusion, a sick joke. I feel condemned to a lifetime of captivity. I cannot fly, will never again soar. I'm a hollow soul, robbed of my life, of my spirit. Physically, I know this place. I remember it all: the sights, the sounds, the smells. I feel the warmth of the sun beating down on me. A burst of nostalgia and comfort floods over me, but I am unable to truly absorb it. Like an automaton, I am somehow able to put one foot in front of the other.

Keep moving forward.

Every threat in that robotic voice replays over and over again in my head. *We know where your family lives. Do not bring attention to yourself. Go straight to your family. We will be watching. We will always be watching.*

The child deep inside me is begging for the loving embrace of my parents and for them to say, *It's okay, Nisey. We have you. Everything is going to be all right.*

That scene plays repeatedly. I want my mom and dad.

Mommy and Daddy.

But each attempt to find my family gets thwarted. My mom is not home, and I am unable to get into the house. My next-door neighbors aren't home, and although part of me wonders if I should just stay and wait, I decide I need to keep moving, keep trying.

I leave my bags on my mom's patio, take my purse, and ask someone working on the outside of a home down the street if I can use his phone. I try not to cause alarm, the threats echoing in my mind. I call my mom, then my dad; both go straight to voice mail. So I leave a message with my dad telling him I'm okay, that I'm walking from Mom's house to his, and the route I plan to take.

God, I hope he's home, or my brother, please!

When I get to my father's second-floor apartment, I knock, but no one answers.

"Can I help you?" asks a woman a few apartments down.

"I . . . I—I'm looking for my dad and brother."

"They're not home. They're up north," she says as she approaches me. "I'm so sorry to hear about your sister."

I try to understand what she has just said. My family is in Vallejo, scared and worried about me. They know—everyone knows—there was a kidnapping. And this woman doesn't realize it's me they're looking for.

"No, it—it's not my sister. . . . It's . . . me."

"Oh! Oh, my. Oh, my God, are you okay? What can I do? How can I help?"

I ask to use her bathroom as she gets on the phone, trying to contact my dad.

I take a small moment of peace in this simple freedom, the first time the Voice isn't lurking on the other side of the wall.

When I'm finished and walk back out to the living room, I'm startled as I see two police officers coming through the front door.

I'm immediately frozen with fear.

"Are you Denise Huskins?"

I take a shallow breath, and I respond, "Yes."

ONE OFFICER STANDS by my side as I sit on a small couch answering his questions. The second officer is on the other side of the room, near the door. My voice trembles and I stutter as I tell the police what has happened to Aaron and me.

I start off by telling them the details of the home invasion: being woken by a flashing white light and a voice saying it was a robbery; the red laser pointers I assumed came from guns; that only one kidnapper spoke. I describe the zip ties, the goggles, the headphones, the threats on the recordings, the sedatives, the trunk, the bedroom I was held in.

Although the officers are being respectful and professional, I wonder how long this will take and when I can be reunited with my family. The police keep everyone out, including the woman who lives here. I think she has my dad on the phone, but the officers insist on isolating me, saying they "*really* need to preserve the scene right now." This poor woman's apartment is now a crime scene. *I am a crime scene.*

The officer next to me asks if I need any medical attention and tells me CSI should be coming. In the meantime, he continues asking me questions.

One stops me cold. "Did you ever ask him to let you go?"

My head pulls back, as if somebody slapped me in the face. *After everything I just told you, do you seriously think he would have let me go if I asked?*

I try not to be offended and tell myself it may be an innocent mistake. Maybe he's never interviewed a kidnap victim before.

"I asked him if he was going to hurt me," I respond sharply. "I asked if he was going to . . . kill me. He had said there was no reason for that, they would hold me for forty-eight hours. . . ."

I describe more of the "drop-off" and my captor's reasoning for releasing me in Huntington Beach.

The officer asks if I know what kind of car he drove and what color. I tell him the sound of the exhaust reminded me of a Mustang, and I think the car was white but can't be sure.

He reaches for his phone to show me a map so I can identify where I was released.

As he does, I see he is holding a recording device discreetly by his side.

Oh, God, they're recording me. Will this be released publicly? What if I say something I'm not supposed to say?

I put my head in my hands and struggle to breathe. The officer notices. "Are you okay?"

"I'm just scared," I say, my voice muffled and meek through my hands.

"But you're okay now. We're here. Everybody's going to take care of you. Obviously, we're going to have to ask you a whole bunch of questions and our detectives are going to have to talk to you."

Fear overwhelms me. *I will have to talk to detectives?* I am so horribly conflicted. I want to cooperate but given all the planning and the Voice's absolute arrogance, I just don't believe the kidnappers will be caught. The more I talk to police, the more likely I'll have to lie to protect my family. I don't want to be in this position and I'm starting to realize I need an attorney to help guide me through this.

"I wanted to see about talking with a lawyer first," I say into my cupped hands.

"Well . . . our detectives can help you out with that," he says. "What did you call him? Did he have a name or anything like that?"

I tell the officer my captor mentioned his associates, T, J, and L, and that they came to the house once or twice while I was in captivity.

I give as many details as I can remember, including the drive down here; how the Voice spoke; that I believed he was white with brownish red hair; that I never looked up at the kidnappers' faces during the home invasion, so I didn't know if they wore masks, but the Voice told me they were wearing wet suits in case something went wrong and they had to swim to escape. The officer seems taken aback by this. I know how this sounds, but this was what happened.

"Have you talked to Aaron yet?"

How could I? I tell the officer the kidnapper brought my bags with us, but my cell phone was left behind so Aaron could call in sick for me.

Even if I did have a phone, I don't have Aaron's number memorized, and the truth is, as much as I'd love to talk to him, my only thoughts have been to get to my family.

"So, who is this Aaron guy? Why did this happen to him? Because you seem like a nice person. I don't understand why—"

I sense the judgment in his tone and cut him off, explaining that Aaron is a nice person too. I tell the officer I don't know exactly why they targeted him and Jennifer, but my captor said several times that she was who they were after. I further explain what my captor told me about the organization he and his accomplices are a part of, that they get hired by clients to kidnap someone for money.

The officer says I seem really calm and I must be very strong. "What was going through your head with all this stuff? I mean, were you super fearful?"

"Yeah," I respond as my mind scans through the last two days. "I just kept telling myself, like, it could happen. I could not be released. The end of this forty-eight hours could end up with a bullet in my head. What choice do I have right now? To live this next forty-eight hours s-scared s-shitless, or"—I take a deep breath—"try to stay calm and focus on . . . hopefully, my future and just getting out of this. So I did everything they asked. I just kept my eyes shut. I didn't want to give them any reason to not let me go or any reason to make that decision. So unfortunately, I don't have a lot of information. . . ."

"You didn't give them any trouble," the officer acknowledges.

Oh, good. He understands.

"Yeah, and I had those thoughts in my head—after forty-eight hours, if they don't follow through, then I'm gonna have to change what I'm thinking and have to . . . have some kind of game plan of what to do next. But so far they fed me, they took me to the bathroom frequently, made sure I had water. They said it was protocol, giving me the sedatives. . . . That was the protocol—there was a certain way we did . . . everything."

I hear more officers outside, mixed with barking dogs, circling helicopters, and other sounds I can't identify.

"Umm, I would like to, uh"—my voice is barely above a whisper—"talk to my mom . . . dad."

"Oh, honestly, that's definitely going to happen. All I'm doing right now is just waiting for our detectives to come over. They need to talk to you, and they'll definitely let you talk to your mom and dad. Absolutely. I know they've been worried about you."

"'Kay," I say, softly.

When? I am so exhausted. When will this be over?

"Do I have to talk to the d-detectives right now?"

"Umm," he says, "just . . . just let them talk to you and tell [you] what they need to do. . . ."

In a tiny voice I say, "I'm just still really scared."

"You are? Do you think that there's any chance that this would happen again to you?"

"Umm, *yeah*," I say, "if . . . if I talk too much . . . yeah."

"Did they tell you not to talk to us?"

I put my hands over my face again, scared to answer this truthfully so the words come out in fits and spurts. "They said that I can . . . I have got to be careful of what I say. I guess . . . I . . ."

There is a pause as I slouch, hiding my head in my hands. I need some guidance, some support. I don't know how I can hold myself together much longer.

"I don't even have that much to offer, as far as details go. I don't—I just don't want to put myself at risk of any extra things, like, I just want this to be done. I want to move forward. I have"—my voice breaks as the tears come—"a lot of things I'm looking forward to as far as work."

My voice fades away.

"Oh, absolutely. How old are you?"

"Twenty-nine," I say, my vocal cords straining as I whimper through my tears. "I just don't . . . I understand that you guys have to do your job, but I don't—I don't think that you're going to catch anyone. And I don't want to be put at risk. I don't want to go through that again. I don't want to live my life s-scared that something is going to happen."

"Well, we are going to do whatever we can to help you. Okay? . . . You seem like a really strong person. I just need you to be stronger for just a little bit longer, okay?"

How much strength can one person have?

"If I could talk to my mom or dad . . . ," I say, my voice breaking again. He says they're probably on their way, which I know can't be right if they're up in Vallejo. I just don't understand why I can't speak to them and why it's taking the detectives so long.

Eventually, he gets to the question I'm most afraid to answer.

"I'm going to ask you a question I didn't ask you earlier, but . . . were you sexually assaulted during this?"

"No." I'm flooded with shame as the lie comes out. But I feel like I have a gun to my head, a gun pointed at my family.

He responds cautiously, "I'm happy that didn't happen to you."

I quickly deflect. "It's weird because with all things considered, they treated me really . . . nicely." I cringe as I hear myself say this, but I continue. "Obviously being kidnapped and held against my will is not anywhere nice [*sic*], but I was always asked about my comfort level, thirst, hunger, all of that. And when I went to the bathroom, they gave me privacy; he let me shower. . . ."

He asks how many times I showered and then moves on to more innocuous questions about my life, like what I do for a living, where I grew up, went to school. I respectfully engage in this small talk, but it's a waste of my energy, especially if I still have to speak to others.

Where are the detectives? CSI?

The officer acknowledges that it's taking a while to find out what the next step is. He says they're waiting to hear from Vallejo detectives since they're in charge of the investigation.

"Do you know anything about my parents? If they're coming back?" My voice is a mere squeak.

It's been over an hour. This is now torture. How many times do I have to ask for my family? Something isn't right. They're clearly stalling.

He doesn't respond. After some awkward silence and more small talk, I ask again. The officer says they know I'm fine, and must be so relieved I'm okay, especially since you hear stories like this on the news and it often doesn't end well.

"What stuff will get out to the press?" I ask. "Like, what I talk about with police or with the detective, does that just become . . . public knowledge?"

"No, no, no," both officers say in unison.

"Because it's— You're the victim," the second officer says. "We are treating you as a vic— I mean, you *are* a victim."

That slip bothers me. *Treating* me as a victim? *Do they not believe me?*

"I don't want it public. Anything," I say firmly. "I am seriously still really scared. I just—" I can't keep my composure any longer. I don't think they understand the danger I'm in. "I don't know what they're capable of," I sob.

The first officer tries to reassure me that I'm safe, that there are two officers here with me and they'll do what they can to help me. I know he believes this and means well, but he doesn't get it. The officers will eventually leave, the news reports will go away, and at some point I'll be on my own again, vulnerable to another attack.

I try to reiterate that this was too planned out, these guys know what they're doing, and grow more and more distressed with each word. Suddenly two people rush through the front door and my heart lifts. It's my aunt Jody and cousin Nick!

Oh, my God, finally! Finally! My family!

19

MIKE HUSKINS WAS in a panic after listening to Denise's message, his initial joy at hearing the words "Daddy, I'm okay" quickly replaced by fear. She was all alone, walking the streets, and he had no way to reach her. What if the kidnapper circled back and abducted her again? He knew every second counted, that he had to act fast and get ahold of the Huntington Beach police so they could get to her first.

He called the phone number the Vallejo detective had given him, the one he was assured would be answered 24/7. No one picked up. Next, he called 911 and asked to be connected with the Huntington Beach police, but the dispatcher routed the call to the Vallejo police instead. *Not these dipshits again!* His blood was boiling, and he felt like his heart would explode. Nearly shouting and breathless, he told them he was Denise's father, that she'd been released, and he needed police to go get her to make sure she was safe.

"Can you verify that it's her?" he was asked.

"Are you kidding me?! You don't think I know the voice of my *own daughter*?" Huskins roared back. He might be a big teddy bear in most situations, but you dared not poke him, especially when the stakes were so high. Like now. "It's my *daughter*! Get Huntington Beach police over there!"

He was standing in the middle of the Hilton parking lot, yelling at the top of his lungs. "People probably thought I was deranged," he later recalled.

At that moment his neighbor called; the neighbor's wife had just talked to Denise outside their apartment.

Oh, thank God! Please protect my little girl.

"Tell Annalisa to keep Denise in her apartment and call nine-one-one," Mike told him.

And that was what she did.

JANE HUSKINS WAS beside herself with worry too. She felt awful she'd locked up the house before she left, so Denise couldn't get in, and even worse that she wasn't there herself. She'd had a gut feeling she should have stayed, but reluctantly rushed to Vallejo, thinking she was needed there more, only to find out she wasn't. Those officers robbed her of the chance to hold her daughter when she needed it most. Jane would never forgive them for that. And now she'd somehow missed her daughter's call and couldn't reach her! Instinctively she knew Denise needed loving arms wrapped around her and to be told she was safe. So Jane began making calls.

The first person she reached was Jim Russell, Denise's best friend's father, who lived down the street from Jane. He hurried over to Mike's, but police wouldn't let him past the entrance to the apartment building. Jim knew Denise was alone with the police, and it didn't feel right. It was clear she needed help. And fast.

He called Jane and told her to find Denise a lawyer.

Jane spoke with one of Mike's sisters, who told her Denise's cousin Nick was a newly minted attorney. When he found out about his cousin's plight, Nick and their aunt Jody rushed over, only to find the building surrounded by cops. The media was beginning to gather outside as well.

At first, the police refused to let Nick inside. He kept telling them he was an attorney until they finally relented and let him and Jody go to Denise.

There she was. Alone. Distraught. With cops forming a half circle around her.

DENISE

"Hi! Hiii!" I whimper in excitement when I see Nick and Aunt Jody. This is the first tone of joy and elation I'm able to express in days.

I finally feel reconnected to my life, seeing members of my family and the undeniable love and concern on their faces.

We move toward one another, arms outstretched, but both cops stop us, barking, "No, no, wait!"

"Oh, yeah, I can't," I say, still trying to be compliant. CSI hasn't come yet.

I just want to hug my family.

A gaggle of uniformed officers and a man in street clothes with an air of authority about him follow closely on Nick's heels. I'm guessing this is the detective I've been waiting for.

Where the hell have you been?

But Nick doesn't budge, telling him he just wants a couple of minutes to talk to me alone. The uniformed officers, who'd positioned themselves in front of the apartment's only door, puffing up their chests, reluctantly leave but take the same aggressive stance just outside the door, which is still open.

Why are we being treated like this?

My aunt and cousin ask me what I need, and for the first time in days, I'm presented with a choice. Nick tells me the police want me to go to the station, but I don't have to right now. I am so exhausted and terrified I say I just want to go somewhere safe.

"Okay," Nick says decisively. "I'll go let them know, and we can arrange a way to get you out of here."

He's two years younger than me, and he's an intellectual property attorney, not a criminal one. I know he's never dealt with anything like this before, but he is intelligent and driven and certainly can hold his own with these officers. If he's nervous or intimidated, I can't see it. The officers are inches taller than he is, their position more powerful, but he matches them eye to eye, chest to chest. He is my knight in shining armor.

His dad, my dad's only brother, passed away from lung cancer when we were preteens. But I know his father is here now, along with my grandmother, looking down with pride at Nick the same way I am, at the man he has become.

Nick's car is about a block away. To avoid the media out front, the police say they'll seal off the back alley from the news trucks and take me to a parking lot about a quarter of a mile away where I can then hop into Nick's car. This diversion will allow Nick to drive me to his mom's house and away from this mess.

The detective comes in and tells us that before we go, they need CSI to come in and gather evidence.

Finally.

The CSI officer quickly takes pictures of my wrists, even though I told them the zip ties didn't leave any marks because I never tried to break out of them. He almost walks away before I stop him, pointing out the circular impressions visible around my eyes, especially my right eye where the goggles dug into my skin. This all seems half-assed and rushed, as if they are just going through the motions but not actually trying to gather evidence.

They don't even take the shoes or the water bottle I told them the kidnapper gave me.

Before we're escorted out, the Huntington Beach detective says he has a Vallejo detective on the phone who needs to speak with me, someone by the name of Mustard. I'm sure Nick can see the desperation and fear I'm feeling because he reaches for the phone.

"I'll talk to him," he says. I am so relieved and grateful. I can't take any more. I feel like I'm going to fall apart.

As he listens, his expression grows first confused and then concerned. *What now?*

"Okay . . . I don't know the details of what happened," he says to Mustard. "I'll relay this information to my cousin. I have your number, but right now we just need to get her somewhere safe."

After he hangs up, he looks at me, worried. I can tell he's trying to be careful with his words; he doesn't want to frighten me.

"So, he says . . . they can offer you a proffer of agreement. It's . . . basically, like . . . immunity."

"*Immunity?* Immunity from what?" I respond.

"I don't . . . I don't know. He said that you should know Aaron's at the station and they're offering it to him in about five minutes. It's being offered to both of you, and whoever takes it first will get it."

"What?!"

"He also said they're sending an airplane down to John Wayne you could fly up to Vallejo in."

"What do I do?"

"I told him we're going to my mom's and then we'll call him. Let's just get you out of here," Nick says as we hear the commotion outside increasing. As I'm escorted down the stairs, I hear the reporters and a crowd out in front of the building shouting my name through the small entryway of the courtyard. I put the hood of my jacket up over my head as if that's really going to hide me.

It doesn't seem like the police sealed off anything because a couple of cameramen and reporters are waiting for us in the alleyway. I jump into the backseat of the police car as the reporters hurl questions at me and the cameras click away.

We get to the parking lot, and I hop into Nick's backseat, afraid that the helicopters circling overhead are broadcasting this scene live. How could the police think this was a good idea?

Nick tells me his mom, my aunt Karen, is up in Vallejo with my dad, along with other family members. They'd arrived there this morning.

"As soon as we all heard, we split the family into forces, half up there for your dad and half down here."

I hold back tears, comforted by this support. I'm not surprised because that's how the Huskins family operates, but I was so removed from everything in my life that actually being back in this reality gives me a surge of empowerment. I am not alone. I was never alone. They've all been here fighting. And we will continue to fight. Together.

WE DRIVE THE few blocks to my aunt Karen's, where the media have been camped out for days. There are dozens of reporters, camera crews, and news trucks outside her town house. "It's been all over the national news," Nick tells me as I try to take it in. "It's been talked about everywhere. We've all been harassed and flooded with calls asking us to go on the morning shows. It's been crazy. Reporters have been banging on the doors and windows, yelling, 'What do you know?'"

I am in absolute shock and don't even know what to say. I didn't think it would be this big of a story. Maybe a local newspaper would report it, but *this*? This is so overwhelming and threatening I can't even think straight. I feel panicky at the thought the press might say something that will prompt the kidnappers to attack me again.

We pull into the back, and I follow at Nick's heels, head down and hood up as he sneaks me in through the side gate. I can still see and hear the crowd out front and am terrified they'll come after me.

Am I safe anywhere?

I'm greeted by a handful of family members, clearly confused, scared, and angry at being hounded by the press. Later, reporters even use a car to block my aunt from driving away from her house, forcing her to drive on the sidewalk to escape. Then they pursue her for miles, following dangerously close behind her.

Why are they so aggressive? Hasn't my family gone through enough?

Paranoid, I ask my family not to talk to the media and I sequester myself in the back bedroom.

NICK GETS IN touch with my uncle Jeff, who is also an attorney and is up in Vallejo with my father. They talk for a while, Nick filling him in. Then Jeff gets on the phone with me.

"Denise, here's the thing," he tells me. "The police simply don't believe you. We're trying to figure this out, but it's clear we need to get you a criminal defense attorney. You absolutely cannot speak to law enforcement anymore. You can't give them any more statements. You already provided one to the Huntington Beach police, so any additional statements can and will be used against you, especially if there are any discrepancies between them. You can't talk to anyone else about it right now either, not even your parents. The only two people you can talk to are Nick and me because our conversations are protected by attorney-client privilege. I am going to try to get ahold of an attorney I know and get his advice on how to move forward."

Oh, my God. How . . . Why? Are the police trying to frame me? Is someone in the department involved with the kidnappers? Is that how the group protects itself?

Nick brings me food, but I can't bring myself to chew. I'm so nauseous, I can barely sip water. I take a shower, thinking maybe that will make me feel better, but it doesn't help. I feel like I'm on the verge of collapse, but I'm so wired from fear and adrenaline that my body feels like it's malfunctioning. I just lie on the bed in the fetal position as a swirl of chaos surrounds me.

Nick comes in after speaking to Detective Mustard again. This time he says Mustard is aggressive, threatening, and accusatory. "He said the story he heard is far-fetched and a hoax on both sides. He said Aaron's sitting in front of him now, so you need to make a decision."

"Oh, my God!"

"And then he said something about not wanting to hear any more about this Navy SEAL bullshit. . . . I don't know what that means, but I told him that we're consulting an attorney."

What the hell is he talking about? Navy SEAL bullshit? What, because of the wet suits?

I briefly speak to my mom on the phone, telling her I can't talk about what happened, but I'm okay. I've been desperate to hear her sweet voice for days, but I am in such a panic that I can find no solace in it now. I'm afraid that by talking to her I'm putting her in harm's way. I feel like my very existence is hurting my whole family.

"I don't understand what's going on," she says. She, my dad, and Devin have been at the Vallejo police station for hours. They've told her it's Aaron's fault, and I tell her it's not. She doesn't believe the police either, but they're so mad, she tells me; the main detective is angry and seems upset that I'm alive. And he said something about not wanting to hear any more about the "frog suits." This is insane!

"Just come here and talk to them," she says. "Maybe we don't have to deal with getting a lawyer. If you just come and tell them the truth, then it will all be okay."

"No. No, Mom, something's not right. Something is very wrong. I can't explain it right now, but based on what I know about the people who did this, I just don't think it's a good idea to talk to the police without a lawyer."

Eventually my uncle Jeff gets in contact with a criminal defense attorney he knows in Orange County. When I speak to the attorney, he asks how well I know Aaron and if I thought he'd take the deal. Despite my assurances that we're both victims, he explains that making a false police report could lead to years in prison, and some people will take immunity to avoid that.

My head is spinning with worry. *We could go to jail? We could go to jail?*

He tells me I absolutely need a criminal defense attorney, someone in the Bay Area, and ultimately refers my uncle to Doug Rappaport in San Francisco.

Nick talks to Devin, who's still at the station with my parents, and apparently Mustard has softened his tone, reminding us that the FBI plane is waiting or I can find my own way up. They just need to talk to me.

After about an hour, we reach Doug. I get on the phone, and he keeps it short. He tells me *not* to take the FBI up on its offer to fly me back to Vallejo.

"I didn't want you to get on the FBI plane for the same reason I wouldn't advise you to get into the mouth of a great white shark," he would later recall. "The further I could keep you away from a predator, the less likely it would be that you'd get eaten. The more you interacted with the FBI without an attorney present, the more likely you'd say something they could twist into something damaging."

He quickly gives me some instructions.

"I'm looking at the news right now, and it hasn't turned on you yet, but it seems like it might soon. Get up here as quickly as you can so you can talk to me first. That's the only way I can protect you. I don't want to hear anything about it until I see you face-to-face. Then we can decide the best strategy for how to move forward."

I hear a baby crying in the background. Everything is so utterly chaotic, I wonder if I'm hallucinating. In fact, Doug's wife just gave birth to their second child the day before, and he was planning to take three months' paternity leave, but he was so moved when my uncle told him about my plight that, after discussing it with his wife, he agreed to talk to me.

He was once a public defender, like his father before him, and still considered himself one to his very core, as devoted to his many pro bono clients as he was to his paying ones. He was selective about the cases he took on because he wanted to give each of them the attention they deserved. Over the past seventeen years, he'd defended dozens of indigent clients as well as professional athletes, a state senator, and even an ambassador from another country, and now, hopefully, me. He'd gone into law to help people, and it was already clear to him I needed help in the worst possible way. I don't know if he'll agree to represent me, but everything is spiraling out of control and meeting with him seems like my only hope for protection, so I agree. Every decision, every movement feels like life or death. We find the next flight out of LAX we think we can make, get in the car—ducking reporters—and head to the airport.

Mr. Rappaport has instructed me to call him at each step: when I get to the airport, when I get through security, when I board the plane, when the plane lands, when my family picks me up from the airport, and when I am on my way to his office.

"I need to know exactly where you are at all times, in case you get detained by the police along the way. I need to speak with you before they do."

Detained?

Now not only am I scared of the kidnappers and the media, but I'm picturing a swarm of officers in SWAT gear coming to arrest me at any moment. Nothing's safe. Everything is a threat.

Once we get on the freeway, we realize that it's rush hour. We are barely crawling, and we clearly aren't going to make the flight from LAX. Long Beach Airport is closer, so Nick finds a flight that leaves at six thirty and books me a ticket.

But when we get to the airport to check in, we realize the flight is for 6:30 a.m. tomorrow. The next flight to San Francisco is at 8:30 p.m. We have no choice. We buy the third plane ticket of the day and wait.

I ask Nick how much an attorney will cost. How will we be able to afford it?

"Whatever it is, we will figure it out. We'll all help you."

I appreciate his saying that, but I feel terrible about how this will affect everyone. It's finally time to head to my gate, alone. I go to the big floor-to-ceiling windows overlooking the runway and slide down to the floor with my knees tucked up and my hood covering my face.

While I'm waiting, I use the cell phone Nick loaned me to log on to Facebook. I see post after post from my friends begging for everyone's help in finding me. I cry silently, drowning in sorrow in the midst of hundreds of people moving around me.

Even as I take my aisle seat, hood still over my head, I keep picturing cops charging in and dragging me off the plane.

The flight takes off and lands and my cousin Carly and her boyfriend are there to pick me up. It's 9:30 p.m. I can't bring myself to look at any TVs as I move through the airport, but even if I did, I probably wouldn't recognize the significance of what was on—at that very moment the Vallejo police are giving a press conference, one that will destroy my life beyond recognition.

20

AARON

DENISE HAS BEEN released—this madness is over! We can start healing; we can move past this trauma into a future that I thought would never be available to us again. I've fantasized about being the first person to see her, taking her in my arms, letting her know she's safe and professing my love. Instead, I find out in a hotel room four hundred miles away from her. But it doesn't matter where I am. She's alive. She's free. And she won't be alone. I'm sure her family is there to support her.

I start running through my head how I can see her as quickly as humanly possible. It won't feel real until I can hold her in my arms. Maybe I can fly down? But I can't go anywhere without my wallet or ID, although I expect the police will give them back now.

Around noon, Amy, Samantha, and I drive over to the police station. All I can think about is hearing Denise's voice. I want to apologize for not protecting her, for bringing this Jennifer shit upon her, for everything. I pray that she wasn't tortured, that she wasn't raped.

We're escorted back to the same conference room as the night before. It's empty, which is surprising but understandable because the police are probably talking with Denise. Hopefully, she'll be able to provide some details to catch these guys.

As we're waiting, we run through the possible true motivations of the kidnappers and why they would release Denise without even a ransom being paid. Samantha explains that many gangs sometimes commit a crime, not for money or drugs but just to show what they can get away with. The crime raises their profile. Our kidnappers may be doing the same thing: demonstrating that the police and the FBI can't catch them. They're building their résumé—like a sadistic unpaid internship.

We sit there for almost two hours before Agent Vinny, Detective Mustard, and a couple of others come into the room. Agent Vinny apologizes for the delay but "there are a lot of moving parts right now." I feel so relieved; they must be pursuing the kidnappers. This is the FBI, for Christ's sake. I assume no one can hide from them.

We agree to come back at five because they'll have more questions for me at that time. I don't want to wait any longer to talk with Denise, but I understand they need to get information from her first. We leave the station and head to Amy's office.

Less than an hour later, I'm told the Vallejo police are holding a press conference at three. Are they really updating the public before they update me?

We gather around Samantha's computer as we livestream the press conference. Lieutenant Park is on the screen. I've seen him only briefly on newsclips, but here's another person talking about my life, my trauma. He starts by reading a brief written statement:

On Wednesday March 25 at approximately 10:30 a.m., the Vallejo Police Department was notified by the Huntington Beach Police Department, indicating that they have located our victim Denise Huskins at an undisclosed location.

Currently, we are in the midst of organizing travel arrangements so that our detectives may meet with Ms. Huskins to further piece together the details of the kidnap for ransom.

From an investigative standpoint, nothing has changed. We are still tenaciously moving forward while evaluating and verifying all information flow and investigative leads.

We will continue to remain guarded with specific information until which time we conclude that we are able to release such information in a responsible manner.

I feel my nails digging into my palms as I reflexively make a fist. *From an investigative standpoint, nothing has changed. . . .* In other words, the police *are still after me.* Denise's release should have changed everything. Park should be saying that they're aggressively pursuing the perpetrators of this heinous crime.

Amy reads between the lines as well.

"You're still a suspect," she says to me as I dig my nails in a little harder.

I want to scream. I want to grab the computer and throw it across the room. Put my fist through a wall, break a table, have some outlet for this pent-up rage. But it's pointless. I need to hug Denise.

Lieutenant Park takes only a few questions from the media. He uses a lot of words but says nothing. I head back to Dan's office and lie on the couch, stuck in a world where everyone controls my destiny except me.

I hope Denise's family is with her.

I hope they don't hate me.

I WAKE UP on the couch. The sun has shifted, so I must have passed out for a while. The short nap restores some of my energy, and I actually feel a little hopeful. But it's a dirty trick, like a dead car battery that sounds like it's about to turn over, only to die again. I'll never be happy for more than that brief mirage between sleep and waking.

Amy comes in and tells me it's past five o'clock and she hasn't heard from the Vallejo police. She sent them a text asking if they wanted us to come down but got no response. We can't just go down to the station because the media is swarming around, and they need to let us in the back. She wants to give them a little more time before she tries again.

Another forty-five minutes, and we still haven't heard anything. Amy and I are both getting agitated. She writes a strongly worded email to the police. What the hell is their problem?

A little after six, Mustard texts Amy: Come on down, we're waiting on you, as if we haven't been reaching out to them.

Amy, Samantha, and I go to the station . . . again. As the car turns the corner, I get a clear view of the front of the station. The number of reporters, cameras, and news vans has exploded. They now take up nearly the entire street.

We drive around the back and park. We knock . . . no answer. We knock louder. Still no response. I'm a sitting duck for cameras out here. Amy telephones Mustard. He eventually comes to open the door.

"Oh, sorry," he says sarcastically.

"You knew we were coming," Amy snaps back as we walk in.

Mustard directs us down the hall to the same conference room. The hallways of the station are less busy than earlier today, almost subdued. Nothing indicates a manhunt is underway. We sit in the only open seats in the back of the conference room. The police occupy every chair near the door, obstructing our exit.

"My client has a few demands," Amy says. "First, he wants to talk to Denise. Second, he needs his wallet and keys back—"

Agent Vinny interrupts. "Have you spoken with Denise?"

"No," I respond. "I don't care if you guys listen in. I just want to hear her voice."

"Well," Agent Vinny replies, "we want to talk with her too, but she's gone and gotten a *law-yer.*"

He drags out the word "lawyer" like it's the stamp of guilt.

Mustard leans back in his chair and puts his hands behind his head.

"We're prepared to offer you a proffer of agreement. Immunity," he says. "We're only going to give it to one of you, not both."

"Everyone, out of the room," Amy snaps.

She files out with all the officers as I sit and wait to try to make sense of this insane situation.

After five minutes or so, Amy walks quickly back into the room. I don't like her energy. She sits right next to me. "I told you that you needed to be completely honest with me." She is angry. "I can't help you unless you tell me the truth. You need to tell me everything right now."

This is a watershed moment, and for the first time, I can tell she doubts my innocence. *What the fuck did they say to her?*

"I have nothing left to give," I croak out, tears welling up in my eyes. I didn't say *I have nothing else to tell*, because I literally have nothing else to give besides my flesh. I'm defeated. They've won.

Through gritted teeth, Amy says, "I promised we'll get back to them by nine tonight. We're leaving. Sam is going to bring you back to the hotel. Dan is going to talk with you later. When we walk out of this room, do *not* say one word. Not one."

The hallway is lined with officers, forcing me to walk by them as they attempt a juvenile form of intimidation. But I've seen this tactic dozens of times when playing sports. I'm half expecting them to break into a chant. I force myself to keep my chin up. I might feel defeated, but I won't give them the satisfaction of seeing me cower.

About an hour later, Ethan calls the hotel room for an update. He tells me the police will be holding a press conference soon. I can tell he's hopeful there's been a breakthrough in the case.

After what happened at the station, I know his optimism is misplaced. Nothing good is going to come out of this press conference.

21

AARON

My parents and I turn on the TV in our hotel room at 9:30 p.m. to see if we can find the press conference airing anywhere. All of the local stations are carrying it live. We anxiously wait to hear what this latest update is about.

Once again Park comes up to the podium.

He starts off by apologizing to reporters for being so "guarded" with their investigative information over the past few days.

"It's confirmed that Mr. Aaron Quinn and Miss Denise Huskins are in a dating relationship, and from this point forward, I will not refer to them as a victim or a witness," he tells the crowd of reporters. ". . . We also know that the statement Mr. Quinn provided was such an incredible story that we initially had a hard time believing it, and upon further investigation, we were not able to substantiate any of the things that he was saying."

My neck and cheeks start burning from anger. *Is he allowed to blatantly lie like this? There's a houseful of evidence!* This is already worse than I expected.

While Denise was initially cooperative, he says, "As of right now we have not heard from Miss Huskins, and we are no longer in contact with any of the family members.

"So over the course of the last few days, if I can kind of put things in perspective, we've had over forty police detectives from the local, state, and federal levels and over a hundred support personnel assisting in the investigation, working around the clock to help locate Miss Huskins. That is a tremendous amount of resources that, in my opinion, was wasted.

". . . I can tell you in the grand scheme of things Mr. Quinn and Miss Huskins has [sic] plundered valuable resources away from our community and has [sic] taken the focus away from the true victims of our community while instilling fear amongst our community members, so if anything, it's Mr. Quinn and Miss Huskins that owes [sic] this community an apology."

It took only two minutes to destroy our reputations.

Park then opens up the press conference for questions. The first reporter asks, "Where's Mr. Quinn right now?"

Park replies, "Mr. Quinn is free on his own."

Another asks if charges are going to be filed against us.

"That's a very good question," he replies. "What we intend to do is this. The investigation is still not complete. There are still some loose ends we need to tie up. At the conclusion of the investigation, if we feel there is sufficient evidence to move forward, we will be requesting criminal charges either from the state or federal level."

I hear my mom gasp.

If I were a reporter I would ask, "How can you say it wasn't real if the investigation is still ongoing?" or "Why isn't Mr. Quinn arrested if he committed a crime?" But no reporter asks that. Instead, they ask only questions that feed his narrative. Eventually, a reporter asks, "Is Mr. Quinn cooperating with the investigation?" and Park immediately replies, "No, he is not." He doesn't even stop to think about it before responding. The hours and hours I spent at the police station have been erased in seconds. The truth does not matter. For some reason Park was sent out to obliterate us, and he's doing his job well. I would scream but I can't even figure out how to make a sound.

A reporter asks how this alleged kidnapping has affected Vallejo, especially with the city recently coming out of bankruptcy.

"If you can imagine devoting all of our resources twenty-four hours a day on what I will classify as a wild-goose chase, it's a tremendous loss," Park responds. "It's disappointing. It's disheartening and the fact that we've essentially wasted all of these resources for really nothing is upsetting."

He hints at the possibility of making us pay for all the police effort on our behalf, though he says he has no idea how much that would be and can't even give a ballpark figure.

Then a reporter blurts out, "Would eighty-five hundred cover it?"

Park and all the reporters laugh. Laughing at our pain, laughing at the lies.

Finally, he reassures the community.

"I can tell you that our investigation has concluded that none of the claims has been substantiated, and I can go one step further to say this: that this was not a random act and that the members of our community are safe and that they have nothing to fear."

How can he say that with a straight face? *No one* is safe! In my mind, all I see are the red laser sights and all I hear is the crackle of the Taser. All I feel is fear.

I'm REELING AFTER he finishes. As much as I want to believe it's just this one cop speaking off the cuff, the press release the Vallejo Police Department sent to the media right before Park's press conference was just as damning: *Today there is no evidence to support the claims that this was a stranger abduction, or an abduction at all. Given the facts that have been presented thus far, this appears to be an orchestrated event and not a kidnapping.*

Dan calls to tell me he's heading to the hotel. He doesn't say anything more than that we need to discuss the case in private, and I can't tell from his voice what he thought about the press conference.

Do Dan and Amy think I lied? Are they going to drop me as a client? If so, where do I go from here?

A few minutes later, I hear a knock on the door. I open it to see Dan's tall frame behind it.

"How's it going, brotha?"

"Shitty."

"You want to know what our answer is to them? Fuck you," Dan says, giving a middle finger to the air.

They're not dropping me.

They're coming out swinging.

DAN BELIEVES THE press conference was a stunt; if they had any evidence, I would be arrested. So we decide it's time to fight back. Dan's firm will hold a press conference around lunchtime tomorrow.

I'm feeling more confident as Dan leaves the hotel. Surely, at some point, the press will see through the police's facade. Park even admitted that the investigation wasn't over; they haven't pressed charges. Nevertheless, I'm still nervous and paranoid. Dan warns me the police may still charge me with filing a false report just to save face.

Park said during the press conference that Denise and her family stopped communicating with them, which plants this deep dark seed of doubt inside me. *Was* the kidnapping a sham? Did Denise plot some twisted scheme to get back at me? Did she go into hiding because the police caught her in a lie? These thoughts keep spinning around in my head.

But ultimately, I know none of that makes sense. That's not Denise. She's the most honest person I've ever met. The police must have attacked her the same way they went after me—she was smart enough to get a lawyer instead of being subjected to hours and hours of interrogation. I'm disgusted with myself for ever doubting her. I'll carry this shame with me for the rest of my life.

22

DENISE

WHEN I WALK into Doug Rappaport's tenth-floor office in a historic downtown San Francisco building around 10:00 p.m., I have no idea the Vallejo police have even held a press conference.

Mr. Rappaport is a tall, lean, bald man with a seriousness that reassures me yet frightens me at the same time. I know nothing about him: his credentials, his experience, or what to expect. All I do know is he's my only hope and I need to convince him I'm telling the truth. I feel like it's my own personal Judgment Day and this conversation will send me on a path either to redemption or straight to hell.

I sit down and Doug introduces me to Lauren Schweizer, a young brunette about my age who is an attorney in his firm.

"So, here's the deal," he tells me. "The Vallejo Police Department just held a press conference, and they completely threw you under the bus. They said you guys made this whole thing up."

What?!

It's just one blow after another, but I'm so maxed out on fear that my only reaction is dumb shock. I feel like I am living in a perpetual state of terror. I can't understand why the police would say we're lying, but to say it publicly like this tells me they're coming after us. *I'm fucked.*

He also tells me the kidnappers made a ransom demand, but it was for only $8,500. I agree it's an odd amount but it's more confirmation to me that this wasn't about money, that this was personal for whoever hired the kidnappers.

"We need to know everything, absolutely anything that the police can find out about you and possibly use against you in a criminal case," he goes on.

So, for the next several hours, I confess every sin I've ever committed, hoping my past transgressions aren't what condemned me to this fate. I tell him I partied, drank, and experimented with drugs when I was younger, but to my surprise, Doug's reply is "Okay, so you had a normal college experience. What else?"

I shamefully admit I've been promiscuous in the past, and he brushes it off by asking, "Okay, but are you on any prostitution websites? Because the police will go through your computer and find out."

"No," I respond, shocked and almost relieved that none of what I'm telling him seems to concern him.

He asks about my finances, and I admit I have nearly $200,000 in student loan debt, but again he dismisses this by saying, "We all have student loan debt. That's nothing. What about gambling or other debts?"

I tell him my credit card has a balance of $4,000, since I took a pay cut for the residency; that I have asked my dad for financial help during this time to pay toward my student loans; and that I plan to pay him back when I start a new job next month. I also have my investments I can always try to access for help.

He asks about my mental health, and I tell him I went into therapy to help me cope with being molested as a child. I give the name of my current therapist and encourage him to reach out to her.

None of it seems to faze him, nothing. He seems more shocked by the behavior of the Vallejo police.

"I can't understand why the police are reacting this way," he says. "I've never seen anything like it in the nearly two decades I've been a criminal defense attorney."

And then I go through every last detail of the kidnapping. After I finish, Doug steps out of the office to make a call. His wife had texted to ask how things were. "She's telling the truth," he tells her, breaking down into tears. And so, luckily for me, she gives him her blessing to represent me, even though he was supposed to be on paternity leave. "She needs you more than we do," she says.

While this is going on, I sit and wait, silently praying he'll take my case.

When he comes back in, he says, "I believe you."

Thank God. I have someone to fight for me.

He tells me I don't have to talk to the Vallejo police or the FBI. In fact, he says he never recommends that his clients speak with police because if there are the slightest discrepancies in what I say, they could charge me with making a false statement to authorities.

There *is* a downside to refusing to talk to them: It might be the only way to catch the man who held me captive and his accomplices. If I don't cooperate, they will be free to target someone else. Yet if I do, they might come after me or my family. No matter what I decide, life as I knew it is now over. This story has been aired all over the world. My name and my face are everywhere. I feel I will never be able to treat patients again, even if I move to another country.

What should I do? I'm having a hard time thinking clearly. My body is on hyperalert and I can't shake the feeling the kidnappers are watching me. In my mind I can see a sniper waiting on the next roof, a red laser dot crossing my body, just long enough to put a bullet in my head. Each time I go to the bathroom, I peek out the window to see if anyone's there. I tell Doug I'm deathly afraid of what the kidnappers will do if I cooperate. I wouldn't be able to live with myself if something happened to my family just because I was selfishly trying to save myself.

"That's what people like this do," he tells me, "in order to have power and control over you for the rest of your life. You can't let them have that control over you anymore. You are safe. The whole world is watching you. They can't touch you. The choice is yours, but if you do speak to the police, you can't hold anything back or they'll use that against you."

This is what I need to hear to take the leap and commit to talking to the police. At about 2:00 a.m., Doug starts making calls to get ahold of the right people at the Vallejo Police Department and ends up speaking with Captain James O'Connell. Doug wants me to rest and I'm assuming he's trying to protect me from the conversation, so he has me lie down in the next room with the lights turned off. I lie on the floor, and he gives me an oversized jacket to use as a pillow. But no matter how hard I try, I can't sleep. My mind is racing. I pick up bits and pieces of the conversation through the door as he talks to O'Connell on speakerphone. Doug tells him I was not only kidnapped, but I was also raped. So the first thing we need to do is get me to a hospital to be examined by a Sexual Assault Response Team (SART) to see if they can gather any evidence of my rapes.

"Well, how do we know she was raped?" O'Connell responds, his tone aloof and dismissive. "She won't even talk to us."

"That's why I'm calling," Doug says, his voice rising. "I'm her lawyer and am speaking on her behalf. I just listened to her for hours, and I am telling you she was raped. She's terrified because the kidnappers threatened to hurt her family if she went to the police, but she is willing to speak to you to catch these guys. She needs to get to a hospital right away for a SART exam."

I'm having trouble believing this conversation is actually happening. I have to convince the police I was raped before they'll set up a SART exam to see if there's evidence of rape?

The police are the ones who can set up the exam, so O'Connell is using the fact that I'm requesting one as leverage to get me in to talk to them. It's despicable! Doug sounds angry too as he argues that it's critical to get the SART exam done as soon as possible to preserve evidence, that the clock is already ticking because it should be done within forty-eight hours of the assaults, which the police know. But O'Connell refuses to budge and says we'll have to wait until tomorrow. After a heated debate, which goes on for what feels like hours, Doug agrees to bring me to the Vallejo Police Department at 10:00 a.m. O'Connell promises him they will keep this quiet so the media doesn't get wind of it.

"Be sure she keeps her same clothes on until then, and that she doesn't shower, wash her hands, or brush her teeth." He says we'll discuss it further, hear what I have to say, and then decide if they'll set up the exam.

I can sense Doug's frustration as he explains this to me, but he remains calm and professional. He can see how sick, paranoid, and scared for my life I am, and I can tell he is handling me delicately.

Doug also says the FBI will probably take over the investigation at some point, which I'm relieved to hear because Aaron's brother is an FBI agent and I respect the Bureau. Doug responds with a dismissive gesture as if he's seen it all and I shouldn't expect much from them.

Finally, around 5:00 a.m., Doug calls my parents and tells them they can come to get me. My eyes well with tears as my dad, mom, and younger brother walk through the door and I rush over to hug them all, finally reunited almost a full day after my release. I've been dreaming of this moment for the last three days, but we have to cut it short and go into Doug's office to discuss the plan. He explains that our first priority is to meet with the police so they can set up a SART exam—a rape test, he clarifies, and before he finishes the sentence, my mom lets out a loud gasp. I'm sure they must have suspected it, worried about it, but hearing it confirmed must be devastating for them. You're still a parent, no matter how old your child is. Doug is kind enough not to bring up payment in front of me; he asks to speak to my dad alone about it. I am sick with dread over how this will affect my family financially.

It's a little past six o'clock when my family and I walk outside to their rental car, the streets slowly becoming lit with the dawn's blue light. I shrink into the backseat with my mom next to me, holding on to me for dear life.

Before my dad and brother get in the car, I hear a motorcycle rev its engine, the rider popping a wheelie as it speeds by. At first, I'm terrified it's the kidnappers.

"That was your lawyer," Devin says.

We're all kind of shocked yet strangely reassured. It's the modern-day equivalent of a hero riding off into the sunset on his white horse.

I GO WITH my mom and brother to their hotel in Vallejo. They're pale with dark circles under their eyes and look like the life has virtually been drained from their bodies.

Damn, they've been through hell.

At first, I lie in bed and just notice all the faint sounds outside. The noise I hear reaffirms my belief that I was held in a remote location, because it feels like every sound is amplified. I hear police sirens miles and miles away and pray that it's the police chasing the kidnappers. All of this could just go away. But I know better. The only suspects they're looking at are Aaron and me. I wonder where he is and how he is and hope he doesn't doubt me like it seems all these people do.

My mom shares the bed with me. I'm turned away from her, huddled into a ball, trying to "rest" for a couple of hours before I go through the next round of hell. My family has always been affectionate. I remember when we'd lie in bed when I was a young child and my mom would tickle my back with her acrylic nails, writing letters to spell out words like "I love you."

I feel she is turned toward me and can sense her amazement that I am lying here in front of her, alive, after two days of horrific uncertainty. She gently reaches out for me, and with the slightest touch of her finger to my back, my whole body reflexively jumps and pulls away. My body can't even tolerate her touch. Although she respectfully backs off, I feel her hand hovering inches away from my back, to let me know she's there.

Her closeness gives me enough comfort to sleep.

23

DENISE

WE MEET MY dad in the lobby of the hotel the next morning. My older brother, Joey, arrives after flying in from Denver. It was his birthday yesterday, the day I was released. Devin tells me they spoke on the phone yesterday morning, and Devin said, "You'll get the best birthday present today. I can feel it. Denise will be released."

Joey and I've always had a strong bond, and I cry as soon as we hug. He has always taken me under his wing and cared for me, ever since we were toddlers.

Trying to lighten the mood, Joey jokes, "Cool shoes," because they're cheap, unattractive tennis shoes. What he doesn't know is they were given to me by the kidnappers. I awkwardly try to explain, but standing in the middle of the hotel lobby, I feel like everyone's watching us, judging. We hurry to the car, and as we drive, my dad answers a call from Doug, who's angry; reporters are swarming the station. The police must have leaked to the media that I was coming there.

We end up meeting Doug at a random dead-end street a mile or so from the station. Helicopters fly overhead as we stand outside our cars, trying to figure out what to do. I feel like a fugitive out of some poorly made action film, the heated suspense building as each scene plays out. I see people who live in the surrounding houses peek out their windows. This is a new kind of danger that I couldn't have possibly prepared for, even with everything the kidnappers put me through.

The whole world is ready to pounce on me and I'm easy prey.

I have to jump in the back of Doug's car, squeezing in between two car seats as I part from my family for the day. In a parking lot we meet a police officer, transfer to his car, then sneak in through the back of the station, where dozens of reporters and cameras await.

When we finally get into the station, the police first have me go to the bathroom and change out of my clothing so they can check it in for evidence. I brought some of my mom's clothes to change into, knowing I'd have to hand these over. In the bathroom, the woman collecting my stuff tries to turn away to give me privacy, but at this point, modesty is the least of my concerns. As I walk through the hallways, I see picture after picture of officers in military gear holding large automatic weapons, posing in front of armored vehicles. I taste bile in the back of my throat as I wonder if I am less safe here than I was in captivity. Thank God for Doug and Lauren. I get this deep, eerie sense that this is a place where souls are lost and never found again.

Lauren waits with me as Doug speaks to someone in charge, and I hear the words "lie detector test." I think, *Okay, fine*, and figure it might even be mandatory. But I hear Doug scoff at the suggestion. "Please. Come on. You know those things are bogus. Absolutely not. We're not doing that." And he walks away. One of the officers milling about casually says only criminals use the bench we're sitting on. Lauren shoots back, "*Alleged* criminals."

It's obvious why he said that. Everyone in this police department knows who I am and why I'm here. That comment shows me they have already decided I'm guilty. Do I have a shot in hell of changing their minds?

Finally, we're escorted to a small interrogation room where an overweight, balding man introduces himself. It's Mat Mustard. He and two other detectives sit in the room, with Doug to my left and Lauren to his, six of us crammed into the tiny, stifling, windowless room.

Mustard sits across from me, with what looks like a tear in his eye, and tells me he is so glad he can sit in front of me after days of wondering if I was alive. His tone is calm, and he's clearly trying to reassure me he is sincere, but this is in such stark contrast with his aggressive behavior with Nick and my family yesterday that I'm not sure how to respond. There is something all too familiar about this pseudo politeness, like he's following a script to forge some kind of bond with me, just like the Voice did. It's unsettling to see the parallels with my captor's behavior.

He shows me two pictures and asks me to identify the people in them.

"Aaron Quinn," and "Jennifer Jones," I answer as he shows me their driver's license photos.

He asks me about Aaron, our relationship, Jennifer, the months, weeks, and days leading up to the kidnapping, what I did, whom I was with, where I went, whom I spoke to. I go through all the events of the home invasion and my time in captivity, telling him everything, including the threats made by the kidnappers and why I had originally denied being sexually assaulted.

Mustard asks me about my prior relationships, drug and alcohol history, and mental health, clearly collecting ammunition. But even worse, he starts to turn the positive things my family shared with him against me.

"Your dad told us you're a marathon runner," Mustard starts.

"Well, I've done a handful of half-marathons, but I wouldn't call myself a 'runner.' I'm really slow." I see where this is going.

"He said you're really tough too. You're a fighter."

"I mean, emotionally tough, sure." I hesitate. Everything feels like a trap. "But I couldn't fight off a man, or outrun a man, especially being drugged."

He then asks me point-blank, "Did you ever think about fighting back or escaping?"

How can someone in law enforcement ask such an ignorant question? Oh, no, I was only taken in the middle of the night with threat of weapons, in fear for my life. I'm sorry. Fighting never crossed my mind!

"Of course I thought about it," I respond defensively. "I'm a very . . . thoughtful person. I thought of the probability of anything I did . . . what could happen . . . if I fought, if I ran, if I screamed. And all led to me or Aaron being tortured or killed. So not fighting was my best defense."

I explain I was silently fighting for my sanity, for my pride, my strength, and I didn't want to give in to criminals who take pleasure in terrorizing people. Mustard doesn't budge in his approach.

He asks me if I've ever been in the trunk of a car before, even "just messing around," to which I answer, "No." *What the hell?*

He makes a point of saying how calm I was and still am, as if it's not normal, and asks if I "urinated" on myself at all, especially in the trunk. I guess because I should have been so scared I peed myself? When I reply, "No," he makes me feel like I've answered incorrectly, and this proves I'm lying, even though I explained to him the Voice let me use the restroom before putting me in the trunk. But it doesn't matter. Whatever I say, it seems wrong. We take several breaks, and during each of them, Doug pulls me aside to say, "You are doing such a great job! Just keep it up. They have to believe you."

At one point, he and Lauren go outside to talk to someone on the phone. They seem excited, but I have no idea why. I wait by myself on a bench in the hallway, and I am approached by a good-looking, clean-cut man with dark hair and wearing a suit and tie. He's maybe a few years older than me.

He has the look of an FBI agent, so I assume he is one, but he doesn't identify himself. He's charming and friendly, but it seems like a facade, like something he uses to set people at ease and get what he wants from them. I'm instantly on guard.

"So, I hear you lived in New York. How was that?"

Again with the small talk. But unlike the Huntington Beach officers, who were trying to make me comfortable, this feels off. He keeps going, asking me where I went to school, what it was like living on the East Coast, and other seemingly innocent questions about my life. I spit out the same superficial responses I give everyone, trying not to be rude, but I'm wary, wondering what his true intentions are. I suspect everything that comes out of my mouth will somehow be used against me.

Is he allowed to ask me questions without my lawyer present?

Finally, Doug and Lauren come in, and we go off to a corner.

"So, I just got off the phone with Aaron's attorneys. They are reputable lawyers I'm familiar with, and everything you're telling the police is what Aaron told them, down to the last detail. They're fighting these charges. We're on the same side. You're doing great. Just go back in and tell them what happened."

I try to go in chronological order of the events in as much detail as possible. During the final hours of the day's questioning I notice the guy who spoke to me in the hallway during the break sitting quietly in the corner. He watches me like a hawk, with a smirk on his face as if to say he can see right through me.

At one point, Doug and the officers check their phones, then say they need to talk to one another outside. There's something going on that I'm not privy to and I can't tell from their energy if I should be worried or excited.

When Doug returns, he says, "I have fabulous news!" Apparently the kidnappers sent an email while I was talking to the police and it corroborates what I've been telling them. My shoulders drop. After two days of threats and fear as I try to convince law enforcement I'm telling the truth, I feel a momentary reprieve. *Maybe I did get through to the kidnappers,* I cautiously think.

Doug encourages me and I continue through the rest of my time in captivity. I get to the part where I start reading the article the kidnapper shows me, the one that quotes my dad. Once again, my voice breaks into a sob. I put my head in my hands as my body convulses. I cry for my dad, my whole family, the thought of what it must have been like for them.

I can feel empathy coming from almost everyone in the room. Everyone except for the hawk, who is still perched in the corner, staring at me like I am his prey. There is a disturbing coldness, a gaping void of soul that reminds me of the Voice himself.

I just hope the others in the room believe me. *Can't they see how much pain I'm in?*

I am humiliated as I go over the details of what he forced me to do, how I was filmed, how I had to perform, and finally, after about six hours of relentless questioning, they agree to take me to the hospital for the sexual assault exam. I guess I convinced them I was raped. Or maybe this is another thing they'll use against me. I can't go to Kaiser in Vallejo, because I work there, and the media will be everywhere. So they set it up for a hospital in Napa, about twenty-five minutes away. As a diversion they plan to have a blond woman who works at the police department be escorted out with officers, so the media will follow her while we leave in a different car.

Down the hallway I can see this woman getting ready to leave, laughing with her buddy officers, putting on sunglasses, preparing to make her acting debut.

It's a joke to them while inside I am screaming in terror.

24

AARON

IN THE HOTEL room the next morning, after barely sleeping, we start watching the news coverage. The press conference is the lead story on every station. "Vallejo PD: Kidnapping of Denise Huskins an 'Orchestrated Event,'" says one. "Vallejo Kidnapping for Ransom 'Orchestrated': Police," says another. The Vallejo police lies are repeated over and over, masquerading as the truth, a free and fair press used as a propaganda machine to destroy our reputations, exposing our lives to strangers' misinformed opinions. And I'm helpless to stop this onslaught. Some newscasters seem to be trying not to laugh as they breathlessly tell viewers about the "hoax." I suppress the unsettling thought that the damage is done.

Ethan comes to Vallejo around ten to bring me over to Dan and Amy's office while my parents take a shuttle to the airport for the trip they had planned for months. I've insisted they go. It's better they get as far away from the stress of this situation as possible. But it was Dan who really convinced them it was the right thing to do. He knew the kidnappers had their address and was worried about their safety, though he didn't tell them that at the time. I'm tempted to speak at the press conference myself, but Ethan, Dan, and Amy advise me against it. I've already given the police four separate statements, and they'll be looking for any little mistake. It's the safest and wisest choice, yet it still feels like I'm letting the police win. Like I'm licking my wounds in the corner because I'm too weak to fight. Despite my internal objections, I reluctantly agree that my attorneys should be the ones to speak on my behalf.

Ethan and I leave the office to head back to Penryn. My brother Matt and my best friend Brandon are going to meet us at my parents' house before we decide on my next move. As we pull up, we see a news van in the middle of my parents' driveway. I feel like I'm stuck in a fishbowl with nowhere to hide. We park around the side to use another entrance. Ethan gives me his San Francisco Giants hat so I can cover my face as we sneak into my own damn home.

We're only inside for a minute before a reporter is knocking on the door. Ethan answers while I hide in another room. I overhear Ethan saying, "I know you are just doing your job, but our family is not making any comments. Please direct any questions to Aaron's attorneys, Dan Russo and Amy Morton." The reporter politely replies that she understands and leaves. I'm grateful to have a family who can handle this new world thrust upon us. I hope that Denise's family is able to do the same.

Brandon and Matt arrive, and we watch the press conference live. Dan is forceful, coming out strong in my defense and blasting the police.

"There seems to be a stream of blatant lies by police" who had a "roomful of evidence" supporting what I'd told them, he says. I'd spent more than twenty-four hours over the last few days being interrogated by the FBI and the police during seven separate visits, he says, and afterward I "looked like he did twelve rounds with Muhammad Ali." He adds, "I don't know what more [he] can do to show he is innocent. Maybe they can start pulling his teeth out next."

The police have controlled every piece of information given to the public—and they've been lying since day one. Finally, we can provide a rebuttal, and it seems the media is a little taken aback. It's encouraging, but I'm afraid it's not going to be enough to change the public's mind. They'll believe that the lawyers are defending me because it's their job, and the police wouldn't say it was a hoax if they didn't have hard evidence. I don't see how Denise and I are going to be able to undo the damage the police have done.

Amy calls me after the press conference and tells me the kidnappers emailed Henry Lee, a reporter at the *San Francisco Chronicle*, claiming responsibility and attempting to clear our names. The *Chronicle* forwarded it to the police, who sent it to our attorneys. I'm skeptical and think it has to be some prank. She emails me with the letter attached so I can read it myself.

As I go through the letter, I slowly come to believe it's actually legitimate. The author says my ex was the intended target. No outside source knows this. The writer says he speaks for the group that kidnapped Denise, that they are a group of professional thieves, "more than 2 and fewer than 8 in number," who started out stealing cars but decided to try kidnapping for ransom to make more money. "We fancied ourselves a sort of Ocean's Eleven, gentleman criminals who only took stuff that was insured from people who could afford it," the writer says.

I keep reading, then read it again. And again. Every last detail screams the kidnappers wrote this and supports what I told police and what I'm sure Denise is telling them. They have to believe us now. I pray the kidnappers will continue to communicate. Each letter will bring the FBI one step closer to catching these guys. They must think the police won't find them, or they wouldn't have written this in the first place but hopefully their arrogance will also be their downfall—and our salvation.

WE DECIDE IT'S best for me to stay at my friend Dan Buljan's house, where the media can't find me. I was the best man at his wedding and have known his wife since they first started dating. Brandon lives near them, so I'll be surrounded by the support of lifelong friends, which is something I desperately need during this time of uncertainty.

On our way over to Dan's, Brandon stops at a restaurant to pick up some food. I wait in the car, too scared of being recognized in our hometown. While waiting, I receive a call from Amy. She tells me they've been in contact with Denise's attorney. They've worked with him before, and he knows what he's doing. So far everything she's told me has been good news. Denise has a competent attorney, our accounts will support each other's, and even the kidnappers are attempting to clear our names. But then I hear a shift in Amy's tone. She pauses before breaking the news to me.

"I'm sorry to tell you but Denise is going to undergo an examination for sexual assault."

Tears well up, and I choke out, "I have to go."

I fall apart as soon as I hang up. I curl into a ball and cry, repeating, "No. No. No."

25

DENISE

I GET INTO A black tinted-window SUV with a female FBI agent, a Vallejo police officer, and Lauren.

We pass by the reporters as I cower in the backseat, hoping they won't follow us. If the media knows I'm going to the hospital, they'll broadcast it, which means the kidnappers will find out and will know why I went there. The whole drive, I look around, paranoid at who may be following us, sick with worry that the kidnappers will discover I disclosed the one thing they told me not to and will kill my family because of it.

I start to doze off, resting my head against the window, and I'm startled awake when Lauren gently touches my shoulder to let me know we've arrived.

We walk through a blocked-off back entrance and a long, winding hallway leading to an exam room. I know it must have taken a lot of planning to make sure this is all done discreetly, and I can't help but worry the people involved may see it as an inconvenience and resent me for what they may think is a waste of time. I can't be sure who knows what or what they may think of me since there's been so much negative publicity.

In the exam room, I am greeted by two nurses who are kind and warm. I don't feel judgment coming from them, and I'm grateful. The female FBI agent, whose name I still don't know, sits in the corner the whole time, and Lauren accompanies me, holding my hand throughout for moral support. Doug is preparing for a press conference he's going to have tonight and said he'd fill my family in on where I am.

For the next three or four hours, I'm forced to recount all the events of the kidnapping and rapes again, down to the disgusting details of what part of his lips, tongue, saliva, and genitals touched which part of me. I tell them the kidnapper used a condom, only penetrated vaginally, and made me shower after each rape, so I wasn't sure if they'd find any DNA. But the nurses say there could be trace amounts and swab my inner thighs, chest, breasts, and neck just in case.

They take pictures of my naked body, noting a sizable bruise on the left side of my back and elbow, and I tell them he dropped me from the trunk, but even worse is the pain I'm feeling in my upper back and neck, an area of chronic pain that gets exacerbated with stress. During the internal exam, they note and take pictures of micro lesions inside my cervix, which they tell me indicate there was sexual intercourse recently. I tell them that Aaron and I had sex Sunday night, concerned the police will use this information against me to say that I'm lying. This type of micro lesion, they say, usually heals within twenty-four to forty-eight hours after sex, so they couldn't have been from Sunday.

Although these nurses are kind, and examine me as respectfully as they can, after everything that happened, after all that I've survived, this is the final tipping point; I feel dehumanized, like I have barely an ounce of dignity left by the end of it all.

The nurses give me medication to prevent pregnancy and STDs. They also offer me one for possible HIV transmission. One of the nurses explains that if I decide to take it, I have to take every dose, every day for a month, for it to work, but the side effects are brutal and make you severely, debilitatingly ill. They look at me, waiting for an answer. I look back at all of them, including Lauren and the awkward female FBI agent in the corner, longing for help or guidance about what to do.

Tears start to well up. I know I have to go back to the police station tomorrow, and God knows how many more days, to recite detail after awful detail of what happened in order to prove my innocence. I'm already sick, in pain, in fear for my life, unable to sleep or eat, hardly able even to drink water or find the energy to move. Yet I'm supposed to take something that makes me feel even worse? But what if he does have HIV and this is my only chance to prevent getting it myself?

One of the nurses, seeing that I'm struggling, says to me, "You have made one impossible decision after the other, so let me make this one for you. The highest risk of transmitting HIV is through unprotected anal intercourse. He used a condom and only entered vaginally, so the risk is extremely low. If I were you, I wouldn't take this."

"Thank you." I breathe a deep sigh of relief. A doctor comes in and prescribes me Valium to help with the PTSD and pain. He warns me this may be similar to what I was given in captivity, so it might be a trigger, and prescribes eight pills only for when I really need them.

Lauren gets us an Uber to take me to where my family's staying. My mom and brother moved to my father's hotel in Berkeley. We know one thing for certain: We all need to stay the hell out of Vallejo.

It's about 9:00 p.m. Doug hoped to wait to do his press conference with Lauren, but the exam took so long that he went ahead and started without her.

When I get back to the hotel, I wait for the news to watch what he had to say.

The nightly news through the cable network at our hotel airs only about fifteen seconds of Doug's press conference, just his line about the police having "egg on their face" and how I am "absolutely, unequivocally a victim."

I am confident he said more and am frustrated the network only aired a short clip.

My dad, Devin, and Joey are all out at a restaurant, picking me up some food as I sit on the bed with my mom. She tells me she and Devin spent the day picking up clothes and toiletries for me to get me through the next few days. She also tells me they all met with Doug for a brief update after I went to the hospital, and he told them about the email the kidnappers sent coming to my defense.

My mom says she doesn't know exactly what it said, but Doug seemed hopeful that it would give investigators more confirmation that I'm telling the truth. We are too. Just then Devin walks in with the food and hears what we're talking about.

"Oh, yeah." He sighs heavily. "That's the worst thing that could happen right now."

"What? Why?" I ask. *How could this possibly be bad?*

He reluctantly points out that everyone believes I fabricated my story, and an email from the kidnappers defending me might seem even more unbelievable. People might think I was the one who wrote it, just to save myself. *Oh, my God, he's right,* I think, feeling defeated. And that, in fact, is exactly what investigators tell Doug they believe. Apparently, there are programs you can use to schedule the sending of emails ahead of time, so investigators argue it doesn't matter that I was at the station when it was sent. And when Doug points out the vocabulary in the email is much more sophisticated than what I use, the FBI goes so far as to insinuate that Doug himself might have helped write it.

Each time I have hope things will turn around, it's quickly extinguished, amplifying my sense of impending doom about how this will all turn out.

26

AARON

I'VE REGAINED SOME of my composure by the time we arrive at my friend Dan's house. His wife, Danielle, greets me with a hug, but my little buddy, their one-year-old son, Dominic, is already in bed. I've spent a lot of time with them, especially after I found out about Jennifer's affair. It feels like a home away from home.

Dan sets up an air mattress for me in the living room. I'm now constantly on alert and see potential danger everywhere, making it almost impossible to sleep. There's a sliding-glass door leading out to the backyard and I can't help but think how easy it would be for the kidnappers to break in.

Maybe because he can see or sense my stress, Dan brings out his laptop for me to use in case I can't sleep. I toss and turn for a couple of hours, but my mind doesn't stop. If it's not the kidnappers attacking again, then it's Denise being raped or crying all alone. After all, I couldn't see my family, so she could be isolated from hers.

Finally, I give up on sleeping and open the laptop. I read through a few articles and comments. All of them contain some iteration of we're horrible people, and we deserve to pay for wasting the town's resources.

There's not a single comment asking why health care professionals like us would throw away their lives and careers for nothing.

Fortunately, I find the uncut version of Doug Rappaport's press conference.

In it, he speaks powerfully and answers each question with skill and poise. "She is absolutely, unequivocally, one hundred percent, *positively* a victim. And this is no hoax. This is no laughing matter. . . . Like a number of women who have been victims of serious physical and emotional assault, she was initially hesitant and reticent to come forward, but she's fully cooperated with law enforcement with the hope to clear her name."

One reporter asks, "What do you say when the police say this was a fabrication?"

Doug responds, "I can say they are absolutely wrong. A lot of people said the world was flat as well."

I immediately feel more relaxed after hearing Doug say those words. I used the same reference earlier in the evening.

He even shuts down a reporter's comment about the ransom demand, saying, "Did they tell you who that ransom request was made to? Mr. Quinn himself. So what kind of criminal is that? . . . Does he go to his own bank and ask for small unmarked bills and then redeposit it into his account? Of course not. That makes no sense."

When another reporter asks how Denise is doing, Mr. Rappaport responds, "Of course she's distraught. She's emotionally and physically broken, and the fact that she's been designated as a suspect only hurts her further." He finishes by saying she's a strong, altruistic person. Just hearing him talk about her makes me feel like there's less distance between us.

As I close the laptop, I am at ease. It's clear that Denise has a strong attorney who will protect her from law enforcement. It brings me enough peace that I'm finally able to fall asleep.

I WAKE UP Friday morning with the sun peeking through the window shades. I've become deathly afraid of the dark, so the sunlight reduces some of my anxiety. Baby Dom is babbling away in his room, entertaining himself by making funny sounds. Danielle gets him out of his crib, and he spots me lying on the air mattress as he rounds the corner from his room. A smile flashes across his face, and he giggles as he does a wobbly sprint toward me.

I sit up, knowing he'll fall when he reaches the edge of the mattress. I catch him in my arms, and he laughs with delight, giving me a hug. I squeeze him while tears spring to my eyes and to Danielle's as well. Baby Dom is just a sweet little boy who hasn't been damaged by this harsh world. He's excited that his friend is here and couldn't care less about the reason. I breathe in this moment, and for a few glorious seconds, I forget that I'm a broken man.

Around lunchtime I speak with Amy, who tells me I cannot talk to Denise until the police are done questioning her. However, if the police decide to charge us, we won't be able to talk until after the trial, which means *it could be years before we see each other.* I find this impossible to contemplate. The kidnappers told me I would see Denise again in two days, and that seemed like an eternity. The same when the police were interrogating me. I know I'll fall into a deep depression if I can't see her soon.

To my surprise, Amy calls again in the early evening to say Denise is done with questioning, but that Doug told her Denise needed more time and would call me when she's ready. I don't know how to feel about that. At least if we're charged, I could rationalize it's the system keeping us apart. But I've put her through so much, I wouldn't blame her for wanting separation from me. I have no idea what horrors she's endured. Maybe I'll only remind her of the kidnapping or of my betrayal. I'm tainted goods.

Being around my best friends helps ease my pain but I'm still in limbo. Not arrested but not free; not guilty but not innocent. She's no longer kidnapped, but we're not reunited.

27

DENISE

I MEET DOUG AGAIN around 10:00 a.m. Friday, this time in the back parking lot of Vallejo's city hall, where we know there are no reporters. Someone from the station will pick us up.

While we wait, Doug asks if I told the kidnappers about being molested as a child, because there's a reference to it in the email they sent. *Really?* Why would the kidnappers mention that, of all things? Nevertheless, he says it's an important detail to disclose to investigators.

He then asks me if I've ever heard of the movie or book *Gone Girl*.

"Have you watched the news? That's what they're calling you—the real-life Gone Girl."

"What? No, I haven't seen it. What does that mean? Is it a bad thing?"

As an officer pulls up, I forget about *Gone Girl*, whatever that is. It's the least of my concerns at this point. There's way too much at stake and I have very little energy or courage left.

Back in the Vallejo Police Department, in that tiny interrogation room, Doug, Lauren, and I wait. The door opens and in walks the handsome, formal-looking man from yesterday, the one who questioned me in the hallway without my attorney present—the one who reminded me of my kidnapper.

"I am Special Agent Dave Sesma with the FBI, and I'll be questioning you today," he says. "There are a lot of other cases and crimes that Detective Mustard needs to take care of, so he won't be here."

He says we're going to go through the events again as specifically as possible, because every little detail counts.

"I know you were blindfolded for most of it, but because of that, your other senses could have given you a lot of information and be heightened, like sounds, smells, touch, just like they do with someone who's blind."

"Okay . . ." *That shit doesn't just happen instantaneously, you idiot.*

He tells me to start from the beginning again, which I painstakingly do. He aggressively cuts me off every few sentences. "Was it from the right or left? Was the blindfold on or off?" The day continues like this, and I spend most of it with my head in my hands, closing my eyes like I'm still wearing the blindfold, trying to get back to that dark place.

I continue on and explain the details of the drive, of the house I was held captive in, even the music that played. I draw on a whiteboard a sketch of what I think the trunk and its opening looked like, what I think the layout of the home is, and the details of the bedroom and bathroom I was able to see.

I describe the big wooden object I always hit with my left hip on the way to the bathroom, the color of the carpet, walls, linoleum, and cabinets in the bathroom, the type of furniture, the details of the pizza my captor had delivered, the clear unmarked mom-and-pop-style salad container, the dining chair, the place mat, the dish and silverware he brought in.

I agonize over every single detail for hours and hours. At several spots I pause, thinking Doug will cut the agent off, or have me not answer because it seems like some of this is a waste of time or a way to trick or confuse me. But he continues to let me talk, and I trust that if there are major discrepancies in what I'm saying, Doug would ask for a break and tell me about them. But I'm struggling, and I tell this agent there are some things I'm having a hard time remembering and I wish I could've paid more attention. He just stares at me dispassionately.

We take a break halfway through the day. There's still so much for me to go through, and at this rate, I'll have to come back another day. If this agent would just shut up and let me talk, it would go a lot faster, and they'd have a lot more useful information. But it's clear he's more concerned with trying to catch me in a lie. Doug reassures me I'm doing a great job, and asks, "Have you always been this hard on yourself?"

I'm a little surprised it's that obvious. "Yes, I have."

But it gives me hope. If it's that obvious to Doug, then it has to be obvious to these guys as well. I'm trying so hard, giving everything I've got to show them they have to do something to find these criminals, how dangerous they are, and if they get away with this, they'll be emboldened to do it again. That thought motivates me to continue on. I can't let the kidnappers get away with what they did to us. If it kills me, I will convince the police they must investigate in order to spare others from the horrible nightmare I'm going through.

A Vallejo officer brings in sandwiches from Subway layered with globs of mayo and fatty meat. I look down at mine, try to take a small bite, and immediately feel horribly sick. I can't eat anything. Can't they see how ill I am? Do they actually believe I'm faking?

After the late lunch break, the questioning resumes. The FBI agent says he needs to ask me questions about the assaults. He says he knows it may be hard, but he needs to know every single detail, down to the position, to what part of my assailant touched what part of me.

He then places a box of tissues on the desk in front of me. I grab one and press it against my eyes as I start to cry, painfully recounting each disgusting detail yet again, second by horrific second. I am barely able to hold myself together. I rest my head in my hands as he pushes me to relive what I tried so desperately to detach myself from at the time. And this soulless figure in front of me seems to be mocking me, the look of contempt on his face telling me all I need to know about whether he believes me.

I describe everything I remember about the Voice: his skin, his hands, his lips, the glimpse of his hair I saw through the tape. I recount our conversations, including telling the Voice about being molested as a child and his claims of having PTSD from his time in the military.

This agent asks several times if there was bleeding or pain, to which I say no, there was just a little soreness. Considering I just had the SART exam yesterday, I feel like he is hoping I will say something that contradicts the evidence that was collected. What's even more sickening is that he even asks me to describe my rapist's pubic hair. The agent knows I couldn't see, so I have to strain myself to try to remember what it *felt* like. It's such an insignificant detail for the investigation, but so degrading to me, and it feels like he's just trying to torment me.

We take another break, and Doug remains positive and uplifting, convinced I've shown them I'm honest. We go back into the room, and I mentally prepare myself for a long night. But maybe twenty minutes in, I'm abruptly cut off by the agent, who tells me he has all the information he needs. The interview is over.

I'm stunned and wonder if this is a good or bad thing. I still have so much more to say.

"There are a lot of inconsistencies in your statement. I'd like to advise you that lying to a federal agent is a federal crime, a violation of 18 USC section 1001," the agent says. "Is there anything about your statements that you want to change?"

I sit for a minute, feeling like any word or noise that comes out of my mouth next will somehow set off a bomb, obliterating my whole life and everyone in it. I scan everything that I've said to investigators, all the details I tried to remember. I know there must be small inconsistencies . . . maybe in the timeline, or little details of the house or cars, or other inconsequential things, but I was drugged and unconscious most of the time, terrified—for my life, Aaron's life, my family's lives—and trying to detach from every moment to spare myself the horror. All of which I explained to investigators over these past two days. So why would he say this?

Doug cuts him off and they both walk out.

I just sit there, my ears ringing as I listen to their muddled voices through the wall.

What kind of fucked-up twilight zone is this? What is going on?!

Doug comes back but doesn't say much. We wait for someone to drive us back to that parking lot and he calls my family to meet us there. As we stand in silence, my fear grows. I can sense from him that things are terribly wrong.

We get into a black car with an FBI agent named Jason. Doug discreetly ribs him about his souped-up undercover car. The agent grins like a little boy but won't admit what gadgets it has, as if it's some type of FBI secret. All the while, I sit in the backseat next to Lauren, frozen in shock.

It's late afternoon, maybe around five o'clock. The agent drops us off and we wait for my family so I can have them there with me for what Doug has to say next. I can tell he is deflated and angry, and for the first time, I feel he's angry at *me*. I feel like my whole world is crumbling around me, and I'm terrified the agent said something that will lead Doug to drop me as a client. I don't know if that's even a possibility, but at this point, I expect only the worst.

My family soon arrives, and Doug tells us what the agent said: "I am ninety-nine percent sure she's lying about this. Have you ever watched the movie *Gone Girl*? It'll explain a lot."

I feel my face go white and I hold my breath, praying the next thing that comes out of his mouth isn't "I can't help you."

Instead, Doug says, "I told him, 'You're *wrong*, and I'll bet my one percent against your ninety-nine percent.'"

My fears are lifted as I realize that Doug is pissed at this agent, not me. He continues. "How could he not believe you after you recounted the facts in such detail with no motive to lie? I don't understand this, but we'll keep fighting for you."

Oh, thank God!

"Thank you," I say quietly. "So . . . what do we do now? What do *I* do now?"

"You do whatever you want to do. They haven't charged you with anything. You're a free woman. You have no restrictions." Doug says he'll keep the pressure on law enforcement to investigate this properly as he builds a defense in the event they decide to prosecute, which it is clear they are planning to do. The thought of my freedom having an expiration date is chilling. I just want this all to be over but am so glad Doug is still going to fight for me!

"Well, what . . . what about Aaron? Can I talk to him now?"

I haven't asked about Aaron before, knowing that I wasn't permitted to communicate with him as long as I was talking to police. Now I wonder if he even wants to talk to me, if he doubts me like so many others do.

"Yeah, sure. You can talk to him. If you really want to after everything."

He seems skeptical this is a good idea, which is understandable, considering everything I told him about our relationship. But he doesn't know Aaron. I do.

"Okay. I don't know how I would contact him. I still don't have a phone and I don't remember his number. I don't know if he has a phone."

Doug tells me he'll reach out to Aaron's lawyers and advises me to stay up here in the Bay Area for a few days in case he needs to talk to me again. I slide into the backseat of the car with my family and watch Doug's and Lauren's concerned expressions as we drive off. What the hell is going to happen next?

LATER THAT EVENING, Doug calls to let me know he's spoken to Aaron's attorneys, and Aaron would really like to talk to me.

"I got a number you can reach him at but told his attorneys you've been through a lot these last few days, and you might need some time before you reach out, if you ever reach out."

I'm happy that Aaron actually wants to speak to me and all evening I stare at the number I jotted down. I long to hear Aaron's voice but I don't have anything left in me to call tonight.

I can hardly sleep as I ponder everything I need to do tomorrow to get my life back. Every obstacle I've managed to overcome so far is immediately followed by another, and I wonder if I'm condemned to eternal punishment like Sisyphus, though in my case I'm being punished for something I didn't do. Just like I did in captivity, I fantasize about seeing Aaron again, holding him, kissing him. I want it more than anything, but in a way, I fear it too. What if he rejects me? I'm damaged goods. But I know I will never be complete without him. I have to believe this will somehow strengthen our relationship rather than tear us apart.

28

DENISE

I SPEND SATURDAY MORNING getting little pieces of my life in order. I have no IDs, no car, no phone, no keys. I'm not sure what information the kidnappers have about me, so I go through all of my accounts and change my passwords. I cancel my credit cards and get new ones. And I get a new cell phone.

I have a passport and my stuff at the apartment, and I get ahold of Heather, one of my roommates, to meet me there that afternoon with my parents.

She tells me the FBI came with a search warrant and ripped my room apart like they were looking for illegal drugs or other incriminating items. They left a receipt for what they took: a pay stub and the first draft of a Christmas card I wrote to Aaron. What do they think that proves? Heather and two friends spent the next day trying to put my room back together again so I didn't have to come home to a mess. Their compassion and consideration are heartwarming.

The following week is the final week of our residency, and typically new residents move in the next weekend to replace graduating residents on their way out. I originally planned to move into an apartment with another physical therapist who was just finishing the orthopedic fellowship that I was about to apply to. She lives in a nice complex close to the freeway, which would have made for an easier commute to Kaiser in Vacaville, where the job opening was going to be that I was hoping to take until that fellowship started in January.

Before the kidnapping, I planned to start moving in boxes and meet her visiting family last Wednesday, the night of Park's press conference. I wonder what she and her family think of me now. Everything is so un-done, so displaced and so uncertain, that I know the only option for me is to gather my things and go back down to Huntington Beach with my family.

The director of the orthopedic fellowship emailed me Wednesday when the news broke that I was released, but since then I haven't heard from anyone from work except for my roommate and one other resident. With these accusations, I doubt that job offer is still on the table. Even if it is, I am so emotionally and physically messed up right now I know I won't be able to work anytime soon.

My family and I go to lunch in Berkeley, where we're seated at a round table in the middle of the open dining room. I'm paranoid that everyone at the other tables recognizes me or my dad, and I can manage only a couple of spoonfuls of the soup I ordered. I can't stop thinking about Aaron, and I tell my family I'm going to step outside and try to call him.

My body trembles as I dial, and my heart skips a beat as his phone rings. A deep voice answers, "Hello?"

My excitement deflates as I realize it's not Aaron, but I say it's Denise and that my lawyer gave me this number to contact him.

It turns out to be Ethan. Although I'm glad to get one step closer, fi-nally talking to Aaron's family, I'm discouraged and wonder if we'll ever reconnect. Ethan sounds relieved, saying Aaron really wants to talk to me, but he's not with him right now. Ethan is just about to leave San Fran-cisco to drive to Penryn to meet with Aaron and tells me to call back in a couple of hours.

Those couple of hours crawl by. My family and I go back to our hotel. My mom and Devin fly back home. Devin has a flight to Australia already planned to spend two weeks with his girlfriend, who lives there. And my mom needs to get back home and prepare for work next week. They're both apprehensive about leaving, but I tell them they should. At this point, there's nothing more to do but to wait for the next move from law enforcement.

I stay with my dad and older brother, Joey. Joey's girlfriend, Danielle, flies in that day, and she is a breath of fresh air. My whole family and I are completely drained, exhausted and stressed, and she brings with her a quiet and positive strength that refuels me.

I mention the whole *Gone Girl* thing that everyone keeps bringing up, and she explains the premise of the story to me: how it's about a crazy woman who fakes her death and pins it on her husband, who's having an affair, and he gets attacked by the media and the public while she hides out.

"It's ridiculous that they're comparing you to that. There's nothing remotely similar."

Finally learning more about the *Gone Girl* story, and how people are so easily convinced that I am equivalent to that character, is a level of betrayal and hurt that devastates me.

I know I'm not perfect and have made plenty of mistakes in my life, but to think I'd do *that* is incomprehensible! People actually believe that I would fake my own kidnapping, put my family, my close friends, my work colleagues, and my patients through that level of hell . . . for *what*?!

Some news reports are insinuating that I want my fifteen minutes of fame. Like *this*?! I've dedicated my life to helping others in any small way that I can. And the public finds it so easy to believe I am an attention-seeking whore willing to throw away her life's work for absolutely *nothing*?

I still fear more than ever that this is specifically designed to make people doubt me, to take the focus off the real criminals and whoever else is in some way involved. This level of cover-up makes me feel that these people are even more dangerous than I could have ever suspected. At this point, the lines are blurred between who it is exactly that I fear—the kidnappers or law enforcement . . . or is there even a difference between the two?

To kill time, I look up a couple of news reports and see how vicious the coverage is.

I also see some nasty comments people left on Facebook about me. I'm encouraged to see some friends or former coworkers come to my defense, but I'm disturbed at the animosity directed at them when they offer those supportive comments. How are people who know absolutely nothing about me so damn sure they have me pegged?

I am even more disheartened to see some people I do know and thought were my friends feeding into and perpetuating the lies, reposting headlines like "Real-Life 'Gone Girl' Allegedly Staged Her Own Insane Fake Kidnapping," rather than waiting and having some faith in me. I can't look at anything anymore. I just feel so let down, so attacked, so utterly betrayed by humanity.

My family had told me several times not to look at anything online. It won't help and will only hurt. Now I know to listen.

Finally, it's time to try to call Aaron again. My dad, Joey, and Danielle are in the hotel room, so I decide to go outside to make the call. I'm so nervous, afraid of what he will think of me. Ethan said that he really wanted to talk to me, but what if he doesn't really trust me? What if he blames me? What if he doesn't want to see me again, especially after what I had to do?

I find a spot behind a dumpster to try to get some cover from the heavy wind that is blowing into the phone from San Francisco Bay. I dial again, expecting to hear Ethan pick up, so I'm caught off guard when it's Aaron instead.

He sounds so beaten down I almost don't recognize his voice at first. As soon as he hears mine, he starts sobbing and repeating over and over, "They thought I killed you!"

The police thought Aaron murdered me? I don't know what to say. I just listen, crying. I knew they were trying to pit us against each other, but to accuse him of killing me? There couldn't have been evidence at the house that would make them think that. Is this how they treat every crime? What if it was just a robbery and we'd both gone to the police? Would they have accused us of lying then?

"Where are you? I'll come to you," he says, his voice breaking as he rushes through each word before I have a chance to reply. "Brandon says he can drive me down to Huntington as soon as possible, if that's okay, if you want to see me, but I know you've been through a lot. Oh, God, I'm so sorry. I'm so sorry. I know you've been through so much. It's okay if you don't want to see me. I can give you your space."

I am so relieved that he wants to see me!

"No, I'm not in Huntington. I'm still up here, staying at a hotel in Berkeley with my family. We have to stay up here for a few days."

"You're in Berkeley? What hotel? Can I come to see you? I want to see you . . . if that's okay."

"Of course." My voice squeaks as I choke on my tears. "Of course I want to see you. Yes! Whenever you want. I'll be here."

He tells me Ethan can drive him down to the hotel. It'll be a few hours, but he hopes to be there around six.

AARON

Midday Saturday I wait for Ethan, who's driving in from San Francisco so we can watch my twin nieces' softball game. It'll be helpful to spend some time with my family, especially not knowing if or when I may speak to Denise. To my surprise, he calls to tell me that he just spoke with her, and she wants to talk to me! It'll take a couple of hours for him to drive up, but he'll set up a call once he gets here.

I'm so excited I finally get to hear Denise's voice. I assume she's down in Southern California, so I make plans for Brandon to drive me down there if she's willing to see me. Now I have a reason to take a badly needed shower.

Once Ethan arrives, he needs to use the bathroom after the long drive, and leaves his phone, wallet, and keys on the counter. Almost as soon as he closes the door, his phone starts ringing. I see the number isn't registered in his phone contacts. I don't want to answer Ethan's phone for him, but I can't handle missing a call from Denise.

"Hello," I say tentatively.

"Hello," I hear Denise reply with a little surprise. Maybe she expected it to be Ethan. My knees buckle and I crumple to the ground. "They thought I killed you!" I burst out, and I can't stop repeating it.

On the other end of the phone, I hear Denise crying. A giant weight is lifted off my shoulders as she tells me it's not my fault. Miraculously, she doesn't blame me for the kidnapping, and she does want to see me. I'm ecstatic to hear she's only a couple of hours away. I tell her that we'll meet her at the hotel, and I'll be there as soon as I can.

I feel terrible asking Ethan to turn around and drive me back to where he just left, but he doesn't hesitate. "We can leave right now."

I hug everyone else, thanking them for providing a safe and loving place for me.

From the moment the kidnappers took Denise, I hoped I would be lucky enough to hold her again. I thought I would have that chance Wednesday, then Thursday, then Friday. With each passing day, it came to seem more fantasy than reality. But today . . . today could be the best day of my life.

29

AARON

I CAN FEEL MY energy rising each minute we drive closer to Denise.
I can't wait to hold her again even though I'm afraid to hear about the
trauma she endured. I'm not sure she'll be able to talk about it yet or ever.
It doesn't matter if she ever tells me, I'll love her and support her as much
as I can, as long as I can.

We arrive at the hotel, a huge, sprawling structure that runs along the
San Francisco Bay. Ethan says he'll wait at the bar for me and gives me
one of his credit cards in case we need it for anything. I call Denise, and
she gives me directions to the building she's in.

I open the door and see a long, winding hallway. "Oh, come on," I
say to myself. It's an overwhelming maze, one more obstacle keeping me
from Denise. I half expect that I'll have to fight a fucking ninja to get to
her. I want to sprint but I'm afraid the other hotel guests will recognize
me. I start walking as fast as I can. There's a left turn, then a right. My
heart is pounding in my chest and I'm beginning to hyperventilate. A
week ago, I thought I'd screwed up so badly that Denise would leave me,
but she gave me another chance. She paid a steep price for forgiving me.
Will she be able to forgive me for that too? Is it fair of me to even ask?

I pass at least twenty doors before I reach the one that will bring me face-to-face with Denise. Somehow I need to show her that she made the right decision. I put my hands on the doorframe to steady myself. Then I knock. . . .

The door opens, I look up, and it's not a memory or a picture on the news that I've seen a hundred times, but her. I grab her and pull her tightly into my body as she wraps her arms around me. We both burst into tears. I can't tell if they're tears of joy or sorrow, but I feel somewhat whole again. No longer able to stand, we fall onto the bed, still in each other's arms.

I TELL HER everything that happened after she was taken . . . the prison clothes, Mustard, the polygraph, French, my phone on airplane mode. I can tell it's a lot for her to take in, but she listens and brushes away my tears.

I let her know that she doesn't need to talk to me about her experience; she can tell me in her own time. We decide to get a room for ourselves, which Ethan graciously pays for. Later that night, she opens up. Hearing each moment of her experience feels like a knife in my gut, deeper and deeper. Eventually, she tells me about the Voice raping her. But she doesn't use the word "rape." She says, "He had to have sex with me."

I don't want to say anything to make her feel worse, but it's painful to hear her have some hint of sympathy for this predator. It's obvious to me he attempted to manipulate her, and I'm afraid she truly believes that he was "forced" to rape her. I keep my thoughts to myself. There's no way for me to understand how she feels at this moment. I can't possibly understand that type of violation. I need to be supportive and, more than anything, let her know I'm grateful that she smartly avoided more physical trauma during the assaults.

Then she uses the phrase again, saying, "He had to have sex with me" a second time, in that strange, robotic tone. It doesn't sound like her; it sounds like what the kidnappers want her to say. Like if they don't call it rape, then it's not so bad. It's bullshit! They forced her to perform while being recorded. Those sick bastards! I can't stop myself from blurting out, "He *raped* you!"

She appears stunned for a second; then I see the truth of the situation hit her. I feel horrible until she says, "That's what I needed to hear someone say."

As she describes the second rape in more detail, she starts crying. "I didn't want to. I didn't want to . . . ," she keeps repeating. "Please don't leave me. I didn't want to."

Her body starts shaking and shaking. I hold her, squeezing her as if my arms are the only things keeping her from bursting apart.

"It's not your fault," I reassure her. "You didn't have a choice. I'm not going to leave you." My soul is crushed into dust. I'm so inadequate at consoling her. How do you help someone in that much pain?

As her shaking slowly subsides, I gently kiss her, saying over and over, "You're my hero." I hold her in my arms, telling her that she never has to feel ashamed or explain herself to me, that I'll take care of all our finances while she heals, no matter how long that takes. I'll sell my house, which will help, and we can find a place of our own. I want us to have a lifetime together, starting now. I mean this with every fiber of my being. I have never loved someone as much as I love Denise. It's not because I feel guilty or I feel I owe her anything. I knew I loved her before this whole thing happened. Being able to hold her in my arms is something I thought I'd never be able to do again, and I'm cherishing every second of it. As the hours pass, I want to act on those feelings, to be intimate with her, to be closer to her. I missed her so much. But I'm deathly afraid of triggering the trauma. Together, we decide it feels right to make love. We keep a couple of lights on low. I need her to see me and know she's safe.

We spend the rest of the night in the hotel room; I don't sleep well, but at least when I wake up, Denise is there.

DENISE

I am sick with anticipation as six approaches. I ask my family if they can go to the bar so Aaron and I can meet alone. They leave when Aaron calls to let me know he and Ethan parked the car and he's on his way to my room.

I wait for what feels like forever. I worry that I gave him the wrong room number, or he's gotten lost, but I try to be patient.

I finally hear a hurried knock at the door and rush over, my stomach churning. I open it and see him leaning into the doorframe with his head tilted down like he's so exhausted he can barely stand. But when he looks up, I see that his gorgeous green eyes have that same look of desperation and relief I know I have right now. This isn't some fantasy that will never come true. He's actually right here!

He sweeps me up in his arms and presses his head against mine, breathing me in. We both cry as he walks me back to the bed, and we fall into each other's arms. He strokes my hair and I rub the back of his head as we kiss like we're long-lost loves who haven't seen each other in decades. I can't believe I am holding him, and I just keep squeezing him to make sure this is real.

Slowly he begins to tell me what happened to him after we were separated, after I was taken, when he called the police, about the interrogations he endured, how he tried so hard to get them to believe him, to look for me, but they wouldn't.

My God. He was kidnapped and tortured too—by the police!

It's mind-blowing to hear him describe the horrible position he was put in, trying to decide whether to call the police, not knowing if doing so would kill me or help me, only to have the police attack him when he did. I don't know who had it worse. I don't know how he managed to stay strong and fight through it.

"We're gonna sue 'em," he blurts out. "After what they did! They wouldn't look for you and they kept saying I murdered you! Fuck them. We're suing them! They can't get away with this!"

"Whoa, whoa, wait." I cut him off, completely overwhelmed by everything he's telling me. There is no way I have the energy to act offensively, to be in a position other than complete defense and retreat. After everything I experienced in captivity, then the abusive treatment of both the police and FBI, and now finding out how they went after Aaron too . . . I need time to think. It sounds like this is something way bigger than either of us can fathom right now.

I'm even more scared than I already was because the media and the public actually *believe* the police. After being released by the bad guys, I could never have imagined the danger I'd be in from the "good guys." I feel even less safe now, like our lives and our families' lives are at even more risk.

We get a hotel room for the two of us. After all that we've gone through, we can't bear to be separated from each other. I feel like my soul has been ripped apart for days, a part of me trampled and lost, and he is my other half making me feel somewhat whole again.

As he tells me he loves me and he'll take care of me while I heal, I am flooded with love for him, but I'm also apprehensive. We'd already been through a lot before this, and I was happy to have reached a good place together, truly committing to each other, but all of this is even more than I am prepared for. "Let's see how things go," I tell him. I don't want him to feel responsible for me, because what happened is not his fault, and I want to make sure that he doesn't feel obligated to take care of me, either emotionally or financially.

I reassure him that if this doesn't work out, it's okay. I can move in with my mom. My family will help me get back on my feet if I need it, so he knows there are other options. The whole point of our conversation the night of the kidnapping was to make sure that he actually did want me, not because he feels he wants *someone*, but because he truly loves me and wants to be with *me*. The last thing I want is for someone to be with me because of pity or guilt.

As we talk through this, I feel how much he loves me and how much he means every word he says. We order room service, something hearty and fattening. Not only do I finally have an appetite, but I'm able to devour the food. We can't leave each other's side, wrapped up in each other's arms. I feel the tighter he squeezes me, the tighter he needs me to squeeze him.

He asks me a little more about what happened, saying he knows that I went to the hospital and I don't have to talk about it if I don't want to, but I tell him I don't want to keep it from him. I can hear myself downplaying what I experienced and, in a way, defending what happened. I tell Aaron the Voice said that he had to have sex with me and Aaron cuts me off.

"He *raped* you. It wasn't sex. He *raped* you, Denise."

He says it so forcefully, with so much anger, that it kind of stuns me. It's like a verbal slap to the face saying, *Snap out of it!*

I know it isn't anger or frustration directed *at* me, but anger that this happened *to* me, how I was treated by the kidnappers, and then the police, and now by what people are saying about me. It's what I need to hear. Until now, even though other people have used the word "rape," it hasn't come out of my mouth.

Why am I tiptoeing around what this man did to me? Regardless of what he said—that it wasn't up to him and that he was forced to do it—he still did it. And he enjoyed it.

I guess I needed to be in denial in order to get through that time. By not putting the label "rape" on what happened, it somehow lessened the severity of it, making it seem less horrifying, so I could manage to stay sane and survive. But I can no longer deny what happened and the deep-seated terror it planted within me, so deep it's impossible to describe and impossible to understand unless you've experienced it yourself.

Although Aaron and I are both in an intense state of trauma, or maybe because of that, we feel closer than ever. We talk about being intimate. He says he doesn't want to remind me of what happened, that he will wait until I'm ready. But I need him and want him. More than that, I love him. I won't let those vicious predators take something special away from me, from us. We make love, and we fall asleep holding each other.

Finally.

30

DENISE

Even under the best of circumstances, it's intimidating and nerve-racking when a boyfriend meets the family, especially the dad and older brother.

The next day is Aaron's first time meeting mine. I love him all the more for going right in for a hug as he greets my dad. For the past week, people in the highest authority have tried to convince my father that Aaron murdered me, his little girl. Although I can tell my dad is a little cautious at first, I know if he spends time with Aaron, he'll see what I see: that Aaron's someone he can trust and will love.

To keep ourselves busy, my dad drives us all around Berkeley, his old stomping ground, to see where he lived when he was in his twenties. We walk the UC Berkeley campus and stop to get coffee. As we wait in line in a small crowded shop, there I am on the TV hanging above us, a close-up of my driver's license photo looking like a mug shot. We glance around to see if anyone recognizes us, and thankfully they don't or at least pretend not to.

At dinner, we go to the restaurant where my dad's been eating every night this past week. To my surprise, they're very accommodating, respectful, and gracious. The manager even comes over to ask us if we need anything. I'm hopeful that there are some people who do believe and support us.

When I'm in the bathroom, my dad tells Aaron, "This is the first time in days I've seen Denise eat," and Joey adds, "She looks more like herself now that you're here."

AARON

Monday, Ethan and I plan to go to my house to pick up some things. It'll be the first time I've been there since the kidnapping.

First, though, we stop at Dan and Amy's office to read the second email the kidnappers sent to Henry Lee, the *Chronicle* reporter, over the weekend. It's longer, around nine thousand words, and runs some nineteen pages.

"There's some crazy shit in there," Dan tells us when we arrive.

I feel my blood boil within the first couple of pages. The kidnappers pretend to want to clear our names but are clearly too chickenshit to come forward. As I read on, I see they're providing an incredible amount of detail. They talk about breaking into homes and describe items they stole and ones they didn't. They talk about drag racing in the middle of the night, which Denise and I heard last fall. Then they describe their expensive drone and a recent memory hits me.

A little over a month ago, Denise and I were coming back to my house after a day out. We were driving through the north side of the island, which is mainly uninhabited. I occasionally saw people flying model airplanes around there. However, this time a small group of guys was flying a large drone. They were almost hidden between two dilapidated buildings. I said to Denise, "That doesn't feel right. That gives me the creeps." But they weren't breaking any laws, so there was nothing for me to do. Now I'm sure I was watching my own predators practicing their attack on us in broad daylight.

It's clear from this email that the kidnappers created and lived in a fantasy, in which they were "gentlemen criminals" who targeted only people who deserved their vigilante justice. It was a craven way to absolve their guilt. But Denise was completely innocent. She wasn't their intended victim, but they victimized her anyway. There's no way they can justify it. Over time, we shattered their fantasy and showed them the truth—no one deserves this.

I'm in a fog after I finish reading the email. There are so many leads for the FBI or the Vallejo detectives to follow, but they haven't asked me a single question since the kidnappers sent the first email. I'm guessing they have some crazy theory that we wrote them. Unfortunately, the public will probably think along the same lines. I can't help but believe that the kidnappers' confession is falling on deaf ears.

However, if law enforcement won't investigate, maybe Henry Lee, the reporter from the *Chronicle* who received the emails, will look into it. The *Chronicle* was one of the main newspapers that received letters from the Zodiac Killer bragging about his murders. Many of his murders even happened in and around Vallejo. So they can't be too surprised that criminals would want credit for their work. Anyone who reads this entire email knows there is a lot to follow up on. Maybe not all reporters have the full email, but Henry Lee does, at least.

I've seen the movies in which the dogged investigative reporter cracks the case and saves the day. I fantasize about someone coming to our rescue, but it can't be the fucking kidnappers.

ETHAN AND I drive over to my house. I'm grateful that it's the middle of a workday, which means there should be fewer people walking around the neighborhood. We park on the street so no one can tell that we're there.

I've seen so many pictures and videos of my house on the news that it feels like I'm visiting a movie set instead of my own home. There's black fingerprint dust caked over the front door and windows. The front door is unlocked and open, letting anyone come inside. I push it wider and see my house is covered in soot and all my belongings are tossed around. There are papers on the floor, cabinets left open, cushions flipped over like they're all pieces of trash. I'm the bad guy whose property doesn't need to be respected. It's the kind of gratuitous punishment that our society loves to dole out. I wonder how these people would feel if it were their home.

As we walk into the living room, I can hear the echo of that *dung, dung, dung* sound in my head. It haunts me even though the camera is gone. Then I see a black plastic box on the kitchen island: It's the portable phone charger that the kidnappers left for me.

"You have to be fucking kidding me!" I shout.

My outburst startles Ethan and I tell him that I've informed the police at least four times about the phone charger.

We search the rest of the house to see what else was overlooked. I see that the police took my Comcast receiver and my PlayStation 4, so they clearly want to search my electronics. (What—do they think I play Grand Theft Auto: *Gone Girl* Edition?) I head to the back patio. The screen is missing from one of the back windows leading into the living room. There are three holes drilled into the window frame, right around the lock. I look around the corner of the house and find the screen lying on the ground. There are clean square cuts by the tabs so as to allow someone to pop off the screen.

I'm starting to lose my mind.

I cannot fathom why the police didn't take this screen into evidence. Another screen has been removed, in the same fashion, from a window at the side of the house. A thick metal wire lies on my gardening table out back. I put on some gloves and bring the wire over to the window with the drill holes. Sure enough, the wire fits perfectly and I'm able to push the lock open. My fury falls into despair. There's no way the police are going to catch the kidnappers if they can't collect evidence that took me less than five minutes to find.

Before we head upstairs, I hear Mr. Rogers meowing at the French doors. He bursts in as soon as I open the door. I pick him up and hold him as he makes the funny little chirping sounds that always greet me when I come home from work. Despite everything, he's still hanging around the house, confused about why I'm not home. It's so comforting to know he's okay, but I know in a few minutes I need to put him outside again.

Thankfully, my neighbors are taking care of him. Their two little girls love playing with him. He is the sweetest cat ever.

Mr. Rogers follows at our heels as we explore upstairs. I see more fingerprint dust and I notice the police have taken my bedsheets. I go to my closet to grab more clothes and I see that a chunk of the carpet has been cut out. It's right where my head was that night. After the Voice forced us to drink the sedative, I intentionally drooled in an attempt to reduce my absorption and leave some evidence. Well, at least the police saw that, but I doubt they'll even test it.

Getting my clothes helps me feel a little more like myself, but it's almost paralyzing to be walking the grounds of my nightmares. Everything is a trigger: the missing carpet, the fingerprint dust, even the post on the hillside that no longer has that metal glare. My head spins, and my skin becomes clammy as I start reliving the horrors of that night. I flop down on my sheetless bed and Mr. Rogers jumps up after me. He curls up beside me, softly purring as if to say it's going to be okay.

My mind keeps flashing back to that night—Mr. Rogers was there when the kidnappers snuck into our room. I felt him brushing against my arms after Denise was forced to the closet. Then the Voice whispered to someone, "Get the cat out of the room. . . . Get the cat out of the room," and just like that my little buddy was gone. He's probably seen their faces and knows their smells. If only he could talk, we could catch these guys and save other people from this trauma.

After I gather myself, I head downstairs to throw out any spoiled food before we leave. Ethan asks me what's in the pot on the stove. I tell him it's steel-cut oats that I had been soaking overnight so Denise and I could have them for breakfast. So far, Ethan has been calm and steady, giving the police the benefit of the doubt for overlooking the charger and the window screens, but he's reached his breaking point.

"Motherfuckers!" he bursts out. "You and Denise were supposedly in a huge fight, yet you decided to make breakfast!? Or wait. You killed her but then decided to make breakfast. What the fuck are these guys doing? Are they even thinking?" he yells.

I'm startled; I've never seen him so angry before. But it's obviously so frustrating to him to watch his family suffer at the hands of investigators who ignore such basic clues. He deflates and slumps down in a nearby chair. Anyone can make mistakes—even FBI agents are only human—but this seems incomprehensible.

I wash out the pot and the smell of the moldy oats fills my nostrils with the truth about this fiasco—the kidnappers and law enforcement together destroyed everything, and we're left to clean up the mess.

As I put Mr. Rogers outside, he looks up at me with his sad round eyes. I bend down and tell him, "I'll be back. I'm going to find a home for you real soon." I can't keep Ethan or Mr. Rogers away from this pain. I can't keep anyone away from this pain.

31

DENISE

FOR THE NEXT few days, Aaron and I stay in San Francisco at Ethan's girlfriend's apartment near Polk Street. We don't want to keep spending our families' money on hotels, and she offers her place, knowing no one would think to look for us there. We call it our "safe house" as we navigate the next week.

On Monday, my dad and Joey come with me to Doug's office while Aaron's at his house with Ethan. I see from plaques on his wall that Doug was rated in the "Top 100 National Trial Lawyers." As professional and pragmatic as he is, I also sense the paternal protectiveness he feels for me, and I know he loses sleep trying to figure out the best way to protect me.

Doug tells me he's working hard to manage the press, to get the word out to the public that the kidnappers have written a nineteen-page "manifesto" describing the kidnapping and their organization. There are things in it that only the kidnappers could know, confirming what we told the police. He tells me another email was just sent as well, this one threatening the Vallejo Police Department and Kenny Park if they don't recant their accusations against Aaron and me. Doug never shows me the emails, and I don't even want to read them. Too much of this information may emotionally break me down. I need to stay numb.

The more I meet with Doug and see how he handles the case, the more secure I feel. Even though we are up against a lot—not just some local incompetent policemen but the entire police force and the FBI—I know Doug is the right person to take this on.

I give written consent for the FBI to go through all of my personal emails, my iPhone, and my computer to prove to them that Aaron and I didn't write those emails. They can search everything. I have nothing to hide. I even ask Doug if he thinks I should talk to the press. The thought of it absolutely terrifies me, but if he thinks it would help, I'd figure it out. He still says it's best for me not to, that he doesn't think it would help and would likely only hurt. So we continue on as is.

Later that night, the local ABC station airs an interview with Doug about the emails, and he's quoted in the *Chronicle*, which finally posts a story about them. We also see news footage of Mr. Rogers sitting on the front doorstep of Aaron's house, waiting for us to return, which is devastating to us. But apparently it's just one big joke to some people. Aaron tells me one person commented, "It was the tuxedo [cat]! He did it!"

ON TUESDAY MORNING, Aaron and I wake up at 3:00 a.m., which is becoming the norm for both of us. We are unable to fall back asleep and find an all-night coffee shop to get us out and moving. There's a lot we need to do, including going to the bank to try to get cash and a new debit card. I need to go to the store to get a new bra and comfortable tennis shoes and makeup since the police took my overnight bag and everything in it into evidence.

Early that morning my dad calls and says Aaron and I should make sure we spend the day in places that have surveillance cameras to show where we've been as an alibi, in case the kidnappers follow through with their threats to harm the police. I haven't thought of that, but I am now even more worried. If Kenny Park or another cop gets hurt, we could be falsely accused of that as well. It's good advice from my dad, but our plan was to be out in public anyway, so we continue with our errands. I just hope and pray that nothing else bad happens to anyone.

We walk the couple of miles to downtown San Francisco. Although it's intimidating to be around a lot of people, something also feels safe about being in a crowd. You're just one of the many faces passing by, and we feel less likely to get attacked if we're out in public. However, throughout the day, Aaron notices that people walking by us or waiting in cars for the lights to change are staring at me.

"Well, she definitely recognized you," he tells me. "She just did a double take with her mouth open."

"Great," I dryly reply. I don't bother looking around. I don't want to know. Aaron's lawyers had him shut down his Facebook account early last week, so the media only has one side-view picture of him, making him hard to identify. But me, well, my face has been everywhere. My brother gave the media a number of photos when I was missing because he wanted to do whatever he could to help find me. How could he or anyone else in that position know that a victim could be turned into a worldwide villain overnight?

The rest of the week is spent packing up my apartment in Vallejo with my dad and Aaron. We plan to leave Friday to drive down to Huntington Beach and stay with my family. When my mom visited me at the beginning of February, she'd driven up in her 1999 Honda CR-V and left it with me because she had just bought a new car. She signed the Honda over to me so I could sell my Mitsubishi Eclipse, the car I'd had since I was a teenager. The maintenance and repairs have gotten out of hand. Thankfully, though, I haven't gotten around to selling it yet; otherwise, Aaron and I wouldn't have a car to drive , because the police still have my Honda.

It hasn't been driven in about two months, so we take it to a friend's husband's auto shop a couple of miles from the hospital, which also happens to be on the same block as Vallejo's city hall. With the kidnappers still on the loose and the police actively against us, every moment we spend in Vallejo feels dangerous, threatening, so we try to be as quick and efficient as possible. At the auto shop, our friend greets me by saying, "Oh, you're still a blonde."

"Why wouldn't I be?" I respond.

As soon as I say it, I realize she thought I might have dyed my hair to be less recognizable. This won't be the last time I'm asked. It's upsetting that there's been so much negative media attention, so many awful things said about us, that friends and family assume I'd try to hide by changing my most distinctive feature, my long blond hair.

Although it might make me feel safer to do it, I decide then and there, and never think twice about it, that there's no way in hell I'm going to change a damn thing about me because of those assholes in law enforcement. It's not about vanity. It's about my identity. It's way beyond hair color. It's about who I am, what I've worked for my whole life to become. I've worked hard to build up my life and be happy and comfortable with who I am. What these people are saying about me, it's not *me*. It's some character they've created that has nothing to do with *me* in any way, shape, or form. So fuck them. All of them. I am who I am, and I'm not going to change. If anything, I'll be even more emboldened about who I am, my roots, my family, my beliefs, and my will.

I'm able to schedule an appointment with my therapist in Vallejo. It takes me three hours to tell Dr. Kelly Land what happened. I ask if the police ever contacted her—I gave them her name—and she says no, but she wished they would because she'd tell them that nothing in her assessment of me would indicate that I would make up a story like they claim.

I'm grateful I already have an established relationship with a therapist. I don't know if I'd have the courage to see someone new, wondering if they believed me or were just analyzing me to see if I was crazy.

OVER THE NEXT couple of days, we make daily trips to the apartment as I pack up and clean. I notice all of my clothes have a strong chemical odor and I assume the FBI sprayed them with something to see if they could find some incriminating item.

By Friday, I get my car from the shop and have finished cleaning out the apartment. I leave a note for my roommates to give to the director of the program with my new contact information, as well as my employee badge, the laundry card, and the final check for the apartment.

That weekend at my mom's, I invite three of my closest friends to come over. Laura is my oldest friend. I've been friends with Cecilia since high school and Taylor since my early twenties. They sit in silence as I spend hours telling them what happened with the kidnapping and the police.

I start crying as I tell Laura I saw her along with Sydney's father, Jim, on the news last week standing in front of my dad's apartment building while I was being questioned by Huntington Beach police. Sydney (who lives in Florida now), Laura, and I have been best friends since we were five, and Jim is like a second father to me.

"I didn't know you guys were there," I choke out, thinking of how different my homecoming could have been if I'd been allowed to see her and hug her, if I'd been greeted by people who loved and cared for me. Instead, I was isolated. And if my cousin wasn't a lawyer, who knows how long that would've lasted?

"I told them," Laura says, her own face streaked with tears. "I said, 'That's my best friend. That's my best friend. Please, let me up there!' But they wouldn't let us through! We didn't know what to do. They wouldn't tell us anything!"

We're both mourning the loss of that moment we so desperately needed at the time.

My friends tell me they spoke to the Vallejo police while I was in captivity, and they shared what they knew of my relationship with Aaron, trying to do anything to help. Wednesday morning, Laura was on the phone with one of the detectives, who asked her if I had any distinguishing marks.

"I was so scared! I thought they had a body and that it might be you, but he wouldn't say. And while I was on the phone with him, a friend texted me that the newscasters said you'd been released and were at your dad's, so I asked the detective if it was true, and he kept saying, 'I can't confirm that.' So I thought, 'Fuck this guy,' and I hung up and sped over to your dad's. That's when I saw Jim."

It's so hard to see my friends hurting, knowing what they must have been through those couple of days, the horror of not knowing if I was alive or dead. As we talk more about the police and the media reports, I hear a little of their experience as well. Taylor tells me that when she watched the press conference, she almost threw her wineglass at the TV when Kenny Park started talking because it was so obscene.

I ask if the police tried contacting them again for follow-up questions to see if they thought it was in my nature to lie or ask anything more about me, and they all said once I was released, they never heard anything from the police again.

You'd think that if the police were dead set on proving that I am an emotionally unstable, narcissistic liar, they would want to get an understanding of my personality from the people closest to me or my therapist. Of course, if they did, they'd discover that their theories didn't hold up, which is probably why they didn't bother. They didn't care about learning the truth. They cared only about what would match their narrative.

That Sunday is Easter, so we go to my aunt Katie and uncle Jeff's on my dad's side of the family. I adore Aaron more than ever for coming, as he meets about twenty of my family members. He keeps introducing himself to people, and at one point he jokes and says to me, "I'm pretty sure everyone knows who I am. I guess I really don't need to tell people my name."

I know he's not surprised because I've told him about my big family and how strong we are as a unit, but I can see he's a little overwhelmed, and we're both exhausted. We leave feeling empowered by the unwavering loyalty and determination of my family, and Aaron tells me his family's the same way. Although we are all lost and confused by the situation we're all in, we're in it together, from both sides, and ready to do what it takes to find justice.

THE FOLLOWING WEEK we stay with my mom's sister Marianne and her husband, Tom, in Carlsbad, near San Diego, and teach Aaron Shanghai, the card game we play every time we get together. The San Francisco Giants are playing the Padres and Aaron's a huge Giants fan, so we go to a game to try to keep our minds busy. As we wait for the Coaster, the San

Diego commuter train, to take us downtown, we hear a voice say, "Aaron? Aaron Quinn?"

I immediately recoil, thinking it's someone who's recognized us from the news. But this guy comes up behind Aaron and hugs him. They laugh, and I meet Pat, a good friend of Aaron's from college. He asks us what we're doing in town, and we try to figure out how to answer him; he obviously doesn't know what happened. He's with friends Aaron's never met, so Aaron discreetly tells him to google his name to get an idea of what's going on. As we ride the train together, Pat tells Aaron what he discovered, quietly, so as not to draw attention from his friends. He feels bad he was oblivious, but we're both grateful that not everyone in the world knows. He invites us to spend the day with them because they're all going to the game too.

And for just a few hours, we hang out, laugh, drink, joke, and feel like we're normal young adults again. In many ways, the fact that it's a small world can work against us, but in this instance, it's a refreshing coincidence and a respite that our souls need.

BUT MORE OFTEN than not, when we try to have some normalcy, we're hit with the reality that we're no longer able to hide in a crowd. We have tickets to see *The Book of Mormon*, which Aaron bought months ago; we almost don't go but we decide we aren't going to hide forever. Sitting in the theater, we laugh so hard our faces hurt. But when the show ends and we stand to leave, we see two women around our age taking videos of us and snickering. I long to be old news, for my face to be unrecognizable again. But I fear this sense of vulnerable exposure will never end.

32

DENISE

AFTER A FEW weeks of trying to stabilize ourselves, it's time to try to get our jobs squared away. Aaron has arranged to be on paid medical leave for the time being, hoping to return to Kaiser in a few months. We're not sure where we'll need or want to live, and we're keeping an open mind that it may have to be out of state. We're hoping he can transfer to another Kaiser and maintain the position and benefits he's built up over the past five years.

As for me, I haven't heard a word from anyone at Kaiser. Nothing. Although my residency was scheduled to run until the first week of April, I haven't received payment for those last two weeks.

True, I wasn't at work because of the kidnapping, but I expected to at least receive a pay stub indicating I worked zero hours. Instead, I get nothing. It's as if I never worked there. I check in with my old roommate to confirm she gave my contact information to Tim Josten, our manager.

Eventually I connect with Tim, and I'm sent the paperwork bringing my employment to an end, but only after I strongly insist I need the proper documentation for legal reasons after being a victim of a very serious crime. I can tell his responses are coming from Kaiser's legal team because of their terseness and the absurdly long delays between emails. The same goes for the director of the fellowship I had hoped to take. It's clear that any opportunities I once had with Kaiser are gone. I still need to take a final exam for the residency, and Tim says that I can come in when I'm ready. I hope that's true.

I don't know when I'll be emotionally able to work again. I fear that I'll be seen only as a fraud, a con artist, someone who can't be trusted, certainly not with someone's health and well-being. That thought crushes my spirit and often brings me to tears. I feel so lost and out of control.

So we try to focus on things we *can* control, like working out or being active on a regular basis. But there are many times running or walking that I'm triggered into panic attacks. Predictably it happens when I pass police. I'm scared this will be the moment they pull up in full SWAT gear, handcuff me, stuff me in their car, and take me to prison. Another time I'm with Aaron near a school that's letting out. I hear someone yell, and I feel so threatened I start hyperventilating and crying, and I need to lean on Aaron to walk back.

And one day I'm jogging in Huntington Beach by myself. I flew down last minute without Aaron to visit because Sydney's dad, Jim, is in the hospital recovering from a stroke. I'm very concerned about his prognosis and I go running to relieve stress. As I jog into the crosswalk at a four-way stop, a raised truck makes a quick left turn, the engine revving, and almost hits me. I jump out of the way to avoid being struck.

I break down on the side of the road and a young mom with a stroller comes over to ask if I'm okay. I can hardly speak as I sit on the curb crying and trying to catch my breath. I want to ask for her contact information in case I need a witness to prove I did nothing wrong. It's so screwed up, this feeling that I have to document everything I do to prove I'm telling the truth. Even though I'm only four blocks from home, I call Sydney to pick me up because I can't breathe. This is no way to live.

I'd always enjoyed my time alone but now I'm scared to be by myself. What if someone breaks in again? What if the kidnappers come after me? If my mom is away and Aaron isn't there, I ask a friend or my brother to come and stay with me until I go to bed. Seeing something as simple as packaging tape like the kidnapper used to keep my eyes shut as he raped me catapults me back to that moment.

As hard as it is for us, we see the toll it's taking on our families, and the concern our parents have for us. One day I can't get out of bed, and my mom tries to give me some words of encouragement in an attempt to motivate me. It's coming from a good place, but what she doesn't realize is, in this moment, it's not a choice. I am virtually paralyzed with extreme anxiety and depression. Aaron's parents also express fear that Aaron's depressed, and this will forever change him. In some ways, we will never be the same. It must be agonizing for them to watch their children, normally so driven, proactive, and successful, acting like mere zombies most days. What we tell them, and even more so tell ourselves, is that right now it's okay that we're not okay. This is a normal response to abnormal circumstances, and it would be more concerning if we weren't affected by all of this. We know, or at least hold on to some hope, that we will get better. At least we have our families here to help us heal, though I know they are struggling as well.

I MEET UP with a friend from college who asks me what I plan to do next. "Are you going to change your name?" she wonders.

"No!" I respond immediately. "Why would I change my name? I did nothing wrong. I'm not going to change who I am because of what they said."

She shrinks in her seat as she listens to me recount the kidnapping and how the police treated me after my release. I can tell this is a lot for her to absorb, but I could never anticipate what she says next.

She tells me the reason she asked if I was going to change my name was because she originally believed what the police said, that the kidnapping was a hoax.

I am so offended and hurt I have to leave the room to compose myself. I had hoped that at the very least my close friends wouldn't have believed what they saw on the news. What kind of person does she think I am to put my loved ones through such hell and risk everything I had worked so hard for my entire life? It goes to show how strongly people put their trust in the words of the police. My own friend initially took their word over mine. I guess she and the general public don't realize that our attorneys wouldn't risk their reputations and careers by proclaiming our innocence publicly if they didn't truly believe in it. They would have hedged. This is a hopeless and frustrating position. It makes me question my whole world. When I return, she tells me she believes me now and feels awful that she ever thought I would fake a kidnapping. She tries to reassure me that even if I had, she always planned to support me no matter what because she's my friend. I appreciate her honesty, but it's still crushing. I wonder who else we know believed the lies as well but hasn't admitted it to us. I feel I can't trust anyone anymore. This is too much, and I need counseling more than ever, but I don't have a therapist down here.

I try to get in contact with someone from victims' assistance, government programs that provide a number of services, including financial support, for crime victims. I no longer have health insurance or an income, so I can't afford a new therapist, and I need the help this program provides. Before I was questioned by the FBI agent at the police station, he gave Doug a card with the name of a person to contact for victims' assistance. But apparently that was a ruse because when I call, I'm told there's no case number or file on me. I'm not in their system. The woman I speak to is not even the correct person to contact, as she works out of a completely different county in a different part of the state, and she can't figure out why I was referred to her. She's kind to me, though, and explains how to fill out victims' compensation paperwork, but without a case number, it's impossible to use these federal resources.

Doug protects me in ways I couldn't have foreseen. Not only does he help me find the right person at victims' assistance, but he also guides my communications with Kaiser. I am notified several times that Instagram and Twitter accounts are being opened under my name or email address, and he has to send legal demands to shut them down. He attempts to get answers or cooperation from the Vallejo police and the FBI agents investigating my case, all the while gathering information that could help my defense because they still threaten to prosecute us.

We try to get the SART exam results, copies of the search warrants, and other pieces of evidence, including a list of who was interviewed by police and what items of ours law enforcement took. We still don't know what they have of ours. The Vallejo police insist the case is in the FBI's hands and most of our requests are ignored or complied with only partially, and every communication indicates that the only thing being investigated is us. There is absolutely no effort being made to find the real criminals. The federal prosecutor assigned to the case, Assistant US Attorney Matt Segal, specializes in white-collar crimes, not violent ones, and he tells Doug he's looking into filing computer crime or wire fraud charges against me. Aaron's attorneys ask for our cars to be returned. They found Aaron's Camry at the VA clinic's parking lot on Mare Island the night of the kidnapping and mine in front of Aaron's house, where the kidnappers moved it. We understand they needed to process both for evidence, but they've had plenty of time to do that. Yet Segal refuses, saying, "Call us when your client changes his story."

I'm horrified at the thought of the harm the kidnappers could be causing—and the threat we are still under—while these so-called professionals pour their efforts into building a case against *us*.

We never get a break from any of this. We are both struggling with nightmares. I dream repeatedly about people at work and school attacking me as a liar; I search for someone I know, a friend, a colleague, who still believes in me, but it's hopeless. Sometimes I dream about people invading our bedroom while we're sleeping, but it always quickly shifts to me trying to get help but not being believed, the police attacking me or the media chasing after me.

I also dream that I cheat on Aaron and ruin our relationship. I still feel guilty for doing and saying the things I did in that second rape. I know I was forced to, but it haunts me just the same. Aaron has to wake me from these nightmares and hold me as I cry for hours, repeating over and over, "I'm so sorry."

Then, in the midst of all this turmoil, we discover yet another betrayal.

Aaron, here at age 2, was an easy child to raise, his parents told police. "Even as a baby, he never cried," said his mom, Marianne Quinn. *Marianne Quinn*

"She's my baby, always was," said Mike Huskins *(middle)* of his daughter, Denise, age 2, with her brother Joey. *Jane Remmele*

The Quinns shortly before Ethan was deployed to the Middle East in fall 2004: *(from left)* Joe, Aaron, Ethan, Matt, and Marianne *Brandon Black*

The Huskins are a tightknit family, always supporting one another, like at a high school baseball function for Devin in spring 2006: *(from left)* Devin, Jane, Joey, and Denise.
Jeff Remmele

Mr. Rogers, the sweet, friendly stray cat Aaron adopted, stayed close to his home after the kidnapping. Neighbors fed and cared for him while Aaron was questioned by the police for eighteen hours.
Brant Ward / San Francisco Chronicle / *Polaris*

Dan Russo and Amy Morton, Aaron's attorneys, have been law partners in Vallejo for more than thirty years.
Eris Wagner

Lt. Kenny Park of the Vallejo Police Department told the media, "Nothing has changed from an investigative standpoint," after Denise was released on March 25, 2015. That evening, he held another press conference, during which he called Denise and Aaron's story a hoax. *Brant Ward* / San Francisco Chronicle / *Polaris*

The house where Denise was held captive and raped by Matthew Muller *South Tahoe Now*

Detective Misty Carausu snapped this photo of Matthew Muller outside the South Lake Tahoe home where they arrested him on June 8, 2015. A few weeks later, FBI agents showed Aaron this photo when he met with them. *Dublin Police Services*

At the April 28, 2016, ceremony in which Detective Mat Mustard *(right)* was named Officer of the Year for 2015, Vallejo Police Chief Andrew Bidou said Mustard defined the "outstanding" qualities of Vallejo's police officers. *Vallejo Police Facebook page*

Denise and Aaron before the San Francisco Giants game they attended in San Diego in April 2015, a brief return to normalcy in the wake of the home invasion, kidnapping, and explosive false accusations made by the police *Denise Huskins*

Aaron surprised Denise with an engagement ring on March 18, 2017, two days after they gave their emotional victim impact statements at Muller's federal sentencing.
Danielle Huskins

Denise walks down the aisle with her father at her wedding at the Monarch Cove Inn in Capitola, California, on September 29, 2018.
Sarah Wendler

Doug Rappaport, the criminal defense attorney Denise hired, has become a close personal friend of the couple and even officiated at their wedding.
Sarah Wendler

Denise and Aaron's first dance was to their favorite song, Dierks Bentley's "Riser."
Katie Kane

Denise and Aaron caught Bentley's attention with this sign at his October 5, 2018, concert in Mountain View, California. *Aaron Quinn*

Denise and Aaron have formed a lasting friendship with Misty Carausu *(second from left)*, the detective who solved their case, and her husband, Dacu Carausu *(left)*, seen here at Misty's baby shower in April 2019.
Misty Carausu

Aaron and Denise with baby Olivia at three months old, on July 4, 2020
Denise Huskins

33

AARON

I ASK DENISE SEVERAL times which FBI agent interrogated her the second day. Her description of him doesn't match anyone I met. She says she thinks his name starts with a "D," and might be Dave, but can't remember his last name. Mustard questioned both of us, and it seems odd for a different agent to question Denise and not me. So I assume we're confusing the law enforcement personnel we interacted with over those crazy days.

Today, in late April, we're back at my parents' house when Doug calls Denise and tells her he watched the movie *Gone Girl* and wrote what he called a "movie review" to send to the agent, pointing out the obvious differences between that fictional story and what happened in our case. Doug knows we're still suspects, because the FBI recently asked permission to go through more of our property, including our electronic devices. I denied their requests. I'm done making it easy for them. If they have probable cause, let them write a damn warrant. But Doug advised Denise to agree as one last olive branch, and while doing so, he implores this agent to look at our case with a fresh eye, saying he has a chance to be a real hero.

Lauren sends us a copy of Doug's email, and we see the agent's name *is*, in fact, Dave. Dave Sesma. And then it hits me. Jennifer told me while she was married she had an affair with an FBI agent named Dave who worked out of the Fairfield office. But that was years ago; it must be a different guy. It can't be the *same* Dave. How could he not recuse himself from the case? It's such a clear conflict of interest. And wouldn't anybody she dated be a possible suspect since she was the intended target? I call Ethan and he confirms what I suspected, telling me an agent must disclose any personal relationship to anyone connected to an active investigation to his supervising agent.

I pull up Sesma's profile on Facebook, and I recognize him from pictures I saw years ago. I ask Denise if this is the agent who interviewed her, and she says yes, it's him. She's certain of it. We're both floored and know we need to get this guy off the case ASAP. In the meantime, Ethan sees that Dave Sesma is currently the acting supervising agent at the Fairfield office. Whom did Sesma disclose his past relationship with Jennifer to? Himself? Or is he hiding it from his supervisor in Sacramento?

I call Amy, and we come up with a plan to gather more evidence. Jennifer's mom sent a supportive email that first day of the kidnapping, saying I was a good person who wouldn't hurt anyone. I was surprised; I wasn't sure if she even liked me when Jennifer and I were dating. Amy reaches out to her, describing the conflict of interest, and she's able to confirm that Jennifer had a prior relationship with Sesma. But she also says that Jennifer was upset to find out she was talking to my lawyers, and to respect her daughter's feelings she will no longer communicate with us.

With some more digging on Facebook, we find a group photo with both Sesma and Jennifer in it, and a picture of him in a Halloween costume that she commented on. Now we have proof.

Ethan and our attorneys are all going to write separate complaints to the FBI and surely, *surely*, they will put new agents on the case. I don't know why Sesma has chosen to stay on the case, but it's obviously impaired his judgment. We need fresh eyes because I don't believe the kidnappers have given up their lives of crime. They got away with it, and they'll do it again.

DENISE

I feel absolutely sick to my stomach when I find out the agent who questioned me is Jennifer's ex. I have been violated and victimized over and over again. I sobbed and described the rapes in detail while he prodded me with all the sensitivity of a robot. I wouldn't have said a word to him if I'd known his secret.

It's unbelievable. After everything we went through, after the way the police and the media went after Aaron because "It's always the boyfriend" and "We always have to look at current and past relationships to rule out the suspect." By that logic, Agent Sesma himself should have been a suspect! Instead, he interrogated me, attacked me, threatened me with prosecution, and he deliberately *didn't* question Aaron, probably because he knew that Aaron would recognize him. This makes me even more fearful and paranoid. *Why? Why are they doing this?*

To compound the insanity, a couple of weeks later we find out that Jennifer's current boyfriend is the Fairfield police officer she cheated on Aaron with. *He and Sesma have worked in law enforcement in the same town for over five years!* It seems impossible they don't know each other. I don't know what to make of all of this, but I wish she would just talk to us, especially since she was the target. Why wouldn't she want to help? Isn't she worried that the kidnappers are still out there? I want to move on with my life with Aaron and stop reliving our past history with Jennifer, but each time we try, something happens to drag us back there. And we still don't know *why* she was the original target and who hired the kidnappers. Each new revelation seems to point to us being pawns in somebody's sick game, but whose? And what's their next move? We have no choice but to wait and see. We're trapped. They say, "The truth shall set you free." If only that were true. Law enforcement doesn't seem the least bit interested in the truth when it comes to our case.

AARON, ETHAN, DOUG, and I meet to discuss a strategy for handling the Sesma situation. Doug plans to write to the Office of the Inspector General in Washington, DC, detailing Sesma's conflict of interest. He also plans to file a complaint with the US Department of Justice's Office of Professional Responsibility to try to get Sesma removed from the case and a new agent assigned, hoping that the new agent will reinvestigate. This will take months. In fact, he's so persistent about this, Sesma's attorney sends him a cease-and-desist letter denying that Sesma failed to disclose any conflict of interest after Doug holds a press conference about the matter in September the following year. Doug framed the letter and hung it on the wall of his office. With all of that work ahead, and the round-the-clock time he's spent with me already, he tells me that the first retainer has been met and he'll need to ask my father for another $25,000.

Another $25,000?

I am blown away. I have never asked my dad how much he paid Doug because I was too afraid to know. I call my dad in tears, sick to my stomach at having to ask him if he could somehow manage a second installment.

Instantly he says, "Of course," because he'll do anything for me. But that money was his inheritance from my grandma that he needs for his older years, especially with his history of health complications. Chunk by chunk, it's being depleted to help me. I feel so guilty I can hardly stand it.

That guilt blends with gratitude as we get deeper and deeper into this process. Ninety-seven percent of federal cases and 94 percent of state cases end in plea bargains because it's too hard and costly to fight back. If you are in that position, it's often safer to accept a deal rather than risk a harsher sentence. If we couldn't afford the lawyers we have, we would have been appointed public defenders, who typically have high caseloads and might have convinced us to take a plea deal as well. Who knows where we'd be if that happened? At least we have a fighting chance.

34

AARON

ONE OF THE reasons I decided to sell my house is that neither of us feels safe in Vallejo anymore, not just from the kidnappers but from the police. What if something happened to us? Would they even respond? It didn't take long for me to get the answer to that question.

It's Tuesday, June 23, and Denise and I are sitting on the sandy shores of Huntington Beach. It's a beautiful day with just the right amount of ocean breeze. We decided to stay in Huntington at least through the Fourth of July. The beach is a good place to take a break from everything. We're there for only about fifteen minutes before my neighbor calls to tell me a car is parked at a crooked angle in my driveway, and he can hear the dryer running inside the house. It didn't look right to him. He's right. My house is currently in escrow. No one should be there right now.

Oh, great, I think to myself. I never want to interact with Vallejo police again, but it sounds like someone broke in.

I have the same horrible powerless feeling I had when the kidnappers took Denise. Actually, we've felt powerless ever since she was released. The federal prosecutor Matt Segal ignored our concerns about Agent Sesma, who remains on the case. Ethan filed an internal complaint against Sesma with the FBI, so between that and the ones Doug filed, we're hoping something will be done, but we understand it will take some time to process them. We try to keep some faith in the integrity of the system, but it's very, very difficult.

For months, Ethan has been trying to help us find a civil law firm to file a lawsuit against the Vallejo Police Department, but most of them don't even call back. I met with one attorney, but he didn't have the means to take on the police. Another attorney, Jim Wagstaffe, met with us earlier in the month. He spent three hours listening to us, and we were hopeful after the meeting. His firm specializes in these types of cases and Wagstaffe literally writes books for judges about civil law. However, we haven't heard anything since. I guess his associates don't want to take on our case. They probably don't believe us and, even if they do, suing the police for defamation is nearly impossible.

I speak to my Realtor, Christie, who goes to my house and decides to call the police. One of the responding officers is Coelho, the same officer who came to my house when I called about Denise. "I know this house," he tells Christie as he walks up to the front door.

There's a young couple in my house who don't have a key or any paperwork but claim an "Aaron Quinn" from Craigslist rented it to them. The doorknobs have been removed from the doors leading into the garage. The attic door is ajar and one of the officers says to Christie, "They're probably looking for valuables." She tells them that things appear to be missing, but she can't tell for sure. The officers order the couple to gather their stuff, which could be my stuff, and leave. The couple insists they've paid rent and they're the ones who are being scammed, which is obviously a lie, but the police don't arrest them. They just wait outside.

Christie has poor cell phone reception at my house, so I'm getting updates in bits and pieces. I can't believe the police won't arrest this couple. We've been too stressed and exhausted to empty the house yet. There are thousands of dollars' worth of woodworking equipment, furniture, and other expensive items still in the home. Christie does her best to convince the police to arrest the couple, but they ignore her pleas. They leave Christie and my neighbors to watch over the couple to ensure they don't go back inside. The police never even call me.

After the couple drives away, Christie and my neighbors barricade the garage doors until she can get a locksmith out to replace the doorknobs. She's able to send me some pictures so I can see if things are missing. I can tell right away that the couple cleared out my garage. All my woodworking tools are gone. Everything. The week before the kidnapping, I was refinishing a rocking chair for my mom and building a large planter box for a lemon tree. Doing those projects was my meditation, a healthy distraction from my depression. As I look through the pictures, I start to cry. Anyone who's been robbed can tell you: Stuff can be replaced but it's the violation that's hurtful. I feel violated by the robbers and by the police officers who are more interested in punishing me than in protecting the public.

Denise and I spend the evening slumped on the couch, thrown right back into the anguish that we experienced a few months ago. We feel sure nothing is going to get better. This is our life now. This trauma has destroyed my body. My hair has thinned dramatically, coming out in clumps when I shower. Despite soaping up five or six times, I never smell clean. My sweat has turned putrid, just like it did after I was interrogated by the police. I've lost weight and my cheeks have sunk in. Exercise leaves me exhausted instead of rejuvenated like in the past. My neck and jaw constantly hurt from grinding my teeth at night. I have no doubt it's taken years off my life. Lying on the beach this morning, I felt hopeful. The sun was warming my bare skin and the ocean air calmed my nerves.

That's all gone now.

Later that night, we hear Denise's mom wailing in her bedroom. I think of how many times over the last few months she must have cried in silence, trying to shield us from her suffering. But she can't hide it anymore. Her pain is piercing, earth-shattering. Denise goes into the bedroom to console her and I hear her mom through the walls.

"Why?" she sobs. "Why are they doing this to my baby girl?"

Denise responds, "I don't know. I wish I knew."

I can't summon the strength to help, and frankly, I don't have a better answer.

When Denise returns, she's drained of what little energy she had left.

She starts crying without any end in sight. "What do we do? Who's going to help us? Do we have to write a letter to Obama?" she asks through the tears. She's seriously asking if our only option is to appeal to the highest office in the land, because every law enforcement agency we've turned to has let us down. I hold her and say, "I don't know. I don't know," because I still don't have an answer.

35

AARON

IT TAKES US a couple of days to get everything together to head back up to Vallejo. I feel exhausted, beaten down by the squatters. Amy called the Vallejo police, and they told me to file a report online so they can "investigate the matter." They're not going to do anything, but I need to jump through the hoops for my insurance policy.

I've had a similar situation with Kaiser, trying to confirm I can have my old job back. They've made me go through the typical worker's comp portals as if I injured my back on the job, and anytime I ask a question, I get vague answers and incorrect information.

I really want to talk with my manager, Tim, whom I've known since starting the residency. I have no doubt he supports me. He's seen me work hard through years of advanced training and would never believe the Vallejo police's claims. But the higher-ups at Kaiser won't let me talk to him. Instead, I have to deal with a human resources supervisor who requires monthly reports from my therapist confirming I'm unable to work. But now my extended sick leave is running out. Denise and I are planning on moving to a small apartment in Benicia, the town next to Vallejo, at the beginning of July. So I've offered to return to work on July 13, but no one has gotten back to me. It's obvious that every written response needs to be vetted by Kaiser's attorneys.

I plan to work in Vallejo only until I can transfer to another hospital. It's going to be hell going back there, where my name tag will identify me to anyone who doesn't already recognize my face from the news. I'm guessing that most people think Jennifer and I broke up because I cheated on her with Denise, adding another layer of shame hanging over me. I don't know if nurses will help me or if families will allow me to work with their loved ones. But we need money. Our attorney fees are piling up. I couldn't protect Denise during the kidnapping, but I can protect her now.

So we're lying on the couch watching TV. We don't have much motivation for anything else. We sit there, numb to the passing images as time creeps by. Then Denise receives a call from Doug. Any call from our attorneys generates excitement about the possibility of a break in the case. So far, it's just been updates about being stonewalled by law enforcement or the prosecutor. It's different this time. Whatever Doug is telling Denise is surprising news.

After she hangs up, she tells me that the FBI reached out to Doug because they've found some evidence that might be related to her. They want her to look at some pictures in order to identify the items. Doug's advice was not to have any interaction with the FBI. Let them link the evidence by other means.

Shortly after Doug's call, I receive one from Amy. The FBI has reached out to her about my looking at some pictures as well. It's an amazing temptation, a piece of bait that could protect the public and clear our names. But it could be just that: a piece of bait that will land me in jail. By now Sesma knows we've tried to get him off the case. He could be determined to charge us with anything to save his job. I tell Amy I'll think about it.

We leave around ten o'clock the next morning to avoid the LA traffic. We're driving Denise's old Eclipse, which needs new window seals, so that makes for a noisy drive. Almost every hour, we receive a call from Doug or Amy, and each time, we have to pull over so we can hear them.

The FBI is insistent. Doug will not allow Denise to speak with them. He needs to protect her. I'm on the fence. I also feel the need to protect Denise and this may be my best chance.

Amy says the agents are willing to come to her office. If it doesn't feel right, she'll kick them out. At this point, we're three hours away from Vallejo and I just want to get to my house before sunset. I tell her no; I'm not going to meet with the agents. I've given them four statements. I have nothing to add. They're the FBI. They can investigate.

About two hours out, Amy calls again; someone from the Alameda County Sheriff's Office wants me to identify my laptop.

Wait. A new agency is involved?

The computer they found matches the description of the one that the kidnappers stole. Like mine, it was bought at a Best Buy in Southern California in 2009 when I was in graduate school.

Amy says the FBI agents are hounding her. We've heard nothing from them for months, but now they won't stop calling. She believes there's a genuine break in the case and it's in my best interest to answer their questions. She'll be there to protect me. I trust her and I decide to take this chance for Denise and my family.

We've made the drive from Southern to Northern California at least half a dozen times the last few months, but never with this much stress. Each mile drags on. We never feel like we're making progress despite driving seventy miles per hour. Denise and I both hear phantom phone calls, auditory illusions generated by the anticipation.

Finally, we arrive at Amy and Dan's office. Denise says she'll wait for me in the car. Her face pale from worry, she looks at me like this is the last time she's going to see me. I tell her it's going to be okay and give her a kiss. I'm confident, or maybe stupid, enough to feel I will handle the situation. Amy meets me at the door.

"They're waiting in the conference room," she tells me. "Sesma is here with Walter. I didn't think he would come. I guess I'll give him some credit because he knows we're going after him."

Of course the prick would be arrogant enough to show up. Whatever. I'm not in jail clothes, and they need my help. I walk into the conference room and immediately sit across from them, eliminating any opportunity for pleasantries.

"Thank you for coming in," Walter says. It seems he's taking the lead, not Sesma, which is encouraging because I felt he believed me the night I heard Denise's proof-of-life recording. "We met before. I'm Agent Walter and this is Agent Sesma."

I look over at Sesma. He gives me a little nod in greeting and I almost return it with the middle finger.

"I know it's probably been a tough few months for you and you had some difficulties with Vallejo," Walter says, "but I want you to know that Dave and I ran with this case. How are you holding up?"

"I'm fine. What do you guys need from me?" I reply. Why the hell would I share anything with them?

"Okay, we'll get to that. I want to make sure you're doing all right—"

I cut him off. "I'm fine. What do you need to ask me?"

"Look, man, I'm trying to build back some rapport and rebuild trust because of what happened," Walter replies defensively. "You don't need to be aggressive."

"My house got broken into again," I reply. "I need to go see what was stolen after I leave here. I don't need the small talk. I'm here to help, so ask me your question."

Are we going to talk about the weather or who won the game last night too? We're not friends. I want information. I want to know what they are investigating. After surgery, the doctor tells the patient whether the operation was a success, not that they're opening a Starbucks down the street.

Walter finally decides to move on and give me useful information. He tells me they found an ASUS brand laptop and shows me a picture of it.

"It looks like the computer that the kidnappers stole but I can't say for certain," I say. "I'm sure you can check the serial number to see if it's the one I bought at Best Buy."

I'm afraid to confirm it, because I don't know if they are setting a trap for me. He shows me a picture of swim goggles with black tape covering the lens. I reply that they look like the goggles the kidnappers made me wear, which they should already know because the goggles were still at my house. He tells me that they're going to show me a picture of a man to see if I recognize him.

It's not a mug shot, as I expect, but a grainy candid photo with sunlight dancing off the right side of his face. His thin lips seem to be caught exactly between a frown and a smile, making an uncanny straight line across his cheeks. He's staring down the barrel of the camera as if he's looking directly at me.

I don't recall seeing him before. He's a generic white guy who would easily blend into the crowd.

I might have said hi to him as we passed on the street or sat at the next table at a restaurant and never given him another thought. Yet I feel as though these eyes have watched me before.

"We found a long blond hair wrapped around goggles at his place," Walter says. "Aaron, we think this is the guy."

Part Three

SURVIVORS

"Denise and Aaron are shining examples of how to find love in tragedy, strength in sorrow, power in reconnection."

—DOUG RAPPAPORT

36

MISTY CARAUSU WASN'T a detective quite yet—that wouldn't start until the following day—but when her boss at the Alameda County Sheriff's Office texted her on June 8 to say she was needed to help execute a search warrant on a home in South Lake Tahoe for one of their cases, she didn't hesitate.

A masked intruder had broken into the home of an elderly couple in Dublin, California, but fled before police arrived, leaving behind zip ties, duct tape, and his cell phone, ultimately leading police to this property 188 miles away. It was an utterly ordinary-looking small cottage with dark gray siding, white trim, and a neatly manicured yard, like so many of the rental properties in the toney resort area, with no hint of the darkness that happened inside those walls.

The man they were there for was Matthew Muller, a thirty-eight-year-old Harvard Law School graduate, ex-Marine, and recently disbarred immigration attorney. He'd barricaded himself inside the home owned by his parents by piling trash, boxes, chairs, and even a massage table against the front door. Carausu and her colleagues had to use a battering ram to break through the front door and push through the debris, only to find Muller standing silently in the hallway. Just under six feet tall with a slender build, auburn hair, and dark eyes, he towered over Carausu. He didn't say a word, not then and not after they handcuffed him and took him into custody, pausing only to kick shut his laptop as sheriff's deputies escorted him out of the home. Carausu followed behind, snapping a photo of him outside in case they needed it for their investigation.

The interior of the house was an absolute wreck, with garbage, clothes, and boxes strewn all over the living room and on the kitchen counters. One of the boxes was filled with license plates. Another held a key maker for several types of Ford vehicles. There was a stun gun on the rocking chair in the living room. But that's not what made the hair on the back of Misty's neck stand on end. Something bad had happened here. She could feel it.

The more Carausu explored the house, the more uneasy she felt. On the floor behind the couch she spotted a huge tub of Vaseline with no lid on it next to the laptop the suspect had kicked shut. Ugh. She didn't want to think about what he'd been watching and using that Vaseline for.

In one of the two bedrooms, a penis pump sat on the floor next to a large bed with a bottle of lotion on top of the fitted sheet, its only covering. Used papers towels were strewn everywhere. The second bedroom looked like it was used for storage, filled with piles of laundry, linens, and garbage.

A search of the suspect's white Mustang that had been parked nearby revealed further disturbing details. The backseat had been removed, which was just plain creepy.

That seat was intentionally removed, but why? And where is the seat?

Inside the car, she found copious evidence tying him to the Dublin home invasion: a Home Depot receipt from a location across the street from the home; a Target receipt from Dublin; duct tape and zip ties like the ones found at the crime scene.

What was in the trunk was even more alarming: a duffel bag containing a blow-up doll dressed all in black that someone had wrapped in thick metal wire; Nerf guns painted black with laser pointers taped to them; more duct tape and zip ties; and several pairs of swim goggles with black tape over the lenses. A black nylon belt with an attached pouch contained another pair of blacked-out goggles.

This pair had a long blond hair hanging from it.

And that was when her suspicions became a certainty.

Oh, my God, she thought. *Someone was wearing those goggles. Who?*

CARAUSU COULD HAVE ignored the hair. She knew it wasn't connected to her case because none of the victims was blond. And she had plenty of work to do sorting through the hundreds of pieces of evidence she collected tying Muller to the Dublin home invasion. Why create more work for herself? But she just couldn't get that long blond hair out of her mind. Whom did it belong to?

She suspected Muller had broken into the Dublin home planning to abduct the couple's daughter and take her to that cottage in South Lake Tahoe, though she would never learn why or how Muller targeted them. Perhaps he had done it before. Successfully. It was a gut feeling more than anything, but when Carausu got back to the station, she put out an all-points bulletin to other local law enforcement agencies, asking if they had any unsolved crimes connected to Muller.

She couldn't just sit there and wait for other police departments to respond to her query, so she ran a check on him in the police database. He quickly popped up as a person of interest in a string of unsolved crimes in nearby cities: a middle-of-the-night break-in and an attempted sexual assault in Mountain View on September 29, 2009; another in Palo Alto on October 18, 2009; and a third in Palo Alto on November 29, 2012.

In each case, the suspect was dressed all in black. In two of them, he forced the women to drink NyQuil or NyQuil mixed with something else. Even stranger, in November 2009 Muller disappeared, prompting his wife to report him missing. But two days later he called from Utah, and she picked him up.

The detective investigating one of the 2009 break-ins had Muller's DNA tested, but it didn't match DNA recovered at the scene. That didn't convince the detective he wasn't involved; he'd told one of the victims he was leaving behind evidence to mislead law enforcement.

Just like what Denise's kidnapper and rapist said to her.

CARAUSU WORKED TIRELESSLY over the next few days and weeks, trying to put these pieces together. She began by calling each of the police departments that handled the other cases.

"It's so funny you're talking about Matthew Muller because I'm staring at a photo of him right now," one investigator told her. "I've always thought he was responsible for a home invasion here, so I've stared at his photo for years, knowing it was him."

She collected the police reports and added them to her case file. The only agency that wasn't calling her back was the Vallejo Police Department. She'd first connected Muller to that town after tracking down the owner of the stolen white Mustang he had been driving. The owner, a student at Touro University on Mare Island, told her he suspected Muller was involved in the home invasion and kidnapping at Aaron Quinn's house and that he and other students believed Muller was the Mare Island Creeper, as they called him: a Peeping Tom who had been looking into people's windows and taking photos the previous summer. Students had followed him to a home on nearby Klein Avenue where he was apparently living with a girlfriend. They called the police, but by the time officers followed up, Muller was gone. The Peeping Tom incidents stopped for several months, then began again. And then Denise was kidnapped.

This is insane, Carausu thought. *Maybe he did move out before police got there, but why didn't they follow up? Witnesses led them straight to a Peeping Tom and they did nothing. I don't understand. Why didn't they do their job?*

She googled the Vallejo kidnapping to learn more. The MO was almost exactly the same: the middle-of-the night break-in, the zip ties, the duct tape. And the female victim had long blond hair.

This has to be the same suspect, she thought. She was shocked to learn the Vallejo police had called the whole thing a hoax on national television.

"It was just heartbreaking the way the Vallejo police and the FBI failed them," she recalled years later.

Carausu reached out to Vallejo detectives many times over the next several weeks, and when she finally did talk to someone, they were dismissive and referred her to the FBI.

The agent who took her call on June 23 was Sesma. At first he didn't sound very interested in hearing what she had to say.

"I introduced myself and said, 'I have a person you may want to meet in the Vallejo kidnapping case you guys called a hoax,'" she told him.

"We never called it a hoax," he snapped back.

A few days later, the FBI showed up at their Dublin office with a warrant and scooped up all of the evidence.

Which was how Aaron and Denise learned there might finally be a break in their case.

37

AARON

EVEN THOUGH I'M staring at the photo of our tormentor, it still doesn't feel real.

After the incident with the house squatters, I gave up hope. We had been branded liars while the kidnappers were free to harm more and more people. But it seemed the FBI had solved the case. Is it *actually* possible we might be able to return to our lives?

My skepticism proves justified.

"You can't tell anybody about this now. I'm writing an arrest affidavit. I'm going to work on it all weekend. I'm not even going to see my kids," Walter says. I thank him and confirm that I'll stay quiet. I'm assuming the suspect is on the run and the FBI needs to stay covert to catch him.

Walter asks if I received any victim assistance to help pay for expenses like therapy.

"No. No one ever acknowledged I was a victim," I reply. "They only said I killed Denise."

"Oh," Walter says, a little taken back. It's almost like he's been living in an alternate universe where I was treated with respect and compassion. Then he gives me a card that I should have received months ago.

I stand up as the agents prepare to leave and shake Walter's hand. I think twice before I extend my hand to Sesma as well. His past affair with Jennifer doesn't matter if he solved the case. I look him in the eye and thank him.

DENISE

A week after Aaron's meeting with Sesma and Walter, we find out that the state of California already has the suspect in custody for a different crime. It's good to know that one of the kidnappers is behind bars, but we're dismayed to learn that before our case can move forward, the state case has to conclude, which could take years. Because of that, we're told that the FBI affidavit for the arrest warrant that Walter spent his weekend writing has to remain sealed for now, hidden from the public. We aren't to say anything to anyone until the FBI agents tell us it's okay. We're at their mercy. All the while, in the eyes of the public, we're still criminals. But despite everything they've put us through, our main concern is doing what is right for the case. So we comply.

One of the kidnappers has been apprehended but we feel no relief, no joy, no hope. Nothing is settled, nothing restored. All I can do is keep fighting for my life, the life I had before this nightmare, but one I feel I've already lost.

If I'm ever going to work again, the next step is to go into Kaiser and take that final written exam and get the certificate of completion. But Kaiser continues to be impossible to communicate with.

It's clear they'd just like me to go away, and they think ignoring me will work. I tried to schedule the test in June; no response. Then again in July; no response. When I persist, they finally offer to just send me the exam to "make things easier all around." I'm not fooled. This is just another attempt by Kaiser to distance itself from me.

I am sick of being treated like an infectious disease, like my mere presence will cause harm and inconvenience to Kaiser. So, knowing that it isn't just Tim I am emailing, but an entire legal department that is monitoring our communications, I write that I expect to be treated the same as all my colleagues and come in to take the exam without further delay. I say:

> For you, or anyone else who reads this or that you have to consult with, please understand that I have been a victim of a horrific crime that has caused me severe emotional, mental and physical trauma. Since then, I have been continuously re-victimized by the very institutions that are in place to serve and protect me. My character and reputation have been falsely and unjustly slandered, causing even more damage in my life and to my well-being. I would think, or at least hope, that for any individual human being reading this, and Kaiser as a whole, would want to avoid at all costs aiding in any further damage or harm to me. The delay so far and any further delay causes me additional significant and unnecessary mental and emotional stress. I am looking forward to hearing from you, scheduling the exam, receiving my certificate of completion and moving forward with my life. Thank you.

I receive a response the next day and the exam is scheduled for the following Friday, July 17. It feels good to finally speak up against this absurdity and get a win.

38

AARON

I THOUGHT THE FBI finding one of the kidnappers would be pure re-lief, but, like everything to do with our ordeal, anything good comes paired with something awful: Denise's proof of life paired with my phone being on airplane mode; Denise's release paired with the Vallejo Police Department's press conference; a kidnapper being caught, but we can't tell anyone. I'm glad that a dangerous man is off the street, but our reputations can't be restored if no one knows the truth!

And it's become increasingly clear how important that is for my pro-fessional future. A couple of weeks ago, I told Kaiser that I was coming back to work on July 13. Part of me is nervous about leaving Denise alone, but another part knows that working will be important for my healing. Besides, we need the income and I've exhausted all of my sick leave.

Unlike Denise, I'm a permanent employee, so Kaiser hasn't completely ignored me, but they won't let me come back unless I undergo extensive questioning about my relationship with her. The prospect of facing an-other interrogation almost throws me into a panic attack, and I suspect that Kaiser is searching for a reason to fire me. Consequently, I'm forced to hire yet another attorney, one who specializes in employment law, which only adds to our financial strain. Our legal fees already top $100,000 and are still climbing. My parents covered the initial $10,000 to Dan and Amy and wouldn't let me pay them back, but I'd insisted on repaying Ethan his $5,000 and picking up the rest of our fees going forward.

On Thursday, July 9, Ethan calls Walter to discuss my employment issues. Walter says he doesn't understand why Kaiser would fire me, inexplicably ignoring the consequences of what the Vallejo police have said about us. Ethan finally convinces him to call Kaiser to tell them the truth, that we've been vindicated. In turn, I hope they will drop this unnecessary investigation and I can start reclaiming a portion of my life. I'm eternally grateful for Ethan's ability and willingness to help us navigate the labyrinth of the criminal justice system. I would be hopelessly lost without him.

OVER THE NEXT three days, I finish my final in-person training for a treatment method that I've been studying over the last four years. I used all of my vacation time for this program, but I didn't mind. It dramatically improved my skills as a therapist, and I know completing the training will be an important step in my healing process. It's the first time I'll be in a large group in which everyone is aware of our case. For the most part, Denise and I have kept ourselves protected in a close circle of friends and family. It's a daunting prospect to step out of that shelter, but I'm determined to complete the program. Yet I don't know how to act when I get there. What do I talk about with my classmates? Do they really want to hear that I'm terrified every second of every day? Are they going to feel comfortable telling me how things are going for them? I would welcome hearing anything about another person's life. It's so strange to have almost every conversation focus on me. But is it weird if I *don't* talk about the kidnapping? There doesn't seem to be a right answer when you are the elephant in the room. And even if I'm able to talk to someone about a lighter topic or, heaven forbid, even laugh at a joke, I'm afraid of appearing too happy. The briefest giggle or smile could undercut my claim to suffering and bolster the portrait the police have painted of us. If I do the opposite and break down, will people think I'm putting on an act to gain sympathy?

If I show too little emotion, will they think I'm a sociopath? The kidnapping and subsequent press conference have become the lens that shapes everyone's view of me. So I will choose disconnection as protection—eat my lunches alone and avoid conversations. Maybe if I hide well enough, people will forget I'm even there. I would rather be unnoticed than judged.

Fortunately, I'm met with kind smiles and warm greetings when I arrive at the training site. No one asks prying questions. I stick to my plan and keep mainly to myself. During one of the breaks on Friday afternoon, Amy calls to inform me that the FBI has decided to unseal the arrest warrant on Monday. I feel a heavy weight starting to lift off me, but I can't let it go completely. I hold on to it, keeping it tethered to me. I'll sever the tie when it's real. Right now these are just words from the same people who called me a murderer and a hoaxer. But if it *is* true, our whole world is going to drastically change again. Hopefully for the better.

For weeks, Ethan was the only family member we told about the arrest, knowing that it could be years until it was announced publicly. We couldn't burden the rest of them with keeping such a secret for years without any release valve. Ethan has a better understanding of how slow the criminal justice system can be. This turn of events is astoundingly quick, and I wonder what made the FBI change their minds. Could it have been because of Ethan's call to Walter?

I guess the reason doesn't matter so long as the public knows the truth.

For the last few weeks, I've felt like I've been sitting on a bomb, hearing the slow tick of a timer that no one else can hear. Now, as I sit in class, I hear the timer clicking away more rapidly. It's accelerating so fast that I almost jump up and shout, "I'm innocent!" Instead, I keep the information to myself, knowing I have no solid proof that law enforcement will keep their word.

Even though I'm not at my full capabilities, I perform well enough to graduate from the program, but I worry that I will never be myself again. I worry that this trauma has wounded me so deeply that I will only be able to loosely scab over the damage. Maybe my potential will always be stunted, cut down by fear and anxiety. Or maybe I can use the trauma to mutate or evolve, like the superheroes I read about in the comic books I loved as a little boy.

39

DENISE

THE AFFIDAVIT IS unsealed early Monday morning, while we're moving the last items out of Aaron's house. He finalizes the sale tomorrow, and that will be it. Chapter closed. We had always talked about moving eventually, maybe in a couple of years, but we were excited about the growth of Vallejo and Mare Island, and we loved seeing it all unfold. It's heartbreaking to have it all ripped away from us.

We decide to hold a press conference in front of Dan and Amy's office in Vallejo at 3:30 p.m. This time Aaron and I will stand beside our attorneys, no longer hiding from the press. I consult with Doug and Lauren about what I should wear. It sounds so trivial, but it's their job to anticipate anything that can be used against me, and the media has basically portrayed me as a conniving seductress who concocted this whole scheme to get back at her boyfriend. So, unfortunately, I could easily be judged by something as silly as how I'm dressed instead of my innocence. Women are constantly judged by their appearance anyway, so I know I have to walk a fine line. I can't wear something too professional or I'll be portrayed as stiff and cold. If I wear something too casual, I'm not taking this seriously enough. But above all, whatever I choose can't be too revealing.

It's frustrating to think about because the focus should be on the case, but we've seen the public pick us apart. I'm sure I'll be sweating, both from the ninety-degree heat and the incredible stress, so I try to pick something comfortable and cool. I decide on a long cotton skirt, a beige sleeveless blouse that covers my chest up to just below my collarbone, and a maroon cotton tank underneath it. I try to keep my makeup modest, and don't bother with mascara or eyeliner because I'm sure I'll cry.

We head over to Amy and Dan's around noon. We've already received dozens of text messages and phone calls from friends and family who heard about the break in the case. As we turn the corner to park behind the office, avoiding the media already camped out front, I click on a news report on my phone. The first thing that pops up is a mug shot of the suspect, Matthew Muller, next to my picture. We are side by side for the world to see, as if somehow we are the same.

There he is. The Voice, that ghost of a man, is actually a real person. I look away, not wanting to see this creature's face next to my own.

We still have a couple of hours before our press conference, so Amy hands us copies of the fifty-nine-page FBI affidavit written by Walter. Before it was released, Walter asked if we wanted our names in it; rape victims usually aren't identified in public documents, but without hesitation we both said yes. We want to confirm the truth to the world; we *must* confirm the truth to the world if we have any hope of clearing our names. Despite our wishes, we aren't named. I'm referred to as "Victim F" and Aaron is "Victim M" throughout the entire document. Now, when we actually *want* our names in the press, our request is ignored without explanation! Victim F could be anyone. It's a generic label that makes me feel like I am no one to them. We are no one to them. It strips us of our identities, in the midst of the most traumatic events of our lives, and reduces us to anonymous nobodies, just blank faces. And maybe that's the point. We don't matter to them. We never did.

But that's not even the worst of it. Doug warned me that reading the affidavit would upset me. He was right.

For one thing, it states that Aaron's Camry and laptop were stolen, yet does not include charges for robbery. Why not?

Even more upsetting, parts of it are written as if we're still suspects!!

The affidavit starts off by saying it will list all the reasons why there's "probable cause" to arrest the suspect, Matthew Muller, as well as include some information that might be viewed as detracting from it due to Vallejo's press conference saying this wasn't a kidnapping. I understand this is meant to neutralize it as an issue for the defense, but the way it's written seems to defend Vallejo's indefensible behavior!

It notes Aaron's house was "neat and clean" when police arrived and "when officers went upstairs they noticed a strong scented odor in the air and that the carpets had recently been vacuumed." These details are irrelevant to Muller's arrest but seem included to justify Vallejo's initial belief that Aaron killed me and cleaned up afterward. Walter left out the documented fact that Aaron's house cleaners had been there the week before.

The affidavit goes on to describe many examples of how the case was mishandled, without coming out and saying so.

It notes that before he reached his brother, Aaron spoke to Ethan's girlfriend, though no one from law enforcement ever interviewed her about that call.

It states "the results are still pending" from the blood sample Aaron gave police. It's been well over three months. There's no excuse not to have tested evidence by now.

It states, "VICTIM M's polygraph had unknown results."

Unknown results? French told Aaron he "failed it miserably." Which is it? I can understand why polygraphs are inadmissible in court, because French was going to say Aaron failed regardless of how he actually did. It's another example of how low investigators will go to coerce a confession.

My heart rate increases as I read: "During SA French's follow-up interview with VICTIM M regarding his preliminary results, which became accusatory at times . . ."

Accusatory *at times?* The whole thing was accusatory!

". . . VICTIM M terminated the interview by requesting to speak with an attorney. VICTIM M left."

As though it was that simple.

It conveniently leaves out that police attempted to use Aaron's own brother against him, and it was hours before Aaron was able to obtain an attorney and leave.

There's nothing in the affidavit regarding the emails sent by the kidnappers to Aaron that first day. These are crucial pieces of evidence. Were they ever even evaluated?

For the first time, we discover that the kidnappers called Aaron's phone *three times* around 8:30 p.m. on Monday, March 23, yet Mat Mustard specifically told him that the kidnappers weren't trying to communicate. Two were missed calls and the other did not connect, which is presumably when someone in law enforcement put his phone on airplane mode. Aaron saw dozens of missed calls from unknown numbers that next night when Agent Vinny finally asked him to try to email the kidnappers. Aaron had always wondered, but had no way of knowing, if any of those were calls from the kidnappers. That's the investigators' job to figure out. And of course, by late Tuesday night, it was too late.

We then read that AT&T quickly cooperated because it was a kidnapping, and they were able to track the calls within two hundred square meters of the intersection of Hank Monk Avenue and Horace Greeley Avenue in South Lake Tahoe, where Muller had me imprisoned.

I feel Aaron's anger steaming from him. "They could have saved you!" he says bitterly. "They should have saved you! It was all *right there!*"

I am already in tears, coming to the same realization on my own. This goes beyond simple human error. This is callous and malicious. They could have traced those calls and found me that *first* night! I realize more than ever that my life was worthless to them, worthless to the very people who were sworn to protect it.

What's even more abhorrent is we realize this information about the phone was originally used to try to incriminate us!

The affidavit says these missed calls were from a TracFone purchased at a Target in Pleasant Hill on March 2. The purchaser is described as "a light-skinned male, with dark hair, medium build, wearing a dark polo shirt, dark shorts, and dark shoes," according to video footage they obtained. In an itemized list of evidence taken from Aaron's home, it included his black basketball shorts and a black top, but we never knew why. And the police and FBI told Aaron's attorney Amy on Wednesday the twenty-fifth, after my release and prior to Park's press conference, that they had video evidence proving the whole thing was a hoax, which is why Aaron thought she was upset with him that day. Of course, they never showed it to her or explained what that evidence was. Now we know. I guess their theory was Aaron bought this phone and I was the one making calls from it in this "elaborate hoax"—one we apparently planned together for a month, in the midst of our breakup, just days after I found out Aaron had been trying to get back together with Jennifer. I mean, what kind of distorted logic is that?

Even if they did believe it was a hoax and thought it was *me* making those calls, they could have gone straight to South Lake Tahoe and caught me. Of course, if they had, they would have found this guy holding me hostage and would have rescued me. Either way, it would have been a win for them. All they had to do *was their job.* Why didn't they?

As I READ on, I notice Walter left out key parts of my statements.

The affidavit states I "believed we were stuck in 'LA traffic' for a while," but omits I told the authorities he hit another car and interacted with the owner. I can only guess they want to limit public scrutiny for not relaying that information then. The owner of that car or witnesses might have been able to identify the driver and gotten him off the street sooner.

Other possible leads I gave are left out, like how we stopped at a gas station in the early morning of my release. They could've asked all gas stations in the surrounding area of the grid coordinates linked to the Trac-Fone if a white man driving a white Mustang came in around two o'clock Wednesday morning; they could have looked at surveillance videos.

The FBI knew pizza was delivered on Monday night, during the low tourist season in Tahoe, so there were probably only a handful of deliveries from nearby restaurants. They could easily have checked with them to find the exact house I was held in.

Just a simple Google Maps search from South Lake Tahoe to Huntington Beach shows two routes: one in front of the Sierras, and the other behind them, which takes about nine hours, as my captor said. He stopped at a bathroom rest stop, presumably at a campground, in the early morning, confirming he did, in fact, take "back roads" to Huntington Beach. These details I told authorities would be important to include in an arrest warrant for one of my kidnappers. Yet they're excluded.

Within an hour and a half of my release, I told Huntington Beach police I believed the Voice drove a white Mustang and gave the exact location of where he released me. There are several businesses in the area with surveillance cameras; video could've been pulled to see if a white Mustang, or other sports car, drove by.

Yet, with the FBI's vast resources and capabilities, there's no mention of any search for surveillance footage. Anything we provided that could've led them to find the kidnappers was apparently ignored. Why? Although they didn't go out publicly and stand next to Kenny Park, they were there behind the scenes. It's clear what they believed and how it drove their "investigation."

Walter writes several times that Aaron and I told investigators the group targets people for money, but he leaves out that we both also told them the group could be hired for "personal" reasons as well. Excluding details like this minimizes that "the operation" was intended for Aaron's ex. This is an important distinction that could weaken the prosecution's case against Muller, especially because of Sesma's prior relationship with her. Sesma's conflict of interest could impact the criminal case as much as Vallejo's press conference and should be addressed in this affidavit. But it's not.

The affidavit also includes bald-faced lies, such as that I agreed to meet with Los Angeles FBI agents who had arranged a plane for me to fly back to Vallejo, but that I "could not be located," and "didn't make any attempts to contact" authorities despite "numerous requests" for me to do so.

"You've got to be FUCKING KIDDING ME!!"

The police knew where I was and how to reach me. My family was communicating with law enforcement the entire time. They told detectives I'd be hiring an attorney since they were threatening me with prosecution if I didn't accept their immunity offer. They knew it would be my lawyer contacting them next, not me. And I never agreed to meet with LA agents. This is the first I'm hearing about it. Mustard told Nick I could take an FBI plane up to Vallejo or find my own way back.

I am so angry that my eyes aren't able to focus, and my vision goes in and out. Tears of sheer frustration stream down my face.

They're blatantly lying to cover for the Vallejo police. And their own ineptitude.

Line by line, paragraph by paragraph, the agents continue to demean and revictimize me.

They state that the female FBI agent present at my SART exam reported there was no "physical evidence of non-consensual sex."

"No signs of nonconsensual sex? Really?" I can hardly speak through my tears.

"How can she *say* that? She didn't perform the exam! She had nothing to do with it—she just sat in the corner! I told them how the rapes happened, how I was threatened! Was I supposed to put up a fight? Encourage him to rip into me and make the rapes more violent just so they would be more *believable*? Aren't these people *trained* in dealing with victims of violent crimes and sexual assault? What is *wrong* with them?"

I sob in Aaron's arms. I'm barely hanging on.

AFTER I REGAIN some composure, for the first time I read the kidnappers' emails to Lee and to Kenny Park, which are included in the affidavit. I am blown away by how thoroughly what they wrote corroborates what Aaron and I told police about the group and the kidnapping. The writer says he and the other two members of their group go by initials, which is what the Voice told me. He even included links to *photos* to prove he was telling the truth—of the fake guns with laser pointers, the zip ties, the blood pressure cuffs they used on us, the portable speakers they used to play white noise so they wouldn't wake the neighbors, which was what we thought was rain; of the room where I was held with my glasses on top of the dresser! Investigators tried to claim to our attorneys that we, or someone we knew, wrote these emails, but there's incredible detail that none of us could have possibly known, like the other break-ins and thefts they were involved in. The first email was sent to Lee on Thursday, March 26, at 2:13 p.m., while I was being questioned by Mustard. And although the first email confirmed I was telling the truth, Agent Sesma still threatened me with prosecution the next day.

The affidavit then goes on to say Sesma claimed I had "inconsistencies with specific details" about my kidnapping and rape, and that it's a crime to lie to a federal agent. Why are they taking such a shot at me in a document that's supposed to be making the case for Muller's arrest, not mine? Other than my originally denying the sexual assault to Huntington Beach police, the only "inconsistency" they noted was that I thought the proof of life was recorded in the evening when it was actually sent by noon the second day. Of course, it fails to report that I *told* investigators I could be wrong about the sequence of events because—between the drugs, the blacked-out swim goggles, the cardboarded windows, and the incredible fear for my life—I was disoriented. It's not like I could have looked at a clock to figure out what time it was. It also leaves out the explanation for why I originally denied the rapes and how severe the threats against me and my family were.

Are all victims treated like this? Or is it just me?

I remember how small and stupid they made me feel during the interrogations, asking me questions as if my answers were somehow wrong, as if what I was telling them didn't add up. But now, as I go over the kidnappers' emails, it appears I was right about *everything*.

When these emails first became public in March, reporters mocked Aaron and me by focusing on the more sensational claims while ignoring the fact that they corroborated what we'd told police. For example, reporters made a joke of how the kidnappers said they used spray-painted water pistols with lasers duct-taped to them, not actual guns; but they failed to mention that the kidnappers admitted we had no way of knowing that, that all we saw when we woke up was "a red dot on [our] faces looking down what appeared to be an assault pistol with rail-mounted illumination and laser sight." Reporters deliberately chose to make us look foolish.

They said the kidnappers coming to our defense was "unheard of," yet captors feel remorse for their actions often enough that the phenomenon has been studied. The emails even explain *why* they sympathized with me. "We are criminals I suppose, but we have consciences and seeing the impact of our actions on someone deeply affected us and caused us to reconsider our lives." That same email says both Aaron and I have "suffered a life-threatening ordeal painful beyond what most people can imagine," and they were shocked and "further ashamed" when we went to the police for help and were threatened with prosecution. Despite their own responsibility for our suffering, the kidnappers thought it was "disturbing how many journalists cast the victims in a negative light," only providing information that led readers and viewers to believe we "were attention-seeking whackos who made it all up."

This is a moral dilemma I've never experienced: agreeing with the very people I disagree with so much. How is it that *they alone*, and not all the journalists or members of the public, can see through the conduct of the police? I guess because they have firsthand knowledge of what really happened. I'm angry at the agents and detectives who put me in this position, where I actually *agree* with the very people who tormented me and threatened my life.

I force myself to keep reading instead of dwelling on that uncomfortable thought. One email says the kidnappers are a group of "professional thieves," mostly college graduates who started out as "occasional car thieves," after a relative "with a colorful background" lured them in with the promise of easy money and a new challenge. They soon joined forces with another group to sell the cars overseas, a much more lucrative market than selling them locally. They hid cars in abandoned warehouses around Mare Island, saying "island custodians" must have noticed their presence because chains and fences they cut had been replaced. One car they'd stolen had even been discovered and retrieved, which they say can be confirmed by the police. They write most cars they stole were off the island, except two—one was the white Mustang I was transported in. The emails explain the technological sophistication required to break into newer cars, and the thieves discovered it was easier to simply break into people's homes and steal their keys.

They then "diversified" into burglary, mainly "for entertainment, like a reality TV show," going through belongings and electronics, finding intimate videos and discovering several instances of infidelity. The emails describe information about the people they stole from, specifically the owner of the white Mustang and his roommates. The thieves also "tested alarm systems and response times and figured out workarounds" so they could be prepared if the police were called.

They claim they generally didn't go peeking into people's houses when they were home and that the Peeping Tom wasn't them; in fact, they say they even scared him off a roof once and called the cops on him from a burner phone, pretending to be a resident, because they didn't need a "pervert" making people more watchful and increasing the police presence on the island.

As if these guys are any better.

Because slipped into that paragraph is a phrase I know is directed toward us: "Close your blinds people, even if you're facing a swamp." The night of the home invasion, we had been intimate on the couch while the blinds that face the vacant wetlands behind Aaron's home were open. How could we possibly have known a drone was filming us? We later learn the FBI found the recording while going through Muller's electronic devices. It's chilling to think about how many moments like that were viewed by unwanted spectators. And how many times they were in Aaron's house. They say it was five, which fits with what the Voice told me.

Yet they delude themselves that they had some sort of code of ethics, saying they never entered the homes of people who had small children, of the elderly or service members, and only stole "stuff that was insured from people who could afford it."

Right, so you guys aren't that "bad."

These Mare Island break-ins were also used to collect false leads, like hair and items with fingerprints, to mislead police. I remember the Voice told me he put DNA in my bag to throw off the police. Now I know how he got it.

The author also describes the countermeasures they took to make sure their DNA wouldn't be left behind, including "full body wet suits (also for purposes of a swimming escape if the island were sealed off), exfoliating, moisturizing, hairnets and balaclava . . . I will pause to note how fantastical this all sounds."

The self-congratulatory narcissism is astounding. Whoever wrote this wants credit for fooling law enforcement.

Walter writes farther down in the affidavit that the Vallejo police confirmed these robberies but also points out that these crimes were posted on a local community blog that Aaron was a member of. I can only assume this irrelevant detail is included to rationalize why law enforcement thought Aaron wrote the kidnappers' emails. It's a half-assed explanation, especially since the blog posts never included the exact make and model of stolen items, items in the home that weren't stolen, or descriptions of the residents, which Aaron couldn't have known.

The group finally settled on kidnapping for ransom to make enough money to retire, saying mine was "a test of methods that would be used later on a higher net worth target, in an environment that was familiar to us and somewhat controlled. There was also a link to someone we thought was a resident there but turned out not to be." Meaning Jennifer.

The emails go on to say there were three assailants, two of whom woke us up while the third stood watch downstairs. Aaron and I both, separately, told authorities we believed this is what happened. This was never made public, so there's no way the author could have known we told police this unless it's true.

The author claims he wasn't the one who had direct contact with "the subjects," and each of the trio had different roles during the home invasion. One collected "biographical information" about us, the second went "through computers and phones," and the third set up "technical items such as the cameras and tracking software" so they could monitor Aaron 100 percent of the time.

However, things quickly went "awry"; they couldn't get access to Aaron's wireless router and the spare router they brought in one of their "packs" broke, along with a camera; the monitoring software they brought didn't work with our iPhones; the team member who was in charge of technical matters and had the computer stopped cooperating, so they weren't able to watch Aaron with the surveillance camera; and various "points of leverage" were "lost" because I was there instead of Jennifer.

Leverage? I wonder what kind of leverage they mean, and if it has anything to do with the affair Jennifer had with the Fairfield cop while she was engaged to Aaron. Maybe the kidnappers knew about that and thought it was a way to emotionally manipulate her and Aaron during the kidnapping. Maybe that was why the Voice asked me if there was anything on my phone I didn't want Aaron to see.

The author writes that the one who held me was now missing, possibly having had a psychotic break, that my captor was apparently so "impressed" by me that he became my "advocate," saying "there could be no clearer case of reverse Stockholm syndrome," and he worried the Voice would go to the authorities as a result.

I am even credited for breaking up a "professional K&R ring before it got off the ground."

The tragic irony doesn't escape me. *Yet here we are, with the press waiting outside and a man in prison because of the harm caused to another innocent family!*

I'm amazed by how clearly it's reiterated this was intended for Jennifer. The writer says one of the team members had been shown a photo of her and "certain features" were the same as mine, so they assumed I was her. They were thrown off by finding my driver's license in my purse when the kidnapping was planned around Jennifer and Aaron. I truly don't understand how they confused the two of us. Although we both have long blond hair, we have very different figures, making me believe it *was* just a picture of her they were going by. They say they saw engagement cards and some of her belongings in Aaron's house, but concede that information was from "some time before" and "stale." The Voice told me the same thing.

The biggest question I have is, why did the Voice tell me "it sounds right" that his group had been hired by that cop she cheated on Aaron with? Was he just trying to muddy the waters and confuse me, or *was he telling the truth?* Why would they state this was all intended for her in these confessional emails if it wasn't true, especially if they didn't think they'd be caught? As far as I know, the FBI has done nothing to pursue this lead, which I gave them during my interrogations.

I'm afraid they'll continue to ignore any possible link to her because if they acknowledge that she was the intended target, it makes Sesma's staying on the case in spite of his prior relationship with her that much more egregious. I hope the Department of Justice and the FBI take our complaints about him seriously. Because if they don't pursue Muller's accomplices, the kidnappers could attack more innocent people and Jennifer could still be in danger.

It's so discouraging that members of the media and law enforcement had everything they needed from the beginning to reevaluate their initial conclusions and properly investigate our case, but instead they took the easy way out and blamed the victims. There's little here in the affidavit that makes me think they'll change tack.

IN THE THIRD email, sent to Park on Monday, March 30, the kidnappers sound frustrated as they repeat they've given enough "corroborative evidence" that police must "know by now that the victims were not lying," yet we continued to be "portrayed as unstable hoaxsters."

"I have spent time doing the wrong thing for the wrong reasons. If you force it I will do the wrong thing for the right reasons," the writer threatens, saying if there is not a public apology to Aaron and me within the next twenty-four hours, they "may be the direct agent of harm."

In the final email, sent to Park the next day, Tuesday, March 31, the author retracts his threats and promises not to cause additional damage. He even offers to turn himself in as he taunts the police with what he might do if he's captured:

> As you can probably tell, I am primarily responsible for this operation going through. If I am convinced that the other people involved can be given immunity . . . I will turn myself in and provide a full confession . . . Now, I am not stupid. I have read all about the ways in which people get screwed on immunity. So, at a minimum this is going to involve

attorneys for all three of us . . . When the time comes, there will be one chance at this . . . It is a serious offer, not lightly made, and one that I hope I will have the courage to go through with after enjoying a few last months of freedom . . .

I don't think you will find us, but if you do, good work . . . you definitely have me looking over my shoulder and jumping at shadows . . . If you manage to pull me out of a hole someday, good job, well-played. I'm not going to hurt anybody. But depending on where I am at that moment in time, I might have another spray-painted squirt gun. Or maybe it will be a real gun, empty. Or maybe not empty. Don't think too hard about that, just aim true and get it done. If it ever comes to that.

How could anyone think we wrote these!

40

DENISE

ACCORDING TO THE affidavit, after that final email from the kidnappers, the FBI did not do ONE SINGLE THING to follow up and investigate anything we told them. For nearly four months! In fact, the authorities did nothing but continue to intimidate and threaten us.

The only reason the FBI caught this guy, Matthew Muller, was because Alameda County Sheriff's detectives did their due diligence and linked him to our case! If they hadn't made that connection, we'd still be considered hoaxers. And Walter had the nerve to tell Aaron he and Sesma "ran with this case," trying to take credit for catching Muller. What a joke!

We read that the home invasion in Dublin, California, occurred on June 5, when an unknown white male entered the home through an unsecured window, went upstairs, and woke the husband-and-wife homeowners with a flashlight shining in their faces. They were told to turn over and place their hands behind their backs. The intruder then approached the husband to restrain him with zip ties and told them their adult daughter in the next room was unharmed. The husband fought back, and the wife ran into the bathroom to call 911. The husband and the intruder struggled for several minutes, and the husband was struck in the head with the metal flashlight. The intruder then fled.

We were told there were a lot of similarities to our case, but the differences are what stand out to us. First off, Muller went there alone, unlike in our case. And why target a husband, wife, and their adult daughter as opposed to a couple with no children? Adding a third victim sleeping in a different room significantly increased the risk of getting caught. Also, instead of having the female tie up the male, the intruder got close enough to the husband that he was able to fight back. No camera, no recording devices with headphones or sedatives? Instead of a TracFone, he brought his own personal cell phone, took it out, placed it on a dresser, and left it?! Why not follow the same protocols that allowed him and his accomplices to get away with our kidnapping?

When the Alameda County Sheriff's detectives tracked down the cell phone subscriber, a woman in Orangevale, California, she said the phone belonged to her adult son, Matthew Muller, who had just told her he lost it earlier that day. She also told authorities he primarily resided at their family vacation house in South Lake Tahoe. This was where Alameda sheriffs found and arrested Muller, along with mounds of evidence linking him to our case, even though he'd had three days to get rid of everything while the detectives obtained search warrants. Was he just being sloppy or was he having a crisis of conscience, like the author of the emails said, and making it easy for police? Or was he falling on the sword for his accomplices?

I'm not sure if I'll ever find out. What I do know is that fucking house is where I was imprisoned and raped, and the Vallejo police and the FBI had the grid coordinates of this location for months!

They could have caught him in March and spared this family, but they refused to follow the evidence! Why?! Because they were more concerned about being right?

By this time, I'm feeling absolutely livid. The FBI, the Vallejo police, the kidnappers—I don't know whom to be angry at. They're all the same to me at this point.

It's time for the press conference.

I go to the bathroom and touch up my lipstick with shaking hands. Sweat pours and my jaw trembles. Thank God I'm not expected to speak; I'm not sure I could put together a cohesive thought, I'm so angry.

Outside, we see dozens of reporters, cameras, and news vans blocking the road. I hear the clicking begin as Aaron and I walk up hand in hand. I'm squeezing his for dear life as my heart races and I try to find any bit of air to breathe. Dan and Doug step up to about a dozen microphones, and we stand behind them. Clenching Aaron's hand with my left hand and grabbing his arm with my right, I look straight ahead as Doug starts speaking, and I tell myself that I'm going to make sure I look every single one of these damn reporters in the eye.

Doug leads off the press conference by proclaiming our "vindication." Unfortunately, it couldn't feel further from the truth. I am so hurt and angry, so disappointed in law enforcement, frustrated with the media, and terribly sad that another family was traumatized, that there is nothing about this day that feels positive. Doug goes on to say we are not only "not guilty but *innocent*" and have suffered horribly. He describes how I was drugged, bound, and put in the trunk of a car until my body went numb. I feel my lips quiver, and I try to hold back the tears that slowly fall down my cheeks. I don't want to do this. I don't want these reporters to see me cry.

Our lawyers say we hope that law enforcement will now do their job and find Muller's accomplices. After Doug and Dan finish speaking and answering questions, it's finally over. We've been out here for roughly thirty minutes, an excruciating amount of time to be standing there on display before the very people who ripped us apart. I feel like it's taken all of my energy just to stand up and maintain my composure. I turn to Aaron and hug him, trying to pull some energy from him before we walk back. As soon as we embrace, I hear more clicking of several cameras.

We decide to head to our friends Dan and Danielle's house, which has been a safe haven for the last several months.

As we gather our things, we see dozens of texts and missed calls on our phones. They're all touching, but the one that moves me to tears is from my cousin: "You did a great job up there. You are so strong! Grandma is watching over you right now and would be so proud."

The one that catches Aaron's attention is a voice mail from the civil attorney Jim Wagstaffe. We hadn't heard from him since our meeting last month. We figured the firm saw our case as too big of a risk to agree to take. But now, with these new revelations, well, I'm guessing they've changed their minds.

On our two-hour drive to Dan and Danielle's, I look up news articles and read them to Aaron. The coverage is more sympathetic to Muller than it ever was to us! Many of the stories focus on his Ivy League credentials. Okay, yes, he went to Harvard, but so did the Unabomber! Yet *our* advanced degrees were never taken into consideration when they called us hoaxers.

We learn that over the previous ten years, Muller was connected to a few other break-ins and was the lead suspect in one of them; was questioned for that crime, then fled the state; was married but then got divorced; was practicing law but then was disbarred. Every aspect of this man's life fell apart. He is *exactly* the type of person who would do something like this, while nothing about our lives indicated we would commit a crime, yet the media seems to be having a harder time believing he could kidnap me than that we could commit a hoax!

I'm so upset I start to stutter, as if my brain isn't computing.

Later, after putting baby Dom to bed, we watch the evening news, hoping there is new information on the case—and curious about what tone the reports will take. We are the lead story on every station. It is surreal to see our faces and names sweep across the screen, channel after channel, once again.

Suddenly, without warning, there he is. The Voice. ABC shows video footage of an old interview with him, from when he was an immigration attorney. As soon as I hear him speak, my body curls into a ball on the couch and I hide my face in my hands. "Oh, my God," I moan, "that's him!"

I feel Danielle and Aaron holding me on either side as I cry, shuddering. "That's him. That's the same voice."

I saw pictures of him all day, but that meant nothing to me. The man who held me captive was a faceless ghost, just a voice with rough, dry hands. But now it's all put together. This creature who tormented and raped me, here he is.

Aaron presses his head next to mine, trying to steady his own breath, and each time I repeat, "It's his voice," he confirms, "I know. That's him. I know."

As THE WEEK goes on, we are stunned to hear the Vallejo Police Department is standing by its baseless, vicious claims, despite the FBI affidavit saying that the kidnapping was real. A reporter asks Captain John Whitney, "Does the department still stand by the statements it made so publicly four months ago that this was a hoax that wasted valuable resources?"

"Yes," he replies without hesitation. "But we are also continuing to investigate it." Vallejo's city manager, Daniel Keen, follows up with "Until that investigation is completed, we don't think any response from the city is appropriate at this point."

Aaron and I are devastated. We're living an Orwellian nightmare in which lies are the truth and truth is a hoax. It's clear that Vallejo is never going to admit any kind of fault—but worse than that, much worse, they will never give up their slander and persecution. Why? Why do they continue to attack us?

OVER THE NEXT couple of days, we see stories quoting Muller's lawyer saying he plans to use his client's mental illness as part of his defense strategy. And not surprising to us, Muller says the same thing in his first "jailhouse interview" with a reporter, Juliette Goodrich from KPIX 5, CBS Bay Area. She wasn't allowed to bring in any recording devices, or pen and paper, so right after her interview she wrote down what he said, noting that Muller insisted certain details be "off the record and for background only." She reports that Muller claims he suffers from "bipolar disorder" with "suicidal tendencies, paranoia, and psychosis," and although he "didn't deny allegations he's the mastermind" behind my kidnapping, he "refused to get into specifics." It sounds like he was evasive, but we wouldn't be surprised either if he alluded to doing this all by himself. Maybe he's scared his accomplices will retaliate against him or his family. It seems so obvious to us that considering the evidence already found at his South Lake Tahoe home linking him to our case, it will be impossible for him to say he wasn't involved. So his only "defense" will be to plead insanity. And you can't be "insane" if you planned and plotted this type of crime with a group of people for more than half a year.

AT THE END of the week, we drive down to Huntington Beach to be with my family. In light of everything that had been happening that week, I'd asked Kaiser if I could reschedule my final exam and, thankfully, they'd agreed. We find out that *20/20* is devoting an episode to our case, for which Dan and Doug were interviewed. As I drive, Aaron starts reading me an article entitled: "So-Called Gone-Girl Mystery: Victim Thought She Was Going to Die."

After hearing the first few sentences, I have to pull over because I can't see through my tears. Doug is quoted as saying, "She had come to accept that she was going to be killed . . . She said to herself, 'I am a good person . . . I have a great family and a great relationship, and if I'm shot . . . ' which is what she thought would happen, that, 'I'm going to be OK.'"

I forgot that I told him that.

When my family gathers around the TV to watch *20/20*, we have to stop several times, either to yell or cry. The worst part is that so-called legal expert Nancy Grace. For the life of me, I can't understand why they would ask her to come on at all. She claims to be an advocate "for victims" but she's one of the most sensationalistic talking heads on television, and she was one of the many reporters who ridiculed me and insinuated I was a fraud. Henry Lee, the *San Francisco Chronicle* reporter who had received the kidnappers' emails but did nothing to follow up on them, is also interviewed.

These two "reporters" were blinded by their own assumptions instead of giving an unbiased account of what happened to us. Nancy Grace played my proof-of-life recording several times on air, including during an interview with Henry Lee, and each time she said "prooooof of li-aaaafe," mockingly using air quotes to indicate she believed the proof of life and the kidnapping were fake. As Lee put it on *Inside Edition*, "I immediately thought, well, how could this be real?" and on *Dateline* said that I sounded "absolutely calm, not terrified, not distressed, as if she was talking to her friend over coffee."

I can't believe these people. *I was DRUGGED, you assholes!* I was being taped; it wasn't a live phone conversation where it would have done me any good to scream and cry and beg for my life, beg for people to find me. If I had sobbed, Muller would have just made me do the recording again, and again and again, until it was done the way he wanted.

Early on we had hoped that Lee could be someone who'd make a difference. But it seems he never cared about the truth, only how our case could help his career. Seeing him jump on any opportunity to do an interview makes me realize he's no better than the police. A couple of months later he gets a new job at a local TV station and writes on Facebook: "How ironically appropriate that my first on-air report . . . will be none other than an update in the bizarre Vallejo 'Gone Girl' abduction case. Recall . . . the suspect sent yrs truly a series of strange emails. . . ." It is sickening to watch someone ride the coattails of our suffering.

The *20/20* episode includes the newsclip of my dad crying and telling me to be strong. It was devastating to read about that in captivity, but it's quite another thing to see his face and hear his voice shaking. They also show a clip of a reporter asking him why it took Aaron so long to call the police, to which he answers, "I don't know. Maybe he was tied up?" Here was a man under the most tremendous strain, yet he makes more sense than the police. I am so proud of him.

After *20/20* we begin to see a few news reports about how poorly we were treated, and people finally come to our defense, but it feels so invasive to have perfect strangers making judgments about something so personal, so devastating, when we aren't allowed to speak to defend ourselves. We have to protect the integrity of the criminal case to ensure this man gets the sentence he deserves. It's a tremendous responsibility for victims to have.

41

AARON

We meet with Jim Wagstaffe at his office in San Francisco in mid-July, nervous yet somewhat hopeful now that his firm is willing to take our case. He greets us warmly with an inviting smile and enthusiastic handshake. He's in his sixties with white hair, a matching white beard, and wire-rim glasses. He sports fashionable sneakers with his expensive suit. He has the energy of a brand-new lawyer despite a long and storied career, and there is something about him that reminds me of Professor Dumbledore from the Harry Potter stories. Wagstaffe guides us into the large, open conference room with giant windows showcasing breathtaking views of the San Francisco Bay. He excitedly introduces us to his two top associates, Ken Nabity and Kevin Clune, his "all-star team." They are young but professional and sharply dressed, with impressive credentials.

After months of being treated like scum, it's almost disorienting to be courted by such a powerful and well-respected law firm. We wonder if things will finally start to turn around for us.

"I have to be honest," Wagstaffe says. "Your case will be very hard to win. It's nearly impossible to sue the police successfully," because they enjoy overwhelming legal protections.

You can't sue the police for doing a bad job, the way you can sue another professional, like a doctor or a lawyer, for malpractice. However, Park defaming us at his press conference along with the violations of my civil rights give us a strong and unique legal claim.

He then goes on to explain the risks we need to consider before moving forward, first and foremost the anti-SLAPP law, which serves as a protection against frivolous lawsuits. It was enacted to protect people's First Amendment rights to free speech against lawsuits by big corporations or powerful people who would bully them into silence. In our case, Vallejo can argue that Park's press conference is protected as free speech under this law and our case could be dismissed before we even got to a trial. If that happens, we would be on the hook for Vallejo's legal fees, which might end up being several hundred thousand dollars.

In other words, we'd go bankrupt.

Wagstaffe knows we'd rather seek criminal charges, or see significant changes made in Vallejo, but that's out of our control. This is our only remedy.

We already know what our choice will be, despite the risks.

Over the last several months, my exhaustion, fear, and stress couldn't stop me from learning as much as I could about the Vallejo Police Department's shocking history. We needed to educate ourselves in the event we're prosecuted, and try to make sense of what the police did. With Ethan's help, what we discovered was worse than I ever expected. It appears we are the lucky ones. We have our lives. We have our freedom. The number of Vallejo police–involved shootings of unarmed citizens is alarming. In 2012 alone, the rate was about thirty-eight times the national average! And these officers are back on the street sooner than what seems reasonable, some even getting promoted! It doesn't appear there are consequences for any misconduct. Instead, they're rewarded!

If we don't challenge the Vallejo Police Department and the city that supported their actions, we're enabling them to continue to cause harm, and thus we would be part of the problem ourselves.

When it comes to powerful institutions like the police that are insulated from lawsuits, negative publicity is one of the few tools for effecting change. So that's what we must use.

We hate what the negative publicity has done to us, our reputations, our safety, our careers, and our families. But if we can use our trauma to shed light on such a dangerous problem, then so be it. We know that Vallejo's lawyers will go after us and try to expose and rip apart every human weakness we have. But we already feel naked and exposed. What more can they do? I guess that's the thing about beating people down to nothing—they've got nothing to lose and will fight tooth and nail to survive.

So, Vallejo: Game on, motherfuckers.

THAT SAME WEEK, we receive a pseudo "apology" letter from the city of Vallejo. It's not public, and it has all the sincerity of a five-year-old's forced apology for hitting his sister: "Sorry your face hit my fist!"

It says that their public statements may have seemed "unnecessarily harsh" to us, but they were correct based on the information they had at the time and so, well, they wouldn't change a thing.

It's a "Sorry, not sorry" written by lawyers afraid of a lawsuit.

Oh, and in order not to "impede" the investigation, this apology will stay private until Muller's indictment. After that, the letter will be made public.

We're still waiting.

DENISE

That week, I speak to Agent Walter on the phone for the first time. He told Doug he had some questions he needs answered because he's writing a search warrant for a red Mustang linked to Muller that was found at the Reno airport. He wants to clarify how many different cars I was transported in and told Doug my statement was "confusing." Doug tells me he assured Walter it was not confusing but very clear, in fact, that I was initially abducted in the trunk of Aaron's car, then transferred to a different trunk and driven to my captor's house.

It's the kidnappers who gave the wrong account about what happened in one of their emails, claiming the Voice switched cars twice.

Maybe the original plan *was* to move me to a third car, perhaps closer to where I was held, and the Voice decided it was too risky. Maybe that was why he left that Monday morning after he put me in the bedroom? Maybe he wasn't supposed to have that car at his home because it was stolen, and he went somewhere to hide it and get another vehicle? Whatever the reason, this error in the email is another indicator to us that Muller wasn't the one who wrote them. He would have known what actually happened.

The fact that Walter is putting more weight on the kidnappers' email than on my account is beyond irritating, but it gets worse. Walter confirms what we'd feared—they believe Muller acted alone, that he had no accomplices, despite the numerous statements to the contrary in those confessional emails and what we told authorities. I just listen, but nothing he says touches my certainty that there are more people involved. We saw them. We heard them.

"How? How do you know that?" I ask.

He mentions investigators found a blow-up doll when searching Muller's property, and he believes Muller had whispered to make it seem like there were others there. His rationale is weak. Ours is not.

For example, Muller told Aaron his car would be left nearby so he could use it to get to the bank, and sure enough, it was found just a half mile from Aaron's house with the keys sitting atop the rear left tire. Yet it was at least a thirty-minute drive to the second car I was transferred to. It doesn't make sense that Muller would risk stalling his getaway by driving in circles just to throw me off, and it certainly would have been too risky to take me out of a trunk in Aaron's neighborhood where someone could pass by. One of the other intruders must have moved it to this closer spot.

And the affidavit described strips of red duct tape located on the roof of the Camry approximately one foot in length and two feet apart. Aaron never knew about the tape during the kidnapping, but in their emails, the kidnappers say they did that to monitor his car with a drone when Aaron went to the bank. How could the Voice control the drone from over a hundred fifty miles away? Why bother putting that on Aaron's car if someone wasn't actually planning on monitoring it?

The FBI hasn't finished searching everything yet, including Muller's electronics, and I want to make sure they keep an open mind. The blow-up doll doesn't explain the two sets of people's legs I saw. A blow-up doll couldn't operate a drill and open drawers while the Voice was upstairs with us. It couldn't remove Mr. Rogers from the room, couldn't simulate footsteps that vibrate through the floor, couldn't flash a Taser from across the room or move past me with the sound of a two-way radio while both of the Voice's hands were on me.

I'm cautious about saying something I shouldn't, or speaking against authority, but I'm afraid they are cherry-picking evidence to try to convince us once again that we were wrong. But what he says next pushes me over the edge.

When Walter says, "I'm ninety-eight percent sure he did it by himself," I snap. I can't believe he's trying to pull that on *me* after Sesma's "ninety-nine percent sure she's lying" bullshit!

I cut him off. "No, no, no, I'm going to stop you right there. I don't want to hear any more of this percentage . . . stuff," I say, stopping myself from cussing even though I want to go off on him. I insist he remain objective and remind him of the many other reasons we know Muller had accomplices. I tell him, "If you really think that he did this on his own, we'll need to see proof. Actual real evidence. You don't want to make another mistake. These people are dangerous, and we don't want them to hurt anyone else."

You'd think they'd want to spend a lot more time exploring every lead before jumping to conclusions. It didn't pan out the last time they did that. I also simply cannot comprehend an investigator not wanting to actually solve a crime.

We get off the phone soon after that, and even though Aaron gave a fist pump when he overheard me respectfully stand my ground, I feel discouraged. They've made up their minds. They've already screwed up so much in this investigation, I can only guess they're committing to this single-perpetrator theory to mitigate the damage. If it's just this one man, well, mission accomplished, they caught him. If it's a group, most of them are still at large.

Why won't anyone in law enforcement listen to us?

42

DENISE

WE'RE BOTH NERVOUS about Aaron returning to work at Kaiser in mid-August but fortunately it's only temporary; he's accepted a job offer at a physical therapy clinic in Santa Cruz, California, with a start date in mid-October.

Still, to break the ice, we set up a happy hour with coworkers at Mare Island brewery, our favorite local spot in Vallejo, before he starts. We haven't been allowed to talk to them for months, and it feels so good to reconnect to the life we had before the kidnapping, to have support, not just from close friends and family, but from coworkers and members of the community. The owner of the brewery knows us from before the kidnapping and greets us warmly when we enter. He literally has goose bumps when he sees us and tells us how he defended us to skeptical patrons when the first wave of negative press penetrated the community.

It's refreshing to sit beside Aaron, hand in hand, as a couple. Before the kidnapping, our relationship was still a secret, although we had planned to tell people about it that very week.

Our coworkers fill us in on what happened the week of the kidnapping, and the weeks that followed. For the first time we hear how Jennifer reacted to hearing she was the intended victim. Apparently, she was most upset to find out via the news that Aaron and I were dating and did little to defend Aaron when there was a lot of office gossip that I was the reason they broke up. Only a few had known the truth: Aaron didn't talk much about Jennifer's infidelity in order to protect her from exactly this type of gossip. It's disheartening to hear she didn't show similar consideration.

They also tell us she had two bodyguards at her side all day long for about a month after the kidnapping, and her boyfriend would walk her up to the hospital every morning and meet her out front when she left.

I can't believe what I'm hearing. She had bodyguards? But Kaiser and much of the rest of the world believed it was a hoax. So who the hell were the bodyguards protecting her from? Us? That very morning I'd taken the written exam to complete my program, but I had to take it in one of the portable office trailers that line the parking lot outside the main building of the hospital instead of in the hospital itself. I couldn't shake the feeling I was being kept away. Hearing this now intensifies my paranoia that people may still think I'm somehow involved. I feel like I've been branded, that "Gone Girl" is tattooed across my forehead and people will always think I'm an unpredictable threat.

Although I should be used to these moments by now, they still sting and cut deep. Just when you think it can't possibly get any worse, it always does.

AT THE END of August, I get a call from Doug and can tell immediately by his tone he has news he's apprehensive about telling me. After obtaining a search warrant for Muller's electronic devices, the FBI was able to retrieve the two videos of Muller raping me in captivity. I am disgusted at the thought of these investigators, especially Sesma, watching the most vulnerable and humiliating moments of my life. But now they know I was telling the truth. These recordings are crucial pieces of evidence that validate my story. And most important, they will help convict Muller, but picturing how it will be used in court is disturbing. The prosecution will say it's rape; the defense team will argue that I enjoyed it. And once again,

I'll have to defend myself for surviving. Even more difficult, we aren't allowed to share this discovery publicly, and all the while people are saying horrible things about me.

One striking example is a man's comment on an article about our case posted on msn.com. He says I was "lying through [my] teeth and sent the anonymous information [i.e., the kidnappers' emails]" to myself so I can "continue playing the victim game," adding, "Her genitals do not validate her story," clearly referencing the damaging phrase in the July FBI affidavit about my SART exam showing "no signs of nonconsensual sex." *Will this stigma ever go away?!*

On top of that, we read in this new affidavit for the electronics that the "jailhouse interview" Muller gave last month was recorded by the jail, and apparently he said "that there was no gang and it was just him." Although we suspected Muller might insinuate he was alone to help his insanity plea, this is a pretty definitive statement to write, especially since nothing Muller said is directly quoted, and it seems to contradict the reporter who said Muller didn't give specific answers about my kidnapping. It's hard not to be skeptical of what these affidavits say now, especially seeing how much information in that July affidavit was either omitted or misleading, like with my SART exam, which steers people to the wrong conclusions.

Sure enough, news outlets pick this up and it's taken as the final answer to the question of whether or not there were accomplices. It's frustrating. Even if he *did* say that, it doesn't mean it's true. Yet it's reported as if Muller was somehow clueless that what he told the reporter "off the record" wouldn't be accessible to authorities, even though the affidavit states that all inmates and the public are told these meetings are recorded. And it's implausible that a Harvard-trained attorney wouldn't know that.

It's peculiar to us how there's more weight put on this one thing he may have said in this one interview, rather than everything that was included in the kidnappers' emails. If he did act alone, why wouldn't he just admit that in the emails when it was obvious the police weren't looking for him? He is clearly egotistical and would have wanted to take all the credit for "fooling" the victims and law enforcement in this "elaborate" kidnapping for ransom.

I continue to be baffled how often people take bits and pieces of affidavits as gospel before seeing all the evidence in court, even though, by their very nature, affidavits are for the purpose of finding out more information.

Years later, we are still unaware of any proof Muller wrote those emails.

AARON

It will be the first time I step into the hospital since the kidnapping. I feel like I'm crossing into enemy territory as I drive into Vallejo's city limits. Denise, her family, my family, everyone I know says they don't believe it's safe for me to go back. They're all afraid that the Vallejo police will find a way to punish me. (I have my attorney's number on speed dial in case I get pulled over.) But I need to go back to work. I need to show everyone that I'm not meekly disappearing into the shadows and I'm going to leave on my own terms.

I thought Kaiser would drop their investigation of me after Muller's arrest, but they dug in their heels just like the police did. They did give me a week of paid administrative leave after the press conference, acting like it was an incredible gift, but they kept demanding I undergo questioning. The employment attorney I hired has extensive experience dealing with Kaiser, and she's baffled by their actions. She's represented clients who were stealing medications or imperiling patient care whom Kaiser never subjected to this type of cross-examination.

She asked Kaiser to specify the exact rules or regulations I'm suspected of violating so I could prepare a defense. They never do. Instead, they said they just want to speak with me "informally." We told them I was interrogated for eighteen hours after being a victim of a violent crime and any more questioning would be traumatizing me again. They responded that I would not be allowed to return unless I signed a letter stating I would not date another "student."

It's a maddening situation. Kaiser clearly wants me gone based on the lies of law enforcement, but they'll never admit it. Perhaps their attorneys believe any admission will expose them to a lawsuit, so they stick to their position that I am at fault. It may be the correct legal strategy, but it's morally repugnant. However, Kaiser is a massive company with all the power; I'm just one guy attempting to reclaim a piece of his life. I agree to sign the letter on the condition that it acknowledges that Denise was a resident and not a student; she's been a licensed therapist for a couple of years. Of course, they never make me sign anything, because it was all a bogus stunt in the first place.

It helps to know I have an exit plan with this new job so Denise and I can move away and start over, start healing. I still feel like a stranger, though, as I begin walking into the building.

After I step out of the elevator on the neurological rehabilitation floor, I start the long walk to my cubicle at the other end of the floor. The hallways are fairly empty in the early morning and I pass only a few of my colleagues, who say, "Welcome back," or "Good to see you." I appreciate their efforts, but it still feels like walking into a room when you know everyone has just been talking about you.

I arrive at my cubicle and I see my desk for the first time. The keyboard is set upside down on top of the computer, the mouse pushed far back from the edge of the table. There seems to be a tiny layer of dust covering everything. It looks like a small memorial to who I used to be. It's a depressing sight; the person who sat there died on March 23 at 3:00 a.m.

One of my colleagues informs me the FBI went through my work computer, which makes sense, though that thought hadn't occurred to me. I sit down and start arranging my things. On my wall are thank-you notes from patients and residents that I had pinned up to remind me on tough days that what I do makes a difference. I read through a few. There are nice words about my dedication to my job, my passion to improve myself. The police and FBI agents surely read them. Would a hoaxer have these kind words written about him? Or do they believe I'm that good of a con artist?

Once again, I'm reminded of the truth: Who I am doesn't matter to the cops.

43

DENISE

In August, Danielle Buljan invites me to a Dierks Bentley concert with a couple of her friends, her sister, and her mom. Danielle and I have established a good friendship over the last few months as we've stayed with her, Dan, and baby Dom. I trust her and know she has good people in her life, but I'm still nervous to go out with a group of strangers. I have this underlying fear that people doubt me, don't like me, see me as a problem, or blame me for what happened. Like most people, I have navigated my share of self-doubts and social anxiety throughout my life, but this new fear is amplified and embedded deep within me. I sometimes feel like I've become a different person, as though the strong, independent, determined Denise I once was has died, and this fearful, timid woman is what's left behind. I used to go to concerts in New York and Boston all the time, travel on my own, make new friends anywhere I went, but now I'm afraid to look anyone in the eye.

I'm also apprehensive about being away from Aaron, even for a few hours. The longest we've been apart since being reunited was a couple of days over Memorial Day weekend when he went to South Lake Tahoe for what he and his friends call "Mancation," an annual guys' trip that started with Dan's bachelor party a few years earlier. I knew it would be good for him to go, have fun, and be around friends who support him. However, it's disturbing to realize now that it was just a week and a half before the Dublin break-in and before Muller was caught. Aaron and his friends had unknowingly stayed within minutes of where I was held captive in South Lake Tahoe—and where Muller primarily resided. In those months before he was caught, we felt like we were still being watched by the kidnappers, or at least one of them, and specifically by the Voice. There were times when we stayed at Aaron's parents that I would get a deeply unsettling feeling he was lurking nearby. They have motion sensor lights around the garage, and they would light up randomly in the middle of the night, but to keep our sanity, we told ourselves it was just wild animals. Also, we'd bought an Amazon Fire Stick to watch TV while we were there, and it went missing. Now that I've read the kidnappers' emails, about how they would break in and take random items from people's homes, I wonder if one of them came in and took it just to mess with us. I wonder how close he got to us again, if he ever really distanced himself from us at all. Muller's family lives in Orangevale, which is only a twenty-five-minute drive from Aaron's parents' house, which we know he knew, since during the home invasion he recited the address.

We told ourselves we were safe because the case was so highly publicized. If anything happened to us or our families, the police and the FBI would be forced to investigate it as a real kidnapping. And we hoped there was some truth to the kidnappers' statements that they didn't intend to cause us further harm.

I still had concerns, however, about the Voice. I worried that he had developed an obsession with me, which would lead me, Aaron, and our families to be targeted once again if and when this obsession flared up.

Even now, with him in jail, we could be at risk. His accomplices are surely worried about the possibility of him turning against them; they might feel it necessary to do whatever it takes to protect themselves, including getting rid of us.

We hope that, because we have no way of identifying them, they'll leave us alone. But no matter what we tell ourselves, we cannot trust that we're truly safe.

GOING TO A country music concert with a group of girls may seem like a harmless event, but not for me. For one, any group social situation triggers some of my PTSD symptoms—anxiety, fear, and self-doubt. But even worse is being in a crowded place where anyone can brush by me, attack me, or kill me without being noticed. However, I don't want to live my life in fear, hiding from the joys as well as the danger. I refuse to let them—the kidnappers *or* law enforcement—have a debilitating, lasting effect on me.

The concert is fun, and as the night progresses, I begin to feel like myself again. We dance wildly just feet away from the stage, screaming like schoolgirls every time Dierks comes closer. Before this, I knew only a few of his songs, but I've instantly become a new, crazed fan. Toward the end of the concert, the crowd gets quiet in anticipation as he starts to sing "Riser," a ballad about overcoming life's challenges, like a phoenix rising from the ashes. I pray that that's me. A Riser. A survivor.

As I listen to the melody and each touching verse, surrounded by all the people holding one another, swaying back and forth, I experience feelings of gratitude to be alive, to be here and have a second chance to experience moments like this, make new friends, take in music that connects the whole crowd—side by side with the horrific memories of captivity, rape, the trunk, the media, and law enforcement. It's too much.

I excuse myself to step away from the crowd, as tears flow down my face. I can hardly breathe and I'm trying hard not to draw attention to myself. I feel lost and unsure of where to go; then I feel a hand on my shoulder.

At first I'm startled, and I turn, preparing for an attack, but it's Danielle's mother. I collapse into her arms and sob, and she embraces me, with the deep, caring warmth of a mom, comforting me as she repeats over and over, "You're safe. It's not your fault."

44

AARON

I'VE BEEN BACK at work for just over a week, although I'm only working half days. My therapist and I agreed that it would be an easier transition to be part-time for the first couple of weeks. It's the right move. My anxiety jumps anytime I think about sitting in the lunchroom with the rest of the staff. Even worse, I hate spending time away from Denise. She's the only constant in my life and her love steadies me, allowing me to occasionally be optimistic.

For months, I've been paranoid about being recognized on the street. At the hospital there is no question everyone knows who I am. I see the little flash in their eyes as they register I'm in the actual room and not on a screen. I have no idea if this is how people react to celebrities, but I can't stand it. I just hope that the novelty wears off soon. I've treated only a few patients so far. They've been what we would call "straightforward" cases, meaning they have more mobility and fewer cognitive challenges than the rest of the patient population. They require less skill from the therapist and working with them has helped me recover my confidence. More important, the patients are a daily reminder of human resilience and put my trauma in perspective. Every one of these patients and their families

has suffered their own version of a kidnapping, yet they persevere. I too
will persevere.

I'M SUPERVISING IN the therapy gym, meaning I'm basically waiting
around in case a therapist needs help. I'm feeling restless because I'm not
busy, and I feel guilty as well, knowing I'm not fully committed to my
work. It's unintentional, but the trauma has taken residence in my mind;
it's like a heavy shadow that I'm dragging along. Before the kidnapping,
I always wanted to take on the most challenging cases. When I worked
with those patients, the bustle of the gym would fade into the background
and my daily worries would be muted. I'd focus solely on connecting
with that person in that moment. Now I don't know if I'm too broken to
be able to do that again.

My colleague Carly asks me to help her transfer a patient from his
wheelchair to the treatment mat. She explains that the patient, in his early
thirties, has a genetic malformation that caused a stroke. He is physically
strong but lacks coordination or control. She needs assistance because the
patient could accidentally throw himself in any direction.

The patient has a positive disposition despite his condition, and I feel
a deep desire compelling me to help him. It's that commitment I've been
missing. Carly may have sensed it because she says, "I would love your
input if you have some treatment ideas." The three of us work together
in almost perfect synchrony. I can see a level of harmony being restored
between the patient's body and his mind. At the end of the treatment, he
has gained enough control that he's able to get back into his wheelchair
with only Carly's help. It's one of those rare dramatic treatment results
that's only happened a few times in my career.

Over the next week or so, the patient improves, from being able to
transfer with the help of only one person, to transferring independently,
to walking. It's a miraculous recovery I was blessed to be a small part of.
I almost burst into tears when the patient thanks me on his last day.

Little does he know how much he helped me.

DENISE

On the mornings when Aaron is working, I spend a lot of time writing and reflecting on what happened, often getting sucked down the dark rabbit hole of the news coverage and comments about our case.

I have only heard short clips of my proof-of-life recording before, but now I find the full unedited audio on the *San Francisco Chronicle*'s website. I'm wrecked hearing the fear in my voice, my distorted tone and drug-induced slurred speech. But my sadness shifts to anger as I think about how the media edited it in such a way to make me seem unreliable. If you listen to it from start to finish, it's obvious I'm drugged, terrified, and reciting a prepared statement that I'm struggling to remember.

I read article after article and hundreds of comments from the first week of the kidnapping saying the most horrible, vicious things about us, and specifically about me. I know why I hid from this information for the last few months, but the truth is, even without seeing them, I felt the weight and magnitude of them all along. Now I want to face it head-on to get a full grasp of what I'm up against.

As necessary as it is, it's devastating to read comment after vile comment tearing down my character, my appearance, my life, saying how I must have needed the money for cosmetic work on my chin or on my breasts, or how I look shady and must be a meth head. Accusations based on nothing but people's own personal judgments and biases. To them, I am a symbol, a story of what's wrong with the world, with women, with "millennials," with society. I'm not a person. I'm just an object to throw stones at.

I finally open and read through the grotesque Facebook messages strangers have sent me. It's shocking how many people put in the time and energy to find me on Facebook, type out hateful statements, and actually push SEND. All because they were so fueled with anger whipped up by the lies told by law enforcement and perpetuated by the media.

Omg . . . aren't you that chick that faked her own abduction? Thank you for wasting taxpayer money, thank you for wasting our law enforcement time. You're gross. Get a life. Coming from an enormous law enforcement family, I hope you get prosecuted.

Liar

Stupid Cunt

You're fucked up!

Fake ass bitch

What a fucking idiot you are. I hope they lock u and ur whole fucking family up. If you ever get kidnap, I hope they throw you in the bay.

You're a fucking dumb ass!

Piece of shit!!! When people actually need help this is what you decide to do . . . hope you proved a point . . . smh

You're pathetic!

You're a fucking joke. To think, people were actually worried about you.

Well played former physical therapist

I can't wait till your in jail you fraudulent bitch. We are going to start making calls to Kaiser demanding your termination.

You're a sick ass bitch for faking your story. I hope you go to prison

Sounds like the authorities have unraveled your sick scheme to make some money. Here's hoping you rot in prison. I wonder how many women were truly victimized while resources were being used to find a liar.

Time for you to get a real SMACKDOWN for your kidnapping hoax stunt!!! What the hell were you thinking doing something like that??? Are you CRAZY??? Some kind of nutjob?. . . . Do you have any idea what you caused? Not to mention scaring your dad so badly he came up here to search for you!! What? you needed 15 minutes of fame??? Attention?. . . . I hope you get your attention in a damn dirty jail soon for what you did and an inmate beats you up!

Show me some pussy. I think you owe it to me after having me search for you for two days.

You're a stupid fucking bitch for that stunt you pulled. I hope they throw you in jail with that piece of shit boyfriend. Burn in hell

Damn hoe, we were hoping you were dead!!!!! Good luck finding a good job now. #meth-headbitch

You Lying Cunt. You and whoever helped you concoct this STUPID Story are going to go to jail, you know that right? And also pay back all the cost for the people that got together to search for you. Even had your dad on TV saying he knows your missing. What a great daughter you are

I hope you get charged and sent to jail you piece of shit. Vallejo doesn't have the money to be wasting on this kind of bullshit you dumb hoe!!!!! I hope you lose your job too!!!!

Stupid cunt. You are what is wrong with society. I hope u choke on a chicken bone. Your fucking dad was on tv crying because he thought you might be hurt or dead. What kind of bitch ass does that to her family?

U R a FUCKING STUPID WHORE WHO NEEDS 2 B SHOT & KILLED IMMEDIATELY!!!!!!!!!

Not all of the commenters are strangers. Immediately after the kidnapping Jennifer's boyfriend, the cop she cheated on Aaron with, retweeted a news story with the headline No Evidence to support the claims that this was a stranger abduction, or an abduction at all. Says #VallejoPD about #Denise HuskinsCase.

Two months later, before Muller was caught, Jennifer posted on her Instagram: My goal for 2015 had been to learn . . . knitting, Spanish, photography, calligraphy, and piano. Life's too short to spend in front of the tv. #grateful #HappySunday. Some people replied with words of admiration and encouragement. Her boyfriend's heartless response? My goal is to keep you from getting kidnapped while you learn all those things, while sitting in front of the tv. #naptime . . .

And that post mocking my pain is still up, months after Muller's arrest, for anyone to read.

The messages go on, and on, and on. I disconnect from this person they're attacking, because whomever they're thinking of, it certainly isn't me, not the real me anyway. These people are angry at a lie. In a way, it protects me to know these statements have nothing to do with *me*, but at the same time, they are all directed at me. They know my name, what I look like, what I do for a living, where both of my parents live. These people who have actively sought me out on social media to attack me could easily seek me out in person and do the same. How the hell can I trust that they won't try to take matters into their own hands? Maybe it'd be better for me to try to work, to get a distraction from all of this. But I can't, even if I wanted to. That option has been taken from me. And I know that for Aaron, it hasn't necessarily been any better. It's just another type of trauma, another type of attack to fight against. No matter where we turn, our fists are up, blocking another blow.

45

AARON

TIM INFORMS ME that Dr. Stricker, the physician in chief, and the area manager, Sandy Rush, are willing to meet with me so I can air my grievances about how Denise and I have been treated by the company. I jump at the opportunity although I expect it to be nothing more than lip service. Nevertheless, they'll have to sit across from me and produce some answers. We set up the meeting for the end of the week.

I've seen Jennifer in the hallway a few times since I returned to work. She avoids eye contact and basically bolts into her office whenever she spots me. However, I decide I need to better understand what happened at the hospital over the last few months before I go into this meeting.

I head down to her office and knock on the open door.

"Is this a good time to talk?" I ask.

I've surprised her, and she starts by saying it's been a crazy and difficult few months for her as well.

She goes on to tell me that when news of the kidnapping broke, she told her manager that I used to come into her office "quite often" to talk and that I would make her "feel bad." But not to worry because she never filed a formal complaint with HR.

I made her feel bad? Because I told her how much she hurt me by cheating on me?

"I'm sure you left out that you were cheating on me for two years and the cop you're dating was being investigated," I counter. She claims what he did was taken out of context, and the police union didn't back him.

As we continue to talk, Kaiser's aggressive treatment of Denise and me begins to make a lot more sense. Jennifer downplayed her indiscretions and played up her victimhood, which fueled the narrative that we were out to get her.

She goes on that she was "so mad" when she found out that Denise and I were dating, and she "knows all about" our relationship—for example, the fact that Denise watched my house over Thanksgiving. There are only a few people who knew that detail and I immediately know who told Jennifer. It was crushing not to hear from these former coworkers since the kidnapping and even more painful to learn that they used our friendship, our confidence, as cheap currency to gain access to the inner circle of the gossip wheel. This betrayal will make Denise and me turn even more inward, afraid that sharing any information beyond our closest friends will be used against us. I'm exhausted from being constantly judged and unsure of whom to trust.

I ask her why she didn't help us get Sesma off the case.

Jennifer responds she didn't help because she was upset we had reached out to her mom. I correct her—it was her mom who contacted us—and she casually brushes it off, trying to minimize the seriousness of the situation. Sesma probably just wanted his name on a big case, she rationalizes, and it didn't matter because Walter was the one who questioned her, not Sesma.

"That's the whole point," I say. *How can she not see the problem?* "He didn't question you, and he didn't question me, because it's a major conflict of interest."

For some reason she feels the need to defend him. Or maybe she's just in denial?

She also tells me that, before Muller was caught, Walter showed her the video of the man buying a TracFone at Target and asked her if it looked like my friend Dan Buljan. So the FBI theory morphed from me buying the phone to one of my best friends jumping on board with our scheme? Maybe I got Ethan to help too. Or I roped in my first-grade teacher or my youth pastor. Or hell, maybe, just maybe, it was a real kidnapping, and this was the kidnapper.

Jennifer says she told Walter it didn't look like Dan and she didn't recognize the man in the video. Then, just as frustrating, she says the FBI told her about Muller's arrest and the unsealing of the affidavit before they told *us*. They updated her at least four times about the case while we heard basically nothing from them.

It's incredible to hear about the support that Kaiser provided her, like the bodyguards and an administrative parking pass so that she could park right next to the hospital instead of in the auxiliary lot with the other employees. It's even more apparent that they viewed her as the only victim.

The more she speaks, the more shocking and hurtful it is. I'll have to share it all with Denise, because I don't want to keep anything from her. But I know it'll crush her. This conversation confirms more than ever that Jennifer's not the person I thought she was.

DENISE

Every day that Aaron leaves for work, I worry. I tell him to always have his phone in his hand, in case he gets pulled over, so he can call me or his attorneys.

I'm constantly terrified they'll stop him, turn off their body and car cams, and beat or shoot him to death, making up some lie to justify it. We even talk about him getting a GoPro to attach to the top of the car so he can record his drives to and from work. I have him text me when he's walking out of work, and when he gets in his car and leaves, so I know when to expect him to get home.

Maybe it's foolish or reckless for us to be here, but we also have to live our lives. Aaron has to return to work, we have to move forward, and we can't let fear dictate what we do. And like with the kidnappers, we have to rationalize that the publicity around the case somehow protects us from being attacked by the cops.

One day he comes home visibly upset. He tells me he spoke to Jennifer in her office. At first, I feel betrayed. He never told me he planned to do this, and it triggers bad memories of our relationship issues from before the kidnapping. But I understand why he did, and I want to hear what her experience was, so I sit and listen as he continues.

Jennifer never thought he was involved in the kidnapping, he reports, but she didn't know me well, so she didn't want to do anything to help me because she wasn't sure if I was crazy or wanted to get back at Aaron.

I can no longer hold back the emotions I'm trying to contain. I start crying tears of hurt and frustration.

How could she say that?! Especially now, now that she knows the kidnapping was real and there's a man in custody?

It was supposed to be you, I think to myself. *They wanted you, but instead this happened to me. I was the one who was raped! I thought I would be killed!*

Everything she said to Aaron maximized her pain and minimized ours. About the bodyguards, she said she was afraid "because the kidnappers were still out there."

But you already said you believed at that time that I was involved. And it's clear by your boyfriend retweeting that article about me faking the kidnapping what you both believed. So, what? You thought I was going to come to the hospital in broad daylight and attack you?

She even made sure to say she read in the affidavit there weren't signs of "nonconsensual sex," as if my experience wasn't that bad. Aaron had to explain to her that nothing about what happened to me could be described as consensual.

I'm stunned to hear that she seems to believe I made up the rapes! *How can anyone say that, especially the woman who was the target? Does she not realize that it could have been her body, her life, her name, her reputation violated and destroyed?*

After Aaron corrected her, he tells me, she began to recognize that she was spared this horror. She said to him, "Someone must have been look-ing out for me."

I gasp. Her insensitivity and lack of empathy astound me.

ALTHOUGH I NO longer have health insurance, Dr. Land graciously is able to do phone sessions every month or so. I update her about every-thing: work, social media attacks, the kidnappers, law enforcement, not understanding why people can be so thoughtless and cruel. Her response helps immensely, and I go back to it again and again as things grow even more unbelievable. She tells me it's actually a good thing I don't under-stand that mentality or behavior, which do not come from a healthy place. If it starts making sense to me, then I should worry.

46

AARON

I ARRIVE TWENTY MINUTES early for the meeting with the Kaiser administrators. Dr. Stricker comes in next, offering me some coffee and attempting to make small talk. I give curt answers, and he quickly realizes this isn't going to be a casual, friendly meeting. We fall into a tense silence as we await Sandy's arrival. Dr. Stricker is a nice man. Everyone at the hospital likes him, and I can tell he's uncomfortable, but I'm now accustomed to awkward silences. I've been on the defensive for months, but this is the first time I get to personally punch back, even if he's not the main culprit.

After a few minutes, Sandy arrives. We exchange pleasantries, and she says, "Tim told us that you have some things you would like to discuss with us. What would you like to talk about?"

Maybe because we've been preparing our civil lawsuit, or maybe because I've fantasized about telling the world the truth over and over again, I take the floor like an attorney giving his opening statement. For about twenty minutes, I lay out the case succinctly, from my initial treatment by law enforcement to fighting Kaiser over nonexistent rules. After each point, I feel Dr. Stricker sinking a little in his chair. It's empowering to actually be heard.

I finish and wait for their response.

"Thank you for sharing that," Sandy says. "You told us a lot of things we didn't know."

I can't help but jump right back in.

"Exactly," I say. "You guys didn't know the facts and you still made judgments."

"You're right," Sandy replies. "We can't change what happened but what can we do right now to improve the situation?"

I finally soften a bit. They didn't blame the circumstances or make excuses. It's the first time an authority figure has shown accountability. I ask them to restore my paid time off because I wasn't on vacation and it was they who were preventing me from working. They agree and my paid time off is restored. It helps ease some of our financial burdens, but more important, it shows me that I, not just my attorneys, can effect change.

DENISE

We're working hard with our attorneys to collect information as we prepare our civil claim against the Vallejo Police Department. So, for the first time, I hear the details of my parents' and Devin's experiences with the police while I was missing. I hadn't asked them before, and I think they wanted to protect me because of how appalling it was. My mom cautiously tells me how Mat Mustard said women who've been molested often want to relive the thrill of the experience. That level of misogyny is disgusting, and I cannot fathom that anyone actually believes it. Even if he does, how could he be heartless enough to say this to the desperate mother and brother of a missing woman?

I also find out the police went to my ex-boyfriend's apartment, hoping to dig up dirt on me. All of their questions were about my mental health. He refused to portray me the way they wanted, so they got frustrated and bad-mouthed him to his neighbors. Vallejo police sought out anyone they thought could malign us or assassinate our character while trying to drag through the mud anyone we were close to.

Our civil attorneys have to make sure our claim is filed within six months of the press conference where my kidnapping was called a hoax, to avoid passing the statute of limitations. They explain to us that the "claim" is the initial notification of the intent to file a lawsuit and gives the party a chance to try to remedy the action before it turns into a suit.

So, on September 17, our attorneys file the claim against the Vallejo Police Department and the city of Vallejo. The filing contains a laundry list of ways our constitutional rights were violated, but the heart of it is that we were defamed by Kenny Park's press conference and the press release the department issued. That night we're at Mare Island brewery with a few people from work because Aaron's last day is next week. *Thursday Night Football* is projected on the wall so everyone can watch. During halftime, local news reports come on and there we are, blown up on the wall.

Well, shit. There's really no hiding from this. This is our new normal.

THE DAY AFTER we file our claim against Vallejo, Muller pleads no contest to the charges in Dublin and gets ten years. A no-contest plea essentially has the same outcome as a guilty plea, except that there is no admission of guilt. What is shocking, however, is that his sentence is *concurrent*: that is, it will be served at the same time as, not on top of, whatever sentence he receives in our case—essentially a wash. He's getting a two-for-one special for his crimes.

47

DENISE

In October, we move to our new home in Santa Cruz, where the towering redwoods meet the breathtaking coastal California cliffs. It's an area with healing and positive energy.

We rent a nice duplex in a quaint neighborhood that's just a ten-minute walk to the ocean. We take walks along the beach and get mesmerized by the patchy clouds that wisp across the skyline, tinted bright pink and orange as the sun sets. There is always a fresh, salty aroma in the air and a cool breeze that perks up your senses, making you feel alive and energized. We take hikes, getting lost in the cool, comforting shade of the giant redwoods. With their deep roots they convey an immense sense of peace and stability. There are birds and wildlife I've never seen before, and different flowers blooming every few months, always giving you a chance to experience awe and wonderment in the persistence of nature's beauty amidst an ever-changing and evolving cycle.

We battle with experiencing these moments of joy alongside our suffering. At times, we feel guilty and confused when we have moments of happiness, as though it means we aren't still in pain. If we're able to smile and joke, does that mean that we haven't really suffered? In the middle of enjoying a wonderful celebration with a family member or friend, I am also always aware of the pain I'm still healing from. But as we read books about trauma, we learn this is normal, that others who've survived trauma experienced similar struggles.

We take comfort in the words of philosopher Friedrich Nietzsche: "He who has a why to live for can bear almost any how." We are fortunate to have many "whys" to live for, which gave us both reason to fight so hard to survive those first forty-eight hours. And we will not give up now or ever.

I AM EXHAUSTED most days, though some are better than others. It takes an extraordinary amount of effort just to get out of bed and not be overtaken by anxiety. Once Aaron starts his new job, he's working four days a week for ten hours, and often eleven or twelve, to support us both. He's taken on an incredible burden without hesitation or complaint, and as grateful as I am, I can't help feeling guilty at times as well.

To keep busy, I clean, unpack, and study feng shui to try to put positive energy into our new home. I work out, go on walks, read or write in my journal, and even start painting. I never considered myself the creative type, but after taking a "Sip and Paint" class with Aaron's mother, I thought it would be a good emotional outlet. And it is. It's also a way for me to show my love and appreciation to all of those who have stood by us. I paint a lighthouse for my mom because she loves them; the sunset on Catalina Island for my dad, who lives a block from the beach; fall foliage in Vermont for Aaron's parents; and for us, a phoenix rising from the ashes.

But a big piece of our lives is missing: Mr. Rogers.

He's been staying with Aaron's parents because our lease doesn't allow for pets. We agreed because we needed a place to live. But after a few weeks here, I ask our landlord if he would allow us to bring our cat, sharing with him what happened and how it would be therapeutic for Mr. Rogers to be with us. He is gracious and understanding, and by November, we have all reunited again.

It makes Aaron feel better that I have Mr. Rogers to keep me company during the day while he's gone. And he truly has become my therapy cat, often lying across my chest, purring as he nuzzles his head into my hand when I am having a hard time. I've tried to find a local therapist, but it's impossible. I have limited finances and no health insurance. I finally did get approved for victims' assistance benefits, but it pays a fraction of the typical fee and requires a lot of paperwork most therapists don't want to deal with. One therapist I called wouldn't work with me because of the pending criminal cases. She said she didn't want to be subpoenaed. I give up.

At least for now, I can still speak over the phone with my Kaiser therapist about once a month. And I have Mr. Rogers. I am doing everything in my power to heal.

AARON AND I are struggling a bit as we try to manage the symptoms of our trauma. Problems that we had before the kidnapping resurface. Our night together before the home invasion was a positive start to rebuilding our relationship, but that process got steamrolled by what happened.

One morning we're standing in the hallway arguing. Our voices aren't loud, but there is tension. Maybe because we rarely argue, Mr. Rogers comes to sit between us, looking up with those adorable, expressive eyes of his, and meows at us with concern. It stops us in our tracks, and we regroup. He may not be able to speak, but his tone rang loud and clear. He manages to be our guiding light, cutting through the noise, reminding us that the three of us are in this together, and we need to support one another through it.

We discussed couples counseling before, but now we know it's time and worth the cost we'll have to pay out of pocket. No matter what, we love each other and want to be together, but we're each struggling with self-doubt and insecurities, and working with a professional will be helpful for our relationship and, more important, for us as individuals.

In therapy, we talk about our upbringings, about how we perceive love and how we receive it. For months after we were first reunited, we were intimate almost every day. I think after the very real threat of losing each other, we felt so bonded we wanted to be connected as much as possible. Everything in our life was chaotic and uncertain, except for our love, which gave us the strength to face our challenges. As other areas of our lives have begun to stabilize, we make love less and less frequently. As we talk it through in therapy, we're finally able to admit out loud that sex can be triggering for both of us. I also think we were still in shock the first few months after the kidnapping, so I didn't associate sex with Aaron with the rapes. But now, as many other symptoms of post-traumatic stress disorder bubble to the surface, so do those stemming from the rapes. Especially now that Muller has been caught and he's no longer just a faceless ghost. I try not to let those memories invade my intimate moments with Aaron, but sometimes they do. And there are times when Aaron wonders if I am reminded of the assaults; he doesn't want to do anything to trigger me or bring me back to that place. Sometimes, even if I am in a good place and not thinking about them, I can tell he is, and he disconnects from me. It's helpful for us to be able to acknowledge these things, so that when it happens, we can come up with strategies to help us reconnect.

We also discuss my fear that Aaron may not really want to be with me, that he is only with me out of obligation. He reassures me that he absolutely loves me and wants to spend his life with me, yet at times he doesn't feel good enough or continues to feel guilty that he has put me through so much. I don't blame him for any of it, the kidnapping, nothing. I tell him that even though certain things he did before the kidnapping were hurtful, and I'm still trying to get past that, I do forgive him.

I tell him that I'm afraid he sees me as damaged goods now, that he'll never be able to see me as anything other than a rape victim and never be able to look at me with desire again. He tells me he loves me even more because of who I am and how I was able to survive it all. He still adores me and is attracted to me, yet he also wants to respect there are things that can trigger me, and he wants to be cautious about adding to them.

So we have a lot to deal with. Therapy helps draw us even closer, and our bond grows stronger as we are able to be open and honest with each other.

48

AARON

THE RAINDROPS TAPPING on the roof of our Santa Cruz home wake me and I immediately know that I won't be able to work today. I'm on high alert—rain means danger. A year ago, I thought the sound of rain was a blessing to the thirsty California soil, but it was cover for the kidnappers' operation. The artificial rain sounds emitting from their white noise machine concealed the danger that awaited outside my home's walls. I paid a heavy price last time I ignored the rain sounds and I can't afford another mistake.

Each drop shoves me backward in time. The panic and fear rise within me, but I make no moves. I can't wake Denise; she needs as much rest as she can get. Yet I'm slipping back to the moments that seem never to let me go. It takes all my concentration to ground myself in the present. I focus on the pressure of the mattress on my back, the sheets draped over my body, the warmth from Denise and Mr. Rogers lying next to me, the tiny vibrations from the raindrops on the roof's shingles. No white noise machine can replicate those vibrations. It's this small recognition that stabilizes me and assures me this is Mother Nature's gift and not an evil cloak. I may have survived this round, but it left me exhausted and my opponent is relentless, ready to strike at any time, and there's no end in sight.

I wait for the sun to rise before calling in sick to work. Thankfully, my new employers have been gracious in providing as much time off as I've needed. I hate that I've called in sick more in the past few months than I did in five years working at Kaiser. After college, I started working full-time and didn't take a vacation for two years. I pride myself on being reliable, consistent, and healthy. But now I'm a flake, and I'm always fighting off a cold. It's embarrassing to feel so weak.

I shouldn't complain; many people have it much worse. I have a wonderful partner in Denise, we live in a gorgeous area with a roof over our heads, and I have a job . . . and my freedom. How many others would trade places with me? A little bit of rain shouldn't break me, but it does.

Thankfully, Denise is the strong one today. She rubs my back and comforts me until I fall asleep for a couple of hours. Over the past several months, we unconsciously fell into a rhythm of trading off who's shouldering more of the emotional load. Through therapy, we developed an explicit strategy, letting each other know the level of our "emotional gas tank." If I have more in my tank, then I'll take on whatever needs to be done and vice versa. Some days we're both running on fumes and then will give ourselves permission to do whatever we need—a walk by the ocean, or ordering takeout and watching a silly movie, or sometimes it's just lying in bed together.

Today, a walk along the coastline pulls me out of my rut. I recognize that I am recovering because my lows aren't as deep and don't last as long as before. After our walk, I'm motivated to make an elaborate dinner, lasagna from scratch. Since we moved to Santa Cruz, the flavors of my food have dramatically improved, which is another sign of healing. For the first six months after the kidnapping, everything I made fell flat, even meals I'd made countless times. Occasionally, the food wasn't even edible, which never happened before the kidnapping. But they say you "cook with love" and it felt like my pain was seeping into the food. Now the lasagna comes out perfectly, and the kitchen is returning to being my place of love and joy.

IN THE MEANTIME, returning to work has been helpful, although it presents its own set of challenges; the most difficult is being away from Denise for twelve hours a day. And I'm so busy that I can barely check in on her. Some days I come home to find her still in bed or lying on the couch, and I feel that I'm being irresponsible by leaving her alone. At least Mr. Rogers is there to help her through the tough days. Thankfully, there are more and more days when Denise has been up taking care of the household chores to support me as I work. We remind ourselves that re-covery is not a straight line. There will be ebbs and flows, but it does seem we're trending in the right direction.

Occasionally a patient tells me he or she is aware of our case. However, more often, I worry that patients know about it but they're afraid to say anything. When I do speak about the case, I struggle to navigate the conversation. All the patients understand that Denise went through a ter-rible ordeal but tend to undervalue or ignore what I went through and, in many ways, am still reliving. Most nights, rain or not, I wake up at 3:00 a.m., my heart pounding with fear, my body's fight-or-flight response already in full gear. Sometimes, I'll even think I see the shadow of some-one standing over the bed. When I do sleep, I have nightmare after night-mare of losing something important, my desperate pleas for help going ignored. Before we leave for any trip, Denise and I take pictures through-out the house so that we can compulsively check that nothing has been moved while we were gone. And everywhere I go, I have to make sure I know where the exits are and try to ignore the security cameras—otherwise, I'll start to panic with the *dung, dung, dung* of that damn cam-era the intruders installed ringing in my ears. It seems no matter what I tell myself, I still feel guilty I couldn't protect Denise that night. A real man would have been able to protect her, right? I can't help but wonder if that's what people think, if they are judging me for that too, though not as harshly as I judge myself.

So I find myself oversharing about my own trauma, as if by *really* ex-plaining it, then the other person will realize it's been awful for me too.

But they can't fully understand. Is it because I'm a man, so I should be able to handle it better? Or because almost everyone inherently compares my trauma with Denise's and judges mine as less bad? After all, I wasn't kidnapped or raped. Except the comparisons don't help anyone's suffering. A person needs to make room for both traumas. What happened to me was bad *and* being kidnapped is horrible. Unfortunately, most of these conversations end awkwardly with me feeling embarrassed.

Mostly, I'm able to go through the workdays without any incidents, but one day I'm told some news that stops me in my tracks. One of the clinic's receptionists tells me that a new patient canceled his session because I have "legal problems." I'm confused, given all the new reports about our innocence. For the first time, I add "physical therapist" to a Google search of my name, and to my horror, all the results are articles from early March saying the kidnapping was a hoax. It's the same when I search "Denise Huskins physical therapist." After Muller was caught, Denise and I were relabeled "Vallejo kidnapping victims" and the media stopped including our profession in news articles, meaning those reports don't show up in a Google search that includes the term "physical therapist."

Before the Internet, if people were publicly shamed and humiliated, they could move to a different town and leave it all behind. But now there's no escaping the digital persona and I can only pray that Google's cryptic algorithms will eventually somehow shift in our favor.

DENISE

For the last several months, Aaron's had to meet with an attorney from Kaiser to prepare for a lawsuit involving a patient who fell a few years back. Aaron was her primary physical therapist, so even though he was not present at the incident, he was named in the suit. This was one of the first things he was faced with when he returned to Kaiser back in August—another situation in which he has to defend himself.

The arbitration is scheduled for late January 2016 in Walnut Creek, an hour or so southeast of Vallejo. An arbitration is like a trial, except it's resolved outside of the courtroom, and instead of a jury, the judge determines the outcome.

We take the occasion to spend the weekend with friends in the area, go to an engagement party, and the next night stay with an old client of Aaron's. She and her mom wrote to Aaron's defense attorneys when I was still missing to say how incredible Aaron is, how much he helped her, and, really, saved her life.

I've been having a hard time emotionally, still anxious in social situations, and even though everyone is kind and warm, I spend part of both nights quietly crying as a couple of his friends comfort me. I'm embarrassed and apologize profusely, but they're understanding and caring.

On Monday morning, we head to the office in Walnut Creek for the arbitration. I drive, knowing how much pressure is on Aaron. I'm nervous for him. If the case moves forward, he would have to report it to the Physical Therapy Board of California and his license could be suspended or revoked, depending on the outcome of the case. And right now I'm not working. If he can't work, I'll have to support us, but I'm not sure I'm strong enough yet. Aaron is shouldering the financial burden for both of us, all because I am too damn weak to move forward. How much more can he take on?

As I'm driving on the freeway, my vision starts to blur, I get lightheaded, and it's hard for me to breathe. I begin to sweat profusely, and my heart races. I take some deep breaths, trying to regain control. *I'm supposed to be the strong one right now, damn it! I'm not about to be put on the spot and questioned. He is! Why can't I pull myself together?!*

But my vision gets worse; my eyes are shaking. I feel like I am looking through a fun-house mirror, and I can't gauge the distance to the cars zooming by me. This isn't safe, and I'm really scared that I'll cause an accident. "I'm sorry. I can't drive right now. I have to pull over," I tell Aaron. "I don't know what's wrong with me."

Even after Aaron takes over driving, my symptoms get worse. My stomach is in knots. I feel every molecule in my body shake, and the blood leaves my skin. I'm covered in a clammy layer of sweat and I feel like I'm either going to throw up or lose control of my bladder or bowels. I continue to breathe deeply, hoping it will pass, but it just gets more intense.

Aaron parks in a garage at the office building. He doesn't want to leave me, but he has to go up. I hope that maybe if I rest, I'll feel better. I take the two Valiums I have left from the eight that were prescribed to me at the hospital after the SART exam. I've taken them only in my toughest moments, and this is certainly one of them.

I call our couples therapist and tell her what's going on. It feels like I'm deathly ill, like my body is abandoning me, revolting against me, against all that I've lived through, and I've lost control. I ask if she thinks I should go to the hospital. I feel so ill that I'm not sure how anyone could help me but wonder if I should be monitored to make sure something more serious doesn't happen. I'm actually terrified that I will die of a heart attack.

She and I talk it through and recognize that the hospital setting may be even more triggering. She recommends I go upstairs to be with Aaron so I'm not alone and call back if things get worse.

Upstairs I apologize to everyone: "I'm having a panic attack and need to lie down," I explain. I lie on the floor of the conference room, curled in the fetal position.

It takes hours before it's Aaron's turn to be questioned, and the whole time he's in there, I feel like my organs are being ripped apart. After about forty-five minutes, Aaron returns with the lawyer, who's smiling like his team just won the World Series. "Yes!" he says, punching the air. "You did incredibly! There's no way this will be moving forward!"

On the drive home, Aaron tells me all about it. When he walked in, the patient and her husband smiled and waved at him. This patient had actually written him on Facebook a couple of months after the kidnapping, after Muller was caught, to express her support and gratitude. I don't think she's aware what this lawsuit could do to him and his ability to practice.

When we get home, I nestle up in bed under a pile of warm blankets and Mr. Rogers climbs on my chest and purrs. I feel at least 75 percent better and am able to fall asleep. I needed to be somewhere safe, and this is my safe place.

Within days we find out that the case has been dropped. Thankfully. One lawsuit done.

I call both our couples therapist and Dr. Land to follow up. Dr. Land specializes in trauma, and her response is reassuring. She tells me it's normal to go through different phases of PTSD. Initially, for months after the kidnapping, I was in a deep state of shock. After being so viciously attacked, I needed to stay numb to survive. But that doesn't mean the effects of the trauma weren't there, lurking deep within me. It was just being contained, so I could somehow find the energy to rebuild my life, and now that things are more secure, my mind and body are finally in a safer space to experience it. People can't avoid feeling trauma, as much as we try to deny, ignore, or suppress it. Eventually, our bodies have to process it. And this is what that looks like for me.

I think about the days leading up to the panic attack. I was away from home for a long weekend, and in social situations with a number of unfamiliar people. We were facing the arbitration, which could have had serious consequences for our livelihood. It all added up to a sense of threat, and my body could no longer deny it.

It encourages me to know this is normal. It was so unexpected and terrifying that I was afraid I was getting worse, and I so desperately want to get better. Dr. Land points out that this *is* me getting better. This is the process I must go through to move forward. But it will likely feel worse before it gets better.

I decide to go on daily antianxiety medication, because the constant underlying stress makes it difficult for me to function or even to think, and I get a new, low-dose prescription for Valium for those extreme moments. I want to go back to work and give my life purpose again, but first I have to get a handle on this.

49

DENISE

SLOWLY BUT SURELY, as we move through the spring of 2016, I'm able to start working again. I start with a couple of clients at a physical therapy clinic. The more I treat patients, the more my confidence returns, and I remember what I have to offer to help people recover. I am encouraged as clients refer their friends and family to me. With the kind of practice I've developed, I am able to dive deeper with my patients, especially those with chronic pain, severe injuries, or complex cases, showing them how the emotional impact of their physical injuries can impede their ability to heal. My own healing process helps theirs, and theirs helps mine.

I also finally find the courage to watch *Gone Girl*. When I finish, I'm angry but it also gives me some sense of closure. For the past year I'd been riddled with self-doubt. I'd obsessively cycle through the home invasion, kidnapping, and rapes, wondering if I should have fought back, if I should have shown more emotion when I was released. Maybe the police would have believed me if I'd had bruises, cuts, and internal injuries and cried hysterically. But the woman in the movie shoved a bottle inside her vagina, hit herself in the face with a hammer, showed up covered in blood, and collapsed dramatically into her husband's arms in front of reporters gathered outside their home. So even if I were more emotional, if Muller beat me, if he ripped me apart inside when he raped me, the police would have just said I was imitating the movie. There was never going to be enough proof to convince them I was telling the truth. I can stop blaming myself now and show myself more compassion. I did what I had to do to survive.

Though we try our best not to think about the criminal and civil cases, they are never far from our minds. Every few months we're confronted with updates, thrusting us right back into it all. When Assistant US Attorney Segal and Muller's defense attorney began talking about a plea bargain in December 2015, Segal met with us to hear what sentence we'd like to see Muller get—while at the same time telling us it didn't matter what we thought, that it was up to him and his meeting with us was simply a courtesy. Segal believes thirty years is enough punishment because studies show sex offense recidivism declines as you age, so Muller won't be a threat to anyone by the time he's released. With Muller, though, it's not just about sex; it's about having power and control over another human being, so he *will* be a danger if he's released, no matter how old he is.

Segal says he's "pretty sure" Muller committed the other crimes he's suspected of and was thinking about having some agents look into them. We can't believe he hasn't done that already. It's been six months since Muller's arrest. Wouldn't you want to find out how many victims there are for sure? Has he or the FBI even checked to see if there were similar unsolved crimes while he was at Harvard?

Not only that, Segal tried to convince us Muller tricked us into thinking he had accomplices by using audio recordings; he has us listen to several recordings found in Muller's possession. Three were recordings we heard through the headphones, including the "Quick! To the window" one Aaron heard. Another was the police radio sounds I heard when I was being moved to the "router room," while the others were ones the kidnappers never played for us. We again have to explain why we *know* there were other people in Aaron's house that night.

It feels like every step of the way they are trying to gaslight us into changing our recollection of events to fit the narrative they've created. Honestly, there have been times we wanted to give in and say, "Fine. He did it by himself." That would be the easiest thing to do: to stop fighting to convince people of what we know to be true. And we wish he *had* acted alone. We'd sleep better at night knowing the person who attacked us had been captured and was now behind bars. But it'd be more dangerous for us to do that. We know Muller's accomplices are still at large. This makes me wonder if other victims are manipulated into changing their stories so they fit what the prosecution wants to present in court.

At the beginning of 2016, we discover that the plea deal Segal is pursuing would require the state prosecutor, Solano County district attorney Krishna Abrams, to agree not to charge Muller in the state court. Segal, as a federal prosecutor, has no jurisdiction at the state level and it's unorthodox for him to even suggest this idea. The federal charge is solely for my kidnapping, not the rapes or anything that was done to Aaron, so the only way we can get justice for everything else he did to us is at the state level. We're furious. Segal has never explained why they're only charging Muller with one crime, and now he's trying to make shady backroom deals without telling us.

Aaron and I and our attorneys meet with Abrams in April 2016 to explain why we don't want her to agree to this bogus deal with Segal. She tells us that she won't, but also that she can't proceed with any state charges until the federal case is wrapped up.

In May, we find out that Detective Mat Mustard is receiving Vallejo's Officer of the Year Award for 2015, the year of our kidnapping and of our civil claim. The Vallejo Police Department proudly displays on its Facebook page a photo of a somber-faced Mustard holding the award. Standing next to him is Bidou, whose mile-wide grin is in stark contrast to Mustard's frown. Bidou looks like he's posing for his high school yearbook photo, while Mustard looks like he's getting his mug shot taken. Mustard's award is also the lead item in the city manager's biweekly newsletter to the public. It's so insanely ridiculous that I laugh out loud when I hear. Of all years, of all detectives. It's like whoever was in charge of this award felt the need to stroke Mustard's ego for some reason. It's amazing how shocked yet not surprised we are by these things now.

Our civil attorneys filed the formal lawsuit against the Vallejo Police Department and the city of Vallejo in March, and in July their lawyers respond, filing motions to dismiss the case. The officers involved give sworn written declarations, including Mustard, who says I "denied being a victim, did not wish to speak with Huntington Beach police," when there are police reports and an audio recording to prove the opposite! How can he lie when we have the Huntington Beach police report in which the first officer who spoke to me wrote, "I asked Huskins if she had been kidnapped and she said 'Yes'"? We also receive a copy of the audio recording of me answering this officer's questions for more than an hour.

Mustard went on. "Strangest of all, when law enforcement arranged to fly Ms. Huskins to Vallejo, where all her family had gathered, she rejected the offer. I found it odd that a recently released kidnap victim would not want to go to her family." This despite Mustard knowing that I flew up to Vallejo the same day I was released, and I asked for my family repeatedly during my questioning with Huntington Beach police.

In his declaration, and in his deposition the following year, Captain O'Connell, who gave my lawyer such a hard time about getting me a SART exam, states that I "did not act like a kidnapping victim" because I was wearing sunglasses and carrying luggage. "She just didn't seem like she'd been through something traumatic," he said. "She looked like somebody who just came home from a trip. These facts were extraordinary. That is not our experience, that victims of violent crimes bring clothes with them or bags." What an absurd statement. Yet he also admitted he is trained to understand that no two crime victims react the same. And he falsely claims I "did not want to speak with police" when in fact there are police reports and audio to confirm I did!

I cannot believe they are willing and able to lie under penalty of perjury. Does an oath not mean anything? Or are cops allowed to lie even when they've sworn to tell the truth?

We file oppositions to their motions and have to wait for the judge to rule whether the case can move forward, which will likely take more than a year.

For months, Muller has been floating an insanity defense without providing any formal medical proof. However, in September 2016, we learn Muller has dropped this contrived defense and accepted a plea agreement in the federal case. It's surreal. We were convinced this would drag on for years. In exchange for Muller's pleading guilty to the charge of kidnapping, the prosecution agrees they won't request more than a forty-year sentence. The next step is the sentencing hearing.

Doug takes this moment to hold a press conference to reveal Sesma's prior relationship with Jennifer. Unfortunately, only a couple of reporters write about his conflict of interest, and it doesn't gain traction. Maybe it's because Aaron and I aren't the ones saying it. Maybe because the bigger story is Muller pleading guilty and this gets lost in the shuffle. Whatever the reason, it's discouraging. The complaints Doug and Ethan filed about Sesma have gone nowhere. Segal claims that Sesma disclosed the relationship to him. Except that's not the proper procedure. He should have told his supervisor. Immediately. It's completely demoralizing, but there's nothing we can do about it.

Sesma eventually gets promoted to a higher position within the FBI. It seems that everyone who abused us is being rewarded, failing upward. Like with everything, one positive is met with another negative, making it difficult to be encouraged about anything in this system.

DESPITE ALL OF this, our relationship only gets stronger. In the fall of 2016, Aaron and I are at a brewery, enjoying a craft beer, sharing a perfect moment on a beautiful day. We are both relaxed, smiling and joking, and I feel at ease in life and with him. For the first year after the kidnapping, when we were in couples counseling, we agreed it wasn't the right time to discuss any future engagement or marriage plans. There were issues from before the kidnapping that needed to be sorted out, and we both needed to be in a better place. We certainly didn't want any good moments like that to be overshadowed by the trauma we were still working so hard to get past. But at this point, we've graduated from couples therapy and both found individual therapists. I've returned to work and am feeling more secure—with myself, with where we're living, with us as a couple, and where I'm at in my recovery.

In other words, I'm finally ready to take our relationship to the next level.

Feeling nervous, I say to him, "So . . . I'm not putting pressure on you or anything. . . . But . . . I just want you to know . . . just in case you weren't sure . . . if you *wanted* to propose to me sometime in the future . . . I'm in a place where I'd be ready to receive that question. . . ."

He smiles at me, clearly trying not to laugh. "Oh, really?"

I chuckle, a little sheepishly. "You don't have to say anything. I don't expect it to happen anytime soon. I just know I told you before I wasn't in a place for that. But now I am . . . and I just thought you should know."

He looks deep into my eyes, with a smile that says everything, and kisses me.

50

DENISE

Sent 12/31/16 5:25 a.m.

Are you that horrible lying woman who faked her own kidnapping???
Oh wow you are such a horrible person. You are going to hell for the
bullshit u have done. I'd lIke to slap u a few times. I'd like to have my
wife beat u up bad too . . . and just so u know, ur not as pretty as u
think. I'd put u at being a 5 outta 10. And I bet ur pussy stinks bad. You
are an ignorant slut and a filthy liar and I'm glad ur going to hell. Eat
shit, whore.

I gasp, "Oh, my God . . . oh, my God!"

It's January 1, 2017, and we're about to go on a hike in Point Lobos
State Natural Reserve to start off the new year with a beautiful walk on
the coast of Carmel and watch the sea lions wiggle on the shore as the
waves crash over them.

But now I'm frozen, sick, and can't bring myself to say anything.
"What's wrong?" Aaron asks worriedly, but I can't speak. All I can do is
hand him the phone as I recoil into a ball on the couch. I try to fight
it—I don't want this guy to affect me—but before I know it, I'm crying.

Aaron doesn't say a word, but I know he's pissed. He grabs his phone and I ask what he's doing.

"I'm going to write him something," he says sharply. He hands me back the phone when he's sure he found the right guy, and I think to myself, *Fuck this guy.*

The only reason I even went on Facebook was because I got a new message from Melanie Woodrow, one of the local ABC reporters who's done a fantastic job reporting and keeping the story alive. She reported on Mustard being named officer of the year, on all of our updates in the cases, and even checked in a few months back about another home invasion involving four guys in the same neighborhood as the Dublin attack, to press the point that there may have been others involved in my abduction who are still roaming the streets.

Her message was simply to wish us a happy new year, and to say she'll see us next month at the federal sentencing for Muller.

I write to tell her we recently got word that the sentencing will be postponed to March 16 and that upon reading her kind message, I also saw the vulgar filth from this guy. I send her a screenshot of it.

Suddenly I am emboldened to fight back. *I am done with this! I am done with people thinking they can say shit to me, that there aren't consequences for their actions. You want to hide behind your keyboard courage and threaten me? If you feel so strongly you can say something disgusting privately, then you should have no problem with having the world see it too.*

I haven't posted anything public on Facebook since the kidnapping because it was drilled into us that it could impact the criminal or civil cases. We've had to be the strong ones, the quiet ones, to be dignified, poised, and professional, to be patient and let the system work.

Well, not anymore. This man's message is not new; it's a combination of everything that's been said before. It's almost two years later, and I'm still getting this shit.

So I start furiously typing:

I don't post this for pity, I post this to increase awareness.

Unfortunately, this is just one example of countless messages like this that I have received. And like the ones before this, unfortunately, this guy won. After reading this I went into one of my many PTSD episodes of terror. My jaw and back are sore from the deep powerful shaking and reflexive tension that my whole body goes into. My eyes are sore and red from uncontrollable tears. I am thoroughly exhausted; every inch of my body is tired from the fit of terror it was battling. This was his goal, and I couldn't fight it. Congratulations, person I have never met, never heard of who hates me so much that he went out of his way to message me this disgusting, demeaning, dehumanizing outrage. I am still disoriented and not sure if I am even making sense. I have to take medication to calm me down. It's almost been two years, a year and a half since it was made public that this was real, that Aaron and I were telling the truth the whole time. All I did was survive, and I was criminalized for it . . . Let's not meet each other with hate and anger. It truly hurts. It has a profound impact on each other's lives, their feelings of safety and self-worth. It doesn't help anyone. We must admit that there are many things that we don't know, even if we so strongly believe certain things. It does no one, especially us, any good to blindly judge, spreading hate and anger. We may be wrong, or misinformed. Please keep that in mind when thinking of new beginnings in this New Year.

After writing to the guy himself, Aaron also writes to the guy's fiancée to inform her how her fiancé spoke to another woman, in case she doesn't know this side of him. And with that, Aaron and I decide that we aren't going to let this ruin our day. We drive down to Carmel and enjoy the first day of this new year, and new beginnings.

As the day goes on, we receive messages of overwhelming support from our friends and family. And then Melanie writes back, saying she plans to do a piece about it, as long as it's okay with us.

We then email our civil attorneys and apologize, afraid this could somehow negatively impact the case. We get a call from Jim Wagstaffe assuring us we did nothing wrong. The most important thing, above all else, is our healing, and if we needed to do this to heal, then that's what needed to happen. He says he's proud of us for what we wrote.

After Melanie's piece is released, almost every major news network picks it up. Even *Cosmopolitan* and *People* write about it. We get a flood of support from the public commenting on our posts, sharing the article, and even trying to contact the guy who wrote the message. We appreciate people trying to fight for us, but I write another post to try to shift the conversation back to the bigger picture:

Aaron and I want to thank all of you for your warm and powerful responses. There have been many unbelievable and awful things about this experience, but what I do know and am so grateful for is that Aaron and I have such an amazing support system. We are surrounded by so many wonderful people, and that is the biggest reason why we are able to get out of bed every morning and continue to move forward rebuilding our lives. I know it's tempting to meet anger with anger, it's something that we have struggled with frequently these past two years. But the battle we are fighting is way beyond this individual man, and his one disgusting statement. There is a much greater cause that goes way beyond him, and way beyond us as victims. Along the way we will continue to dodge these types of attacks . . . We must meet hate with love. We must meet ignorance with empathy. So, thank you, all of you, for allowing us to do that.

FOR THE NEXT couple of months, our sole focus is on writing, editing, and rewriting the victim impact statements we'll read in court at Muller's federal sentencing. We speak with Linda Moore, the probation officer who is writing the presentence report for the judge that will include her recommended prison term. It feels great to finally speak to someone involved in the case who listens to us, who seems to genuinely care about the truth, and who doesn't pass judgment or disregard our accounts based on bias.

She tells me we can write a statement to include in her report that can be longer and more detailed than what we read in court. It can be whatever we need it to be to show the impact this man has had on our lives. I take this opportunity seriously and write a fourteen-page, single-spaced account of the first forty-eight hours and the days, weeks, and months that followed, to also show what we have been up against with law enforcement.

I write that it's difficult to know where to begin in describing how Muller's actions have affected my life, and that it's no secret the actions of law enforcement revictimized us and escalated our trauma. "It feels impossible to separate the two, one significantly affects the other, and attempting to try does not provide justice to anyone . . . but what is true and undeniable is that it is all centered around this man, Matthew Muller."

I write that I know he wasn't there alone, that this was not the act of a single man who simply had a mental breakdown or moment of insanity like he is claiming. Muller's role was only one part of a methodical plan by an organized group that plotted this for over half a year.

I describe how Muller, the voice that spoke to me in those forty-eight hours, repeatedly said things to acknowledge the horror he was putting me through yet continued, knowing the pain and suffering he was causing. He even went as far as to say that he would never do this again, yet less than two months later, he was linked to another home invasion.

I write about my SART exam and recall asking the prosecutor where it was or what the results were; Segal looked blankly around the room, clueless, and actually said to me it didn't matter because they had the recordings of the rapes! Not only was this incredibly insulting and demeaning, but it was shortsighted.

The SART exam is the most vulnerable thing a woman can do so soon after a sexual assault, but you go through it in hopes that the information they collect could help find the perpetrator and prevent other women from this horrific experience . . . You hope that by making that sacrifice and opening your legs to strangers to pick, prod, examine and picture you, it could possibly save others.

What if the data processed with my SART exam can link him to other open rape cases in the state? This would not be the only situation of serial rapists that happened. That was my understanding of the purpose of SART exams, so they can . . . find the perpetrators and protect the public from more attacks, not just a means to prove whether a woman is telling the truth or not.

I describe how the media and police claimed how I was treated by the kidnappers was just too "bizarre" to believe, saying things like "'That's not what kidnappers would do.' 'Why would kidnappers be so nice?' Simple. To throw off the police, blame the victim, and not get caught. This is not new. This has happened in many cases before this one. . . ."

I mention a high-profile case in which a young woman was charged with lying to police about being sexually assaulted, only to be vindicated when her assailant was caught—and proved to be a serial rapist. Then there was the *Dateline* special on our case, which included an interview with a victim from one of the 2009 cases linked to Muller. I was in and out of the bathroom dry-heaving while she talked about her experience; what the intruder said to her, and how he said it, told me immediately it was the same man who kidnapped and terrorized me.

I explain that this poor woman "went to the police and their initial reaction was *'Are you sure it wasn't a bad dream?'* . . . I am still in awe that police officers continue to receive victims this way."

I conclude by saying it's clear the safest thing for the public is for Muller to be sentenced to life in prison, because someone with his track record will likely strike again.

I know the statement I give in court must be much shorter and will be focused on Muller rather than the conduct of the investigators and the prosecutor, so I'm grateful for the opportunity to at least let the judge know how these so-called professionals handle their cases and the victims affected the most by them.

51

AARON

I T ' S   H E R E.

Nearly two years later, we are at the finish line, with the criminal case at least. Denise and I are up before the sun rises on March 16, 2017, waking in a Hyatt hotel room in Old Town Sacramento, only a couple of blocks from the courthouse.

We've thought about this moment endlessly, and there's a sense of relief combined with extreme anxiety. As we mentally prepare, our bodies reproduce that strange sweat, trembling, and sickening churning of our stomachs that we endured for months after the kidnapping.

This will be our first time speaking publicly in front of reporters we've watched talk about us for two years. They've seen us standing with stoic expressions on our faces while our lawyers spoke on our behalf, or they've heard from our parents. But today the spotlight is on us.

Muller's plea agreement is for thirty to forty years. With a plea agreement, the defense will argue for the lower number. The prosecution will argue for the higher number, but ultimately the sentence is determined by the judge. So there's still a chance the judge could rule for life. Federal criminal cases use a point system based on the crimes committed and how they were carried out. In his sentencing memorandum, Muller's attorney, Thomas Johnson, incorrectly calculated Muller's offenses as coming to forty-one points, which would be equivalent to thirty years. But the numbers actually add up to forty-seven, and anything above forty-three points nets a life sentence.

We have arranged to meet Doug and the victims' assistance advocate for the US attorney's office at a back entrance of the courthouse to avoid getting bombarded by the media.

The hallway outside the courtroom is filled wall to wall with friends and reporters. Everyone turns to look at us, and reporters move in to swarm us, but we evade them by bolting into the jury room adjacent to the courtroom. Our immediate families and other attorneys join us shortly thereafter. Everyone is clearly anxious.

Linda Moore, the probation officer we spoke to regarding her presentence investigation, comes in for a minute to introduce herself in person. She warmly shakes our hands, being sure to make eye contact. I think she wants to show us that she sees us as human beings and not just a case number. I often think about this moment when I'm frustrated with the criminal justice system. It's a heartening reminder of the many professionals who are truly dedicated to justice.

DENISE

Waiting is always the hardest part. I hate that the kidnappers were right about that. Sweat pours from my armpits, and I have to stuff tissues there temporarily. I jokingly apologize to everyone in the room, but I know they don't care. Everyone in here has been with us through the hardest times, and I'm not afraid of being honest or vulnerable with how the trauma is affecting me.

I can't believe I'm going to see him, actually see the body, the face, the man the Voice came from. I've seen him in pictures, and in snippets of video news reports. But being in his presence, feeling his energy again, even from the opposite end of the courtroom, is going to be nerve-racking. I know that I'm safe, that he can't hurt me, but no one and nothing can take away the power and control he had over me and my life in that forty-eight-hour period.

And those emotions all come flooding back.

It's time, and we start to file in from the door on the right side of the courtroom. We sit a couple of rows behind the prosecution, protected by our attorneys at our sides, and our families are in the rows directly behind us.

I'm a little concerned by the size of the courtroom, just four rows of bench seats on either side, because we have about a hundred expected family members and friends. I assume Muller's family will also be there to support him, and there's a lot of media as well.

Aaron's mom even called the court a couple of weeks ago to ask if the courtroom was big enough, in her persistent mama-bear kind of way. They dismissed her concerns, but I can hear people being asked, "Are you family? We can't let everyone in," leaving me frustrated and stressed.

I see my childhood best friend, Sydney, sitting in one of the last seats. She smiles at me and my eyes well up. We're surrounded by so many people who love and care about us, who've traveled from across the state and even from out of state to show us support. Most of the defendant's side of the room is filled with our family and friends as well, and I am hopeful everyone got in.

Next, reporters file in and are escorted into the jury box. Every seat in the courtroom is full, and the heavy wooden doors shut. A collective silence descends on the room.

Matthew Muller enters through the door next to the judge's bench on the opposite side of the room, shuffling stiffly as he slowly makes his way to his seat. He's dressed in an orange jumpsuit, his hands and feet shackled. His gaze is distant, his skin pale, lifeless. The angles of his face, cheeks, and chin are sharp, hidden behind thick dark-rimmed glasses. His posture is rigid. It almost looks like whatever deep disturbing evil lives within him is trying to escape his physical body. I can tell he isn't trying to look at any specific location other than his seat, showing no emotion. He looks different from the photos and videos I've seen and is now sporting a childish bowl haircut.

Doug nudges me. "What's with his *Dumb and Dumber* haircut?" he quietly scoffs. "He's just trying to look crazy and gain sympathy."

This causes me to silently chuckle, but I quickly stop myself because I know all eyes are on Aaron and me right now.

For the next couple of hours, we listen as the prosecution and defense each make their case.

Muller's lawyer tries to play up the mental illness angle, saying Muller was diagnosed with bipolar disorder in 2009, and comparing him to a homeless woman who lives near the courthouse, pushing a grocery cart of her belongings and constantly mumbling to herself.

Segal actually gives a legitimate rebuttal. Mental illness is not something to take lightly, but to use it as a defense in a case like this, with the amount of planning involved, is just reckless and insensitive to those who truly do suffer.

I have no doubt Muller's actions have taken a serious mental toll on him, especially now that he's facing the consequences of those actions. That would make anyone anxious, depressed, perhaps even suicidal, yet where's the proof he's bipolar?

After he was brought in for questioning in the 2009 Palo Alto case and he supposedly "went off the grid" because of a manic episode—was it truly mania? Or was he just worried about being caught for a serious crime?

After hearing from each side, Judge Troy L. Nunley discusses the point system, noting that Johnson's math was incorrect. The points add up to life, he says. Johnson argues that only a painted squirt gun was found, not a real weapon, so it shouldn't be counted against his client. Yet the judge cites several cases ruling that the reasonable appearance of a weapon with a deadly threat is sufficient.

Finally, someone in a position of authority who makes sense. In the dark, the appearance of a gun with a laser sight attached to it is a clear enough deadly threat to unsuspecting victims. It's been infuriating to hear people downplay and even joke about what we went through, just on this fact alone. What were we supposed to do, ask our assailant to shoot off a couple of rounds before we complied just so we knew that the damn gun was real?

Judge Nunley also says that in the presentence report the probation officer recommended "not thirty years . . . and not forty years . . . but *life*."

He turns to each respective party as he says this, with a conviction that drives home his point.

Aaron nudges my leg, with a small shred of hope that a life sentence is still on the table.

AARON

It's finally time for our victim impact statements, and we've decided I will go first.

This whole day I've been running on adrenaline after getting only four or five hours of sleep, but I've been able to keep a level of calm and focus that I've never experienced before. I revised my statement twenty or more times, read and reread it so much that I could recite it from memory.

Sitting in the courtroom, I am so acutely focused that everyone feels like they are a hundred yards away yet still crystal clear. I am an eagle hovering above the chaos, preparing to strike.

Before I stand up, I turn to Denise and kiss her. I can tell she's somewhat surprised. I'm not afraid of public displays of affection, but this is certainly the most public of forums. The whole courtroom is watching but it puts us both at ease. I'm telling her, "We got this." I walk past the prosecutors seated on the right, and Muller and the defense seated on the left. I stand with Amy at the podium in the middle of the courtroom to face the judge. I can feel the audience's undivided attention behind me, and I see the rows of reporters sitting in the jury box to my right.

I purposely begin softly. Puffing up my chest would only play into the stereotype that a man should be loud and angry to make his point.

"'We're going to take Denise for forty-eight hours. Pay the money, get her back, and you can move on with your lives.' Forty-eight hours . . . and we can move on with our lives. Forty-eight hours . . . It's been over 17,370 hours since you said those words to me. . . . When does this forty-eight hours end?"

I go on to talk about how they turned my home into a prison, destroying the memories I created there with my father. I start to cry but I keep going, emphasizing the impossible dilemma over calling the police. For the first time, I think the media is questioning their initial skepticism of me. Prior to this moment, they emphasized the "bizarre" circumstances of our ordeal, but now they must see that Denise and I behaved logically.

Then I talk about Muller:

"You like to feel that you are in power and the rules do not apply to you. That's what makes you so dangerous. You are smart enough to manipulate situations to get away with crimes but not humble enough to seek help. . . .

"I hope you find some meaning in your life, that you use your intelligence and law degree for some good. Maybe you provide legal counsel for other inmates that cannot afford it or have been provided a seriously overworked public defendant? For I have personally seen the necessity of legal representation because I have experienced the unchecked power of the law. . . ."

I share how for the past couple of years, my eight-year-old nieces have my brother and sister-in-law check their bedrooms to see if someone is hiding there.

"They are not checking for the boogeyman. They're checking for a man. They're checking for *you*. My other brother is an Iraq war veteran. The military was off-limits in your 'gentlemen criminal' code but I guess military families are fair game. My father is a retired doctor. My mom is a retired nurse. They are both over the age of fifty-five. That was another cutoff in your code, an arbitrary age limit. Instead you created one of the worst scenarios for a parent, feeling absolutely powerless when your child is in danger. That is the rationale of people who will create any justification to cause harm."

I talk about my own daily struggles with anxiety and how it's a battle that I'm afraid I'll never win. I hear crying all around me. At that moment, everyone in the room knows this wasn't just the *Gone Girl* case. Denise did not suffer alone. They feel my pain.

"I would not have the capacity to stand here without the unwavering support of my family. I truly do not know how to express the sheer depth of my gratitude for them. All I can say is that I love you all so much.

"I saw a quote that read, 'In the end, be your own hero, because everyone's busy trying to save themselves.' That person never met Denise Huskins. She sacrificed her mind, her body, her spirit to save those she loves . . . to save me. . . . Denise convinced the devil to let her free only to be demonized by self-proclaimed saviors. Nevertheless, she is a woman of beauty and warmth serving those in need. Denise, you are my favorite person. . . . You are my hero."

I hit my crescendo as I finish loud and proud, telling Muller he has to be held accountable for what he did because society is safer with him behind bars. I know that I have done what I set out to accomplish. After Denise gives her statement everyone in this courtroom will know that a long sentence is fair . . . including Muller.

I stare at Muller for a few steps as I walk back to my seat, hoping for some level of acknowledgment, but he looks straight ahead, like a wax statue placed in a courtroom scene. I give up quickly, knowing Denise is going to begin speaking and this is her time. I've already said my piece.

Denise and I exchange our positions as she moves to the front of the courtroom. From my seat, I watch, awestruck by Denise's power, her courage, her grace as she looks Muller in the eye at the beginning of her statement. It's the stuff that legends are made from and I will tell our children and our children's children about it until my last breath.

DENISE

I'm moved as I watch Aaron give his statement. It's emotional and compelling. He bravely allowed his pain to show so everyone would know how hurtful and damaging all of this has been. I am so proud of him. Muller hasn't been charged for the crimes against Aaron, so we had to ask for Aaron to be allowed to speak today. People have almost entirely disregarded what he's been through. I'm grateful that they can hear it today.

After Aaron returns, I follow behind Doug, with my packet of paper in my cold, sweaty hand. I feel every eye on me and am wondering if Muller has the courage to look at me. I know I am going to make him, one way or another. He *is* going to look at me as I say what I need to say.

I take a deep breath at the stand and whisper to myself, "Oh, God."

I start by thanking Judge Nunley for the opportunity to speak today, to have a voice and a role in this process.

"As you know, I have sent the court a more detailed account of the events of my experience with this man," I say. "For healing purposes, please understand . . . I will speak directly to the defendant."

The judge acknowledges this with a hand gesture toward Muller, as if to say, *by all means.*

I take another deep breath, close my eyes to center myself, preparing for the moment that I've waited for for so long. I turn back around, away from the podium, and face Muller. I feel myself stand taller, my chest open, bold, and powerful. I look directly at him, and say with force:

"Matthew Muller."

I hear my voice command the attention of the room. I am almost shouting his name. I'm turned away from the podium, and the microphone, and I want to make sure that not a single person in this room misses a word I say. I feel my heart flutter and a slow tremble of anger build up from God knows where. I've never been so ready for something in my life.

As soon as I say his name, I see his eyes dart to the right, focusing on me. His face remains expressionless, but he refuses to turn his head toward me. But I see him, and he sees me, and that's all I need. I keep my eyes locked on his, knowing what I'll say next, having practiced repeatedly. I speak forcefully, taking deliberate pauses between each sentence to catch my breath, and to make my points vivid and clear.

"So the Voice has a face. . . . It has a name. *Now* we meet. Face-to-*face* . . . eye to *eye*. *I* am Denise Huskins . . . the woman behind the blindfold."

Again, I almost shout my name, proudly. I shout it to all the lies said about me, the people suggesting I change my name. I am not Victim F, "the real-life Gone Girl," a "hoaxer," just a body to take, a random life to threaten because "this wasn't meant for you; this was meant for Jennifer Jones." *No, I am none of those things.*

I am Denise Huskins.

I feel the power surge within me. I have never felt so strong.

"The woman you *raped*, drugged, tortured, and attempted to manipulate." Every time I look at him, he stares right back at me.

I remind him of all the things he said to me during captivity, how he acknowledged Aaron and I didn't deserve this, yet for two days he continued "drugging me, holding me captive, raping me, and forcing me to record a proof of life, still hinting at all the ways I would be punished if I didn't comply. . . . But you didn't kill me. So you're not *all* bad, right?"

I tell him I've read the character references that some people wrote to the court, saying they had positive experiences with him and saw how he had struggled in his young adulthood. But criminals like him put on a facade for the people in their lives, "keenly aware of right and wrong," which is "why they keep these actions to themselves and from loved ones."

I tell the court, "I could see right through it with every moment I was with him but developed a rapport with him in hopes that some bit of the 'good' in him would choose not to kill me."

Turning back to Muller, I remind him of what I shared with him about my own struggles after being molested as a child, how therapy helped me recover.

"I was trying to connect with this voice who was hardly human, in hopes it would spare me from more torture, spare my body, spare my life.

"After sharing that, you still made the decision to rape me, and not just violating my body, but forcing me to perform, act, and have it recorded. . . . You couldn't just take my physical body and let me be detached from it, like I was in the first rape as you flopped me around the bed like a rag doll. This second time, you made me perform, 'let's pretend like we are with other people, the people we love, to get us through it,' as if this were happening to the both of us. I saw right through all of this, but knew I had to appease you."

I pause before this next line, as I can feel my anger fold into deep pain, regret, and shame.

"The only way I got through it . . . was to picture that it was Aaron that I wa—"

My voice cracks and I can no longer hold back. I bend in half and sob, covering my face with my hands. Doug puts his hand on my back, and I can feel most of the room crying with me.

Behind me I hear Segal say, "Aaron—you can go up there!"

Aaron must have jumped over the wooden gate, that's how quickly he's at my side, his arm wrapped around me.

The judge is patient and kind, asking me if I need a break. Doug whispers, "If you can, try to keep going. You're doing great."

I've already decided I won't stop. I will keep going. I've got this. And with Aaron at my side now, I'm able to pull myself together and push on.

"No, thank you, Your Honor," I respond, patting my face with tissues as I take another deep breath.

I repeat: "The only way I got through it, was to picture it was Aaron that I was with. That will haunt me for the rest of my life. I know you did that on purpose, to leave your mark on me in the most special and intimate moments of my life.

"I know that you have made countless excuses, from military to bipolar disorder to even vaccines. Be a man, the so-called powerful man that you try to fool yourself into being by tormenting others. Own up to your actions, take accountability, tell the *truth*. You finally pled guilty here, but what about the others? I know you think you have the public and the system fooled . . . but *not* Aaron. *Not* me."

I turn to the judge and direct the rest of my statement to him, declaring that Muller knew what he was doing, that the crime was thoroughly planned, and he was well aware of the pain he was causing. I go on to talk about how I was treated like a criminal, a liar, and was afraid not only of law enforcement but the kidnappers who I knew were not being pursued.

I talk about how I live with guilt and shame for not speaking up when I was molested, which could have possibly spared another child that trauma.

I say I'm grateful to be alive, but the toll on our lives, and on my body, has been severe. If I come home alone, I have to check every corner holding a knife, and I sleep with a hammer next to my bed in case we're attacked again. I find myself reaching for it during the worst of my daily nightmares.

"Sleep is not rest for me; it is a trigger. There's not a moment in the day that I don't remember this. It's not that I want to focus on it, but the depth of the terror is so deep I have had to learn how to live side by side with it. I am humbled in that reality, this new reality. I am at that point in my life where Aaron and I talk about marriage and a family. But I am so scared of bringing a child into this world after the horror Muller has put me through, put my family through. . . .

"I thank God for the attorneys Aaron and I were able to find but ask why innocent victims should have to hire lawyers to shield them from the very people who are sworn to protect them. Above all, I am so grateful for Aaron standing by my side and giving me strength and support as I continue to struggle. . . . He knows exactly how to calm me, care for me, how to hold me in the midst of my nightmares. The thought of returning to his arms during those forty-eight hours helped get me through it, and I never want him to let me go. He gives me peace, love, laughter, and hope in humanity.

"I still can't make sense of any of this, and I accept that I will never know. But what I do know is that Matthew Muller willingly, thoughtfully, participated in this hell we have survived. He had every opportunity in that forty-eight hours to do something different but chose not to. He said he was remorseful and would never do it again, yet two short months later, he still attacked another family.

"Hopefully, for the sake of his own soul he will rehabilitate himself behind bars, but I have no doubt that this man should not be free to walk amongst the rest of us. I don't say that because I believe in revenge, in an 'eye for an eye,' but because of my experiences with him. I know, without doubt or hesitation, that as long as he walks free, there will be more victims."

I feel hopeful as we walk back to our seats and await the court's decision.

Judge Nunley looks directly at Aaron and me. He tells us that what we went through was awful, and no matter what happens today, nothing will be able to take that away, as much as he wishes it could. He says the molestation wasn't my fault, none of this is my fault, and I shouldn't blame myself, that the love we clearly have for each other and our families will continue to help us recover.

For the judge to speak personally to us, as if no one else is there, fills us with gratitude: At least there are some people in power who are kind, pragmatic, and empathetic. He and the probation officer have given us hope that not all is lost in this system.

With bated breath, we hear his ruling, sentencing Matthew Muller to forty years in prison.

I exhale with a mixture of relief and disappointment.

We understand this was the best decision, given the constraints of the plea deal. If he'd sentenced Muller to life, the defense could file an appeal. Judge Nunley made it clear throughout the hearing that he felt a life sentence is merited. But I assume he can deal only with what's presented to him.

As he strikes the gavel and court is dismissed, one reporter runs out of the courtroom before the others, which seems insensitive to me. So he'll get his story out there ten seconds before everyone else? How absurd. But most of the reporters quickly follow, and we make our way to the jury room, where our civil attorneys approach us, wide-eyed and excited.

"That was amazing! You both did fantastic!" they crow. "I don't want this to come off wrong, but we couldn't have paid people to deliver that better! And Vallejo's defense attorneys were sitting in the front row next to us. Of course they came to see what they're up against, and you guys crushed it!"

Their youthful enthusiasm is uplifting. As always, it's difficult not to be self-critical or think of how things could have gone differently. We were editing our statements even last night. But as I think back, there's not a thing I'd change about what either of us did or said.

We did it, and a huge weight feels lifted.

We're escorted out of the room again, and some guy, presumably a reporter, follows, filming us with an iPhone. The usual circus. But strangely, we're unfazed. We're about to reunite with our loved ones and celebrate the fact that this huge milestone has been passed.

52

AARON

A SEMICIRCLE OF REPORTERS, with microphones ready and cameramen standing behind them, faces the courthouse's front doors. They're hoping for a sound bite from one of our attorneys, or a family member or friend, or ideally us. But we leave through the back and we've told everyone not to speak with the media. Denise and I want our victim statements to stand on their own.

There are more obstacles for us to tackle, including our civil case and the possible state charges against Muller, but speaking at the sentencing was a major accomplishment. When Denise spoke about the second rape, she doubled over, gasping, "I can't . . . I can't," as if she were literally being torn apart. I was afraid she wouldn't be able to continue, and I sat paralyzed at the edge of my seat, unsure of what I was allowed to do. When Segal turned around and said, "Aaron, you can go up there . . ." I was already on the move before I heard the end of his sentence. I took Denise in my arms and whispered, "It's okay. It's okay." Denise steadied herself and continued. Truly, the stuff of legends.

As I stood next to her, I realized those antiquated ideas of men being the protectors of women are nonsense. Everyone, man or woman, will need protection at some point. But what we really need is support, a person to stand next to us and say, "This sucks, but we'll do it together." Denise didn't need me to come to her rescue or take over; she needed me to stand witness.

WE GATHER WITH our friends and family at a nearby restaurant; many of them weren't allowed into the courtroom because it was too full. People keep pouring in over the next hour, including our attorneys. Everyone greets us with hugs and words of encouragement. Even more touching, some of them share their experiences during the sentencing. Denise's father, Mike, tells me that my mom kept passing him tissues because they were both crying uncontrollably. It was the first time they had ever met. Danielle, Denise's soon-to-be sister-in-law, shares that she'd never seen Joey so emotional; he cried throughout his sister's statement.

All around the room, I see groups of my friends finally meeting Denise's friends, and my brothers talking with her brothers. There are Denise's cousins on both sides of her family, aunts and uncles, some who haven't seen one another since before her parents' divorce. The awkwardness of cocktail party conversation doesn't exist; the shared trauma has brought everyone closer together. A sense of peace permeates the room.

Denise's family is spending the weekend with us before she and I leave for Maui for a week's respite. I've been planning to propose either this weekend or in Maui, depending on how everyone reacted to the sentencing. My first choice would be this weekend. It would mean a lot to have everyone together celebrating the closing of one chapter and the beginning of another. But I just wasn't sure if the timing would be right. That was what the kidnappers wanted—to invade our lives and keep us locked in trauma. They wanted to control us, make us second-guess ourselves, put our lives on hold even long past the actual event. They wanted power over us for the rest of our lives. I step away from everyone to take a moment for myself. I look around the restaurant and see smiles and hugs, jokes and laughter, connection and empathy, the antidotes to terrorism. I know what I'm going to do.

Denise and I call it an early night, exhausted by the day's events, while a small group continues the party at the hotel bar. As we're getting ready for bed, Denise says to me, "It kind of felt like an engagement party, huh?"

"Yeah, it kinda did," I reply. And we reflect that we are blessed to have an amazing support network. Their unified strength has kept us alive.

WE'RE WIDE-AWAKE BY 5:00 a.m. Too much has happened for our bodies to rest any longer. We walk down the street to one of the few breakfast spots open so early. There's only one other customer in the place, a man reading the newspaper. When we sit down, I see the sentencing is the front-page story.

He sets down his paper when the waitress brings his coffee, sees us, looks down at the article, looks back up in disbelief, then decides the best course of action is to continue as if nothing happened. I would do the same.

I whisper to Denise, "That's got to be one of the strangest ways to start your day." But I don't mind this recognition; he's reading about our strength and not law enforcement's lies.

THE FOLLOWING DAY, now back in Santa Cruz with Denise's family, we take advantage of the beautiful spring weather and go wine tasting. I'm trying to get everyone together at a winery that sits on the foothills of the mountains with a view of the ocean in the distance. But Denise's mom and stepdad are with their close friends, Rich and Ruby, in another part of town. I tell Denise, "We should all be together today."

"It's fine. We'll see them later for the barbecue at Rich and Ruby's," she says.

"I just think it's important that we're all together today," I insist. Denise gives me a little side-eye look, clearly confused by my persistence. I'm afraid I blew it—I'm not the pushy type—so I quickly drop it.

We enjoy ourselves at the winery. Later as we get ready to go to the barbecue, Denise wants to change into more casual clothes.

"No, you should stay dressed the way you are," I tell her.

"Why? It's just my family. They don't care," she replies.

And I'm a little stumped. I know she won't want to be in sweatpants when I propose but it's true that her family doesn't care.

"Uh . . . maybe we'll take a group picture because everyone's together," I say. *Smooth move, Aaron,* I think to myself. Denise reluctantly agrees and I'm sure she knows by now.

We head over to Rich and Ruby's. I'm wearing a jacket even though it's not cold. I'm holding the ring in my pocket; the box feels like it's ten times larger than when I first bought it.

Denise suggests that I take my jacket off, but I insist that I'm fine even though I can feel beads of sweat forming on my forehead.

After we have some appetizers, I start to gather everyone together on the back deck before the sun goes down. I suggest to Denise she put her boots back on.

"Why? Who cares?" she says. I can tell she's already a little confused that I'm so insistent about taking this picture. I'm never the one to suggest a group photo. But I convince her that it'll look better if she's wearing her boots.

We take a few pictures, and before anyone can break away, I turn to face the group.

"I want to thank you guys for supporting us through everything and accepting me into your family. Denise and I joked that after the sentencing it kind of felt like an engagement party. But that's not good enough for me—I want the real thing."

Denise puts her hands to her cheeks and starts to cry as I reach into my pocket. As I bend to one knee, I can hear Mike saying, "Oh, he's doing it now. He's doing it now!" I asked for his permission the day before the sentencing. I'm sure he thought I was going to ask her in Maui.

I get out, "Denise, will you marry me?" just before she drops onto both knees, tears of joy streaming down her face. She wraps her arms around me and squeezes me tight. I help her to her feet and slide the ring onto her finger.

"You know, you need to say yes," I joke.

"Yes," she gets out, and thankfully, the ring is sized perfectly. It looks exactly how I imagined on her finger.

We have faced hardships very few couples have endured, but we've worked through them together. We've developed a strength that's greater than the sum of its parts. And now we'll continue our partnership for the rest of our lives.

53

DENISE

We have just arrived in Maui, still worn-out from the excitement of the past week, but also elated to celebrate so many wonderful turning points in our lives. In a few days, it will be two years since the kidnapping, and we've come such a long way. Last year, we came to Maui for the one-year anniversary, making a pact that we would create new memories around this date. They don't get to own this time.

On that first anniversary, at 5:00 a.m. on March 23, 2016, we got up to watch the sunrise at the edge of Haleakala's volcanic crater. It's the highest point of the island, where you get a 360-degree view to the ends of the earth. Exactly a year earlier we were under the control of those unpredictable intruders, not knowing if it was the last day of our lives. Now we were floating up in the heavens, watching the breathtaking sight of the glowing rays of sunshine piercing the clouds, exposing bright yellows and oranges that created a halo in front of a translucent blue sky.

As soon as we walk off the plane, Maui's atmosphere gently blankets us with a silky coat of warmth that lifts and revitalizes. I could think of no better place to try to find peace and celebration.

It's great to be back, with so much to look forward to.

I had no idea Aaron was going to propose. Looking back, it's comical how all the signs were there, but it never crossed my mind. We have been living together ever since the kidnapping. Things have been solid in our relationship, and we've talked about our future together, knowing that marriage was inevitable. So I wasn't shocked that he proposed but was blown away by how it happened, when it happened, and was completely overjoyed to experience it with my family there.

I can't believe I didn't pick up on all the signs that seem obvious now, like how adamant he was that everyone be together, or even suggesting what clothes I wear. He's never one to say we should take a picture. He is never that opinionated about these trivial details, but I didn't think twice about it because I was enjoying the moment with family.

When we were all lined up, and had taken a couple of pictures, he stepped forward to give a little speech, which was when it finally hit me. Before he finished the first few words, I was thinking, *Oh! Oh, my God, this is it! He's going to propose, isn't he?!*

It was hilarious, because at the same time I was thinking that I heard my mom to my left say, "Oh, my gosh, is he proposing?" and my dad to my right saying, "Oh! Oh! He's doing it now!"

My hands reflexively covered my face and I giggled as he got down on one knee and asked me to marry him. I fell to the floor with him, and we hugged and kissed each other, surrounded by family, overwhelmed with joy.

It was so thoughtful, so sweet, and everything I could have hoped for. After what we've overcome together, and the depression, trauma, and self-doubt I experienced before meeting him, I wasn't sure if I'd ever get to this place. There were so many times when I genuinely believed I'd never find a true partner I loved and adored who actually loved and adored me back. Someone who completed and complemented me perfectly. I just felt for most of my life like it was unrealistic to hope for, that this wasn't meant for me and I'd go through my life independent and alone, or simply settling for something different. I can't believe I get to have it: true love, true companionship, and a real partner who loves me unconditionally. It just goes to show, as hopeless as life can seem at times, there are plenty of reasons not to give up. Life is wonderful, and the unpredictability, the not knowing what's to come, the ever-changing and evolving phases are all actually a good thing.

AFTER ARRIVING IN Maui, we stop at a restaurant and sit outside, befriend one of the many island roosters that scavenge for food, admire my ring, and acknowledge the hope of new beginnings and a positive future.

Most of my family went home the day before, but my brother Devin stayed to house- and cat-sit for a few days while we're gone. Now Devin texts us that Mr. Rogers brought in a dead bird as a present. We call him on FaceTime, and he shows us Mr. Rogers in the background, licking himself so proudly. I tell Devin that he should take it as a compliment—it's Mr. Rogers' way of showing his love.

So we have a good laugh, call to our kitty over the phone, and settle in for a bite to eat.

WHEN WE GET to the hotel, I'm alerted to a new post on Nextdoor.com: "Dead Tuxedo kitty on the corner . . ." naming our cross streets.

My heart stops. *Oh, God, no! No, it can't be! It can't be him. It just can't. That cannot happen. We just saw him!*

Before Aaron can even ask what it is, I'm already calling Devin. Mr. Rogers usually does his twilight rounds outside but comes in for dinner before it gets dark.

I can hardly breathe, hardly speak. "Is Mr. Rogers there? Did he come in yet?"

"No," my brother says, a little surprised. "I let him out again not long after I talked to you, but he's not back yet."

I start to panic. I tell Devin about the post I just saw on Nextdoor.com. Aaron hears this for the first time, sitting at my side with a look of horror.

"Please, can you go to the corner and check? It can't be him. It can't."

I can tell my brother is trying to keep calm, to keep me calm. I stay on the phone with him as he walks down the street, and the whole time Aaron is at my side, saying over and over again, "It's not him. It's not him," his voice shaking.

And then my brother says, "Oh . . . oh, no. Oh, God . . . it's him. Oh . . . I'm so sorry. It's him. He's . . . he's dead."

I start wailing as I fall over on the bed, and Aaron folds over me. "It's not him," he repeats. "It's not!"

I squeeze out, "It is, it is," and he falls to the floor, sobbing.

"What should I do?" asks Devin.

"Go back, grab a towel, and get him. Then FaceTime us so we can see him, so we know that it's him, and we can see him one last time."

I feel so awful he has to manage all of this, especially with me on the phone. It looks like maybe Mr. Rogers got hit by a car. He has a little trickle of blood coming out of the corner of his mouth, but the rest of his body doesn't seem to be injured. We assume that he was struck as he was crossing the street. People often run that stop sign.

But we also can't help but let our fear and paranoia take over as we wonder if it was an accident. We just spoke publicly for the first time, and in our statements, which are available for the world to see, we spoke of how we know that Muller did not act alone. What if they're still watching us, know where we live, know that Mr. Rogers is our cat, know his evening routine, and know that killing him will be a message to us—"We're still here"? It looks like he was struck in the face, dying instantly. It could have just as easily been from a blunt object as a car. And if it was someone sending us a message, it would be too obvious to place his dead body on our doorstep.

Our minds spin and we hold each other as we mourn. We wonder if we should even try to stay the week. How can we stay in paradise after losing our sweet little boy, the third member of our little family? We decide to give it a day before we make any decisions.

After about an hour, we decide to go down to the ocean to cleanse and freshen our puffy, teary faces. Within minutes of our wading into the sparkling, clear blue sea, a man points out a sea turtle swimming right next to me.

It pokes its head and fin out of the water as if to say hello, then swims off. We sit on the shore a little later and see the turtle float back through, swimming without a care just feet from the shore, weaving among dozens of people wading in the water, floating without fear, making friends. He has the spirit of Mr. Rogers, and he's showing us that he's still with us.

Soon everyone gathers for a perfect view of the sunset, and like in a movie, a man stands on the cliffs above playing what sounds like a Scottish funeral dirge on his bagpipes. He's clearly honoring a lost loved one.

Aaron and I sit silently, holding hands and resting our heads together as we watch the big orange sun gently meet the water. Right before the last sliver of the sun melts into the horizon, a whale breaches directly in front of it, exposing his glorious belly. As he disappears into the water, so does the sun. It's magical, a once-in-a-lifetime sight. The crowd cheers in gratitude at the beauty we just witnessed. I start crying and say to Aaron, "I was thinking of him, and saying good-bye. . . ."

"I was too," he responds, wiping tears from his eyes.

Maybe these are random occurrences. But we choose to believe that it's one of many miracles we've encountered over these last several years. Our kitty is here with us, telling us that everything will be okay.

He was our guardian angel, coming into our lives in our time of need. He showed up on Aaron's doorstep to be his companion right before Aaron found out about his ex's infidelity and his father's battle with cancer. He quickly adopted me when I came into the picture. He experienced that initial night of trauma with us, and our spirits all mended because of our bond. There's something profound about an animal's spirit, their intuitive nature, and a wonderful brilliance to their unclouded clarity about what's important.

As long as we're together, with the people we love around us, we can face all of life's challenges as well as embrace the celebrations. We certainly have opened our hearts to the power and energy of the world around us, being face-to-face with life's greatest joys and most horrific tragedies. We continue to get uplifted by that energy as long as we can remain open to receiving it.

Despite living through our fair share of trauma, we know that we aren't immune to more. It's a part of living, of being human. Some of our happiest moments are rebounded off our saddest. But if we hide from the bad, we'll never experience the good. Was this all destiny? Was this all meant to be, to get us to this moment? Was this the only way we get to have our happy ending, to overcome the impossible? To suffer through pain? One of the most magical gifts of life is not having answers to all these questions, but to be able to ask them in the first place.

54

AARON

WE RETURN FROM our trip more determined than ever to ensure Muller faces state criminal charges. I even called the Solano County DA from Hawaii, hoping the publicity from Muller's federal sentencing would put pressure on her to do the right thing. Although Muller is sentenced, our fear is there's a perception that the case is wrapped up, closed, and nothing has been done to find his accomplices. Despite our relentless attempts to get new agents on the federal case, Sesma remained the acting supervisor overseeing what and how everything was evaluated. And Segal, the assistant US attorney who originally entered the case to prosecute *us*, stayed on as well. We just can't trust they investigated anything in depth. So maybe this is our chance to get more answers.

The DA tells me she's waiting to get the case file from the feds before making a determination. Over the next few months, her responses to my emails become more delayed. Eventually, she stops responding altogether. I guess she's hoping the silent treatment will make us give up.

However, I am the persistent type and ignoring us is unacceptable. Her decision will be on the record, one way or the other. So I take it upon myself to locate the FBI agent who is responsible for sending that case file to the DA's office. In June he emails me, confirming he sent the case file about a month earlier. After I confront the DA with this information, she finally responds, saying she's evaluating the case.

In December, we meet with Sharon Henry, the prosecutor from the DA's office assigned to the case, along with some of her staff. We all acknowledge the peculiar circumstances of this criminal case, particularly the Vallejo police's behavior and our civil lawsuit against them. Because of that, she tells us she doesn't plan on calling Vallejo police officers to the stand and will have to rely solely on our testimony. It feels like it's her way of saying she's aware of Vallejo's misconduct, but we, the victims, will have to take on the burden of rectifying it. She tells us they really won't have a case unless we speak, and it may be too emotionally difficult for us. The subtext is clear: If you want charges, you will have to pay the price of admission.

So this prompts us to lay into the DA about Vallejo's actions. I begin by stressing the implications of Mustard lying in a sworn declaration during our civil suit—it potentially calls into question every case he's worked on. Defense attorneys should and will attack his credibility on the stand. How many other times has he lied under oath? What other evidence is he willing to alter? Yet he continues to be the lead detective in Vallejo!

Henry expresses concern about Mustard's conduct, and she says she'll look into it. Unfortunately, I've learned by now the DA's office would rather turn a blind eye than cross Mustard. As president of the police union, he has a lot of power, especially when it comes to the DA's reelection campaign.

Denise presses Henry about what is being done to hold Vallejo accountable. They violated my civil rights, they defamed us, and they lied to cover all their actions up. They let criminals get away: first the kidnappers, then the squatters. Denise tells Henry what these officers have done is borderline criminal. So who polices the police? Apparently, it's the police. Henry, sounding a little defensive, says no one is above the law, and if it's brought to the DA, they'll investigate.

Denise points out that we're bringing it to their attention *now*. Shouldn't this be enough to warrant an investigation? Henry says they allow the police to do their own internal investigations before the DA's office gets involved. *Seriously?* Vallejo is clearly not making any changes, Denise points out. They've proven to be unreliable at self-discipline, so isn't it the DA's job to step in?

It's clear there won't be any resolution in this meeting; Denise astutely backs off and returns the focus to Muller. We still need to work with them on the criminal case, so we can't alienate them, but they certainly know where we stand. I'm so proud to be Denise's partner at this moment. For months, I've been taking the lead on pushing for state charges and I bet the DA believes Denise is a passive observer. She now sees what I've known for years: Denise is a *warrior.*

Once again we've demonstrated we're a formidable team. And we did it on our own. No lawyers. Just us. A month later the DA charges Muller with two counts of forcible rape, robbery, burglary, kidnapping for ransom, and false imprisonment.

He will finally be held accountable for raping Denise. And for what he did to me. But that doesn't mean we aren't feeling some trepidation about a possible trial. His defense team will attack our credibility. They'll try to portray the rapes as consensual. It would be safer for us to accept the long federal sentence and move on. But we can't. Muller is dangerous, even if he isn't released until he's seventy. So we'll muster our courage and do our part to ensure this predator never has a chance to hurt anyone else again. The Solano County DA finally came through and now we need to hold up our end of the bargain.

IN THE MEANTIME, the civil case continues to creak along. Our civil attorneys pursue discovery from Vallejo as we await the judge's ruling on whether the case will proceed to the next phase. Inexplicably, Vallejo produces only a few emails and four text messages from the entire investigation, stating that almost all communication about our case was verbal. It's an obvious lie yet impossible to prove unless someone on the inside comes forward and admits evidence was destroyed.

In May 2017, we sit quietly in the conference room at Wagstaffe's office while one of our civil attorneys, Kevin Clune, deposes Chief Bidou. Bidou has the air of a politician at a casual meet and greet rather than at a serious legal proceeding as he enters the room with his attorney. We politely stand and look him in the eye as we awkwardly shake hands. I try to hide my disgust as we get started and he admits he can't cite a single piece of evidence for calling the kidnapping a hoax or a single instance where we lied. He insists it wasn't just one thing, but a totality of reasons that made them doubt our story, although we can counter each thing he lists: the "lack of evidence" to prove it was legitimate (there was plenty of evidence that could have led them to the kidnappers); the "bizarre story from the onset" (it really wasn't; everything the kidnappers did was designed to make sure they wouldn't get caught); my delay in reporting the crime (I was passed out from the sedatives the kidnappers gave me and Denise's life was threatened if I did go to the police); that the kidnappers used such a "small" piece of duct tape to bind me, a "strong human being" (the "small" piece of duct tape was cut, so it was actually long enough to wrap around my ankles); that I went through something traumatic yet fell asleep (because I was drugged!); culminating with Denise's discovery and her "not cooperating" with the Vallejo Police Department (which is pure fiction).

We just sit there, silent. Instead of looking at the facts and then drawing a conclusion, they had a theory of what happened and looked for information to fit the theory. It's classic tunnel vision.

Incredibly, Bidou also admits they didn't follow up on anything that would have proved we were telling the truth, because the FBI took over the investigation the day after Park's press conference. Yet publicly, after Muller was caught, Vallejo stated they were working alongside the FBI the whole time. Basically, it seems he'll say anything to cover their asses. And he still insists there was nothing wrong with the way they handled our case.

We didn't expect anything different from him, but it is still jarring to hear out loud. I'd been hoping it would be like a TV crime show where he slips up and reveals an extraordinary fact that gives us a huge advantage.

But as an experienced police officer, he's testified in court countless times, so he knows just what to do, bobbing and weaving as Kevin asks question after question, hoping to paint him into a corner.

In the late afternoon, we catch the break we've been hoping for. Bidou says he wasn't at the police station during Park's press conference the evening of March 25, 2015, because he was in Napa for a leadership training retreat. But strangely it wasn't a leadership training conference for chiefs or captains from other local departments; it was for Vallejo officers only. Almost all the top brass left for Napa hours before the press conference, leaving a skeleton crew behind. Bidou himself was gone by two o'clock that afternoon. Before that, he held a meeting at the station in which everyone, including the FBI, agreed that the kidnapping was fake. But Denise didn't start speaking to Huntington Beach police until around 11:00 a.m. This means that, within three hours, they'd decided it was a hoax. We never had a chance.

The three-day getaway was held at the Silverado Resort and Spa, home to two golf courses, luxurious pools, and high-end restaurants. It's less than twenty miles away from Vallejo; why did they have to stay overnight? So they could party until the wee hours while we were being thrown to the wolves? Bidou provides vague descriptions of what was covered at this crucial training, which he claimed couldn't be rescheduled because it had been "planned for months." Even O'Connell attended this training session despite retiring the following week. Who attends seminars just days before retirement? I can only conclude it was a farewell party for O'Connell. And *we're* the ones who wasted Vallejo's valuable resources?

In the past two years, I've tried to curb my worst opinions of the Vallejo police. Maybe they'll learn from their mistakes; maybe they'll change for the better. But I'm now confronted with the chief of police admitting their handling of our case was worse than I suspected. It's difficult to grapple with the prospect that this police incompetence is good for our lawsuit, because it's terrible for society.

Our attorney starts asking Bidou follow-up questions like, if Bidou was in contact with Park before the press conference, where exactly Bidou was when the press conference aired, and since he was at a resort, if he was drinking beforehand. It's important to know if the chief of police making critical decisions about such a big case was under the influence. Vallejo's attorney explodes, saying the line of questioning is ridiculous, that they've been here all day answering questions for this "stupid" case, and even throws in a "Jesus Christ!" It feels like the room is about to break out into a shouting match, but Kevin stays calm and professional.

Bidou seems unfazed, but he's clearly not prepared for what Kevin hits him with next.

"Do you recall anyone saying any words to the effect of 'burn that bitch' with respect to Ms. Huskins . . . once it had been determined that the matter had been a hoax?"

Bidou's ears turn red as he shrinks down in his seat and his voice lacks conviction when he responds, "I have never heard anybody say that."

You never heard anyone else say that, because you're the one who said it, you prick!

A few weeks earlier our attorneys had received an anonymous tip telling them to ask all Vallejo officers being deposed, and specifically Bidou, who it was that told Kenny Park to "burn that bitch" prior to his press conference. Sadly, we weren't really shocked when we first heard about this. It was clear the Vallejo police were on a witch hunt when it came to Denise and wanted to burn her at the stake. They seemed intent on mob justice, not real justice. That much was clear from the malicious nature of Park's words that night and in the ensuing press release. In my head I can actually picture them all hanging out at the bar of the resort, yelling, "Burn that bitch!" as they watched Park speak. It shows who they are and how they feel about women.

More than three years later, Captain John Whitney, whose defense of the Vallejo police to the media after Muller's arrest so upset us, files his own civil claim against Vallejo for wrongful termination. He says his firing was retaliation for expressing his opinion on several horrific instances of misconduct within the department, including Bidou telling him to deny he told Kenny Park to "burn that bitch" prior to his now infamous press conference and to delete text messages related to our case so we couldn't use them in our civil suit. No wonder our attorneys were given so few texts and emails. Unfortunately, our case is already settled by the time we learn about Whitney's claim. I wonder if he was the anonymous source and was too afraid to go on the record. If so, I can see why—he was fired without his pension or medical benefits after twenty years of service. This is why "good" cops stay silent.

However, right now we have no proof, just that anonymous tip, so Kevin can take this line of questioning only so far. My jaw aches from clenching it so tightly throughout the deposition, anger being my only protection from the pain. I can sense that Denise feels the same way, but we stay quiet. Society is apparently offended by too much raw emotion from victims, so we keep ourselves contained, act according to everyone else's expectations, or we'll face being labeled "too emotional" to be taken seriously.

Fortunately, it's only a month before Judge Nunley rules in our favor, refusing to dismiss our case. He writes, "A reasonable jury could find that the defendants [the Vallejo police] engaged in conduct that was extreme and outrageous." It's a landslide victory for us, meaning our case can now proceed to a jury trial. The judge's ruling legitimizes our plight. He broke through Vallejo's disinformation campaign and saw the truth. It feels like the momentum is in our favor.

But before we're able to depose Mustard, Park, or Sesma, Vallejo appeals Nunley's ruling, bringing the case to a screeching halt. All discovery and depositions stop until the Ninth Circuit Court of Appeals weighs in, which could take another year or two. "Hurry up and wait" seems the hallmark of the legal system, and we continue moving forward with the rest of our lives.

55

AARON

A FEW MONTHS INTO the appeals process, our civil attorneys notify us that Vallejo wants to schedule a mediation hearing. We agree to meet in January 2018, although we don't expect to reach a resolution, thinking this is just another stunt. But early on in mediation, we realize they came to get this settled. And after a long day of back-and-forth, we agree upon a $2.5 million settlement.

However, we have to wait until March for the city council to finalize the agreement. In the meantime, the stress of whether or not this is the right decision takes its toll. Denise's immune system is shot, and she gets a case of shingles. It's not about the money; settling means no more discovery, no more depositions. No trial. Is it irresponsible to accept this without having Mustard, Sesma, and Park take the stand and answer for their conduct? We did discover the Silverado trip during Bidou's deposition, so it's possible something else will be exposed, but to what end? After seeing the way Bidou answered our attorney's questions, we expect the others will respond in a similar fashion, saying anything to avoid accountability. If we don't take this settlement, a trial could be pushed back for years. People need to know the truth now, before those men cause more damage. And there's no guarantee we'll win. So this feels like the right decision. A civil suit's only real resolution is monetary, but it's an amount that will show people how malicious and egregious their actions were.

As the date approaches, we discover that the details of the settlement, including the exact amount, have been leaked to the press with the spin that it will burden the taxpayers and that the police did nothing wrong. We wouldn't be surprised if it was Mustard himself putting it out there. Will this new smear campaign work? We haven't spoken publicly about any of this because we wanted to uphold the integrity of these cases, but with Muller behind bars, we're no longer bound by silence. Last year we found our voices during our victim impact statements, so now it's time to use them. We reach out to the producers of ABC's *Good Morning America* and *20/20*, who have been asking us to do an interview for years, and sit down with Amy Robach on the day of the city council meeting. The public will see us and hear us. They will witness our pain and perseverance. They will be shown the truth.

Denise and I are inspired by the #MeToo movement. Those two words create a powerful message that tells survivors they are not alone, and together, we can build a force that can break down any system of oppression. Hopefully our interview will be another small contribution to support the other brave victims speaking out against abuse and injustice.

A COUPLE OF weeks later, we finally have a chance to meet Misty Carausu, the detective in Dublin who caught Muller. For years she's wanted to reach out to us but wasn't sure if she could, given the complicated circumstances surrounding our case. And it's something we've wanted since this all started—someone in law enforcement to thank, someone to call our hero.

We end up talking with her and her husband for hours. Denise and Misty cry and hug each other, while in those funny "small world" ways, I discover her husband also works in law enforcement and has crossed paths with my brother Ethan many times over the years. We listen intently to Misty's story of pursuing Muller and her husband's support during those long days and nights, a united team that reminds me of us. Without Misty, Muller would be in a jail cell but never connected to our case. We would still be living under the stigma of Vallejo's lies. Although the trauma will never fully disappear, it has started to fade because of her.

Occasionally during dark times, I fall into a deep hole of cynicism and apathy. I believe I can't make a difference. The criminal justice system is too entrenched in its ways to change for the better. In those moments I remember that there are many Misty Carausus in the world, putting their lives on the line and making sacrifices for the greater good. And though I may feel knocked down, I am not broken. Like many others before me, I need to climb my way out, dust myself off, and continue fighting.

DENISE

We are excited and energized, immersed in finalizing the last details of our wedding, when another bomb is dropped on us. Sharon Henry, the Solano County prosecutor, tells us Muller has been transferred to the Solano County prison and his preliminary hearing on the state charges has been scheduled for Tuesday, September 25. Which is next week. Just four days before our wedding.

Not only that, but he's chosen not to hire a defense attorney and is representing himself, which means *he's allowed to cross-examine us*! Henry also tells us that Muller said in court he was willing to plead guilty if Aaron and I give half our civil suit settlement to the Innocence Project, an organization that helps exonerate the wrongfully convicted. To us, it's just another ransom demand, which is exactly what Doug tells a local reporter when he's asked to respond to Muller's statements. "Quite frankly, they didn't pay it the first time, and they're not going to pay it the second time," he says.

We're surprised yet not surprised. Bombshells seem to be par for the course in our lives. But we're thrown into another panic as we try to manage our emotional reaction to this revelation at the same time we're preparing for what should be the happiest day of our lives.

In the state of California, Proposition 115 allows investigators or police officers to provide hearsay testimony at a preliminary hearing on behalf of victims who would be retraumatized if forced to testify. Yet Sharon Henry tells us we will be the ones testifying. We'd agreed at our meeting last year to testify at trial, but it never occurred to us Muller would be able to cross-examine us himself. I believed that in violent crimes such as these, in which a perpetrator had violent, life-or-death power over his victims, there should be special considerations and laws to protect those victims from further harm. Proposition 115 is one such protection, but it's unclear why it will not be used in our case. I can only assume that no Vallejo officer would agree to do it. But there's always the FBI.

That Thursday, we talk with Henry on the phone so she can prep us on what to expect when we testify. She casually mentions that Muller could play "the tapes" at the hearing. She doesn't see why he would, but it's a possibility.

She keeps talking, but I cut her off. She can't mean what I think she means!

"What tapes?" I demand.

"Of the rapes."

I lose it. I've tried *so* hard to be cooperative and accommodating throughout this agonizing process, but this—this is too much. A whole courtroom full of strangers could watch the most traumatizing and degrading moments of my life? I'm fuming with anger and sick with disgust all at the same time.

"How is this possible?" I ask her, trying not to yell but barely able to restrain myself.

I've already come to terms with having the judge, the defense, the prosecution, and the jurors viewing the tapes. Even Muller himself gets to watch and rewatch the videos. That is disturbing enough to have to live with. But for just anyone attending a public hearing to be able to observe these vile acts is appalling.

"There must be *some* way to put a protective order on the recordings," I say, "to prevent them from being shown to just anyone, like in the federal case."

She tells me federal courts have different rules.

I raise my voice, insisting she do something, anything, to keep these from being played in open court. She agrees to see what she can do. I call Doug to tell him about this exchange. I'm so flustered and angry, and in such a hurry to get to the wedding venue for the walk-through, my heel slips off the edge of the carpeted stairs, and I slide down several steps, leaving a rug burn running the length of my left forearm that will be caught in several of our wedding pictures. Another physical representation of the emotional trauma that stains even the most joyous moments of our lives.

Henry ultimately files a motion to make sure the tapes won't be played, and they aren't.

Around the same time, Muller does his first TV interview ever, closely followed by two more. He says it was a mistake to demand that we give half our settlement to the Innocence Project in exchange for pleading guilty, but that he was upset that he was transferred out of the federal jail because he was trying to help other inmates, and thought we had some control over the timing of his transfer. It's clear from the way he talks that he has passive-aggressive animosity toward Aaron and me, and I realize he will do anything to fight us. A few days before we're supposed to face him at the hearing, we learn he plans to hire a defense attorney after all, which pushes back the date.

Even though we're shaken, we refuse to let any of it get to us. No one—not the kidnappers, law enforcement, or the jaded justice system— will ruin our special day.

56

DENISE

THE FOG THAT blanketed Monterey Bay for two weeks finally lifts the morning of Saturday, September 29, 2018. I wake to the early dawn light at the Monarch Cove Inn, a Victorian-style bed-and-breakfast that sits on a cliff overlooking the bay, not far from where we live. It's a perfect fall day. The main house and guest cottages, which date back to 1895, are surrounded by eucalyptus trees that host the thousands of monarch butterflies that migrate this time of year, while in the distance dolphins and whales dance in the sparkling sea. The venue represents everything we love about our adopted home. It's a gorgeous and peaceful place, and we want to share that with the ones we love.

Everything about this morning is going smoothly and on schedule, but I'm sweating, my stomach is churning, and I feel a deep, underlying bubble of anxiety. Wedding-day jitters may be normal, but mine seem to be interwoven with the trauma of three years ago. It's like even "good" nerves remind my body of the attack, sending it careening into the fight-or-flight response. As much as I try, this anxiety never fully leaves me. So I've learned to manage it quietly and continue to focus on all the good that surrounds me.

And there is so much of it, especially on this day of all days. I'm brimming with happiness and gratitude as my father walks me down the aisle, a moment we've dreamed about all my life and one we weren't sure we'd get to experience, between his health scares and my abduction. I hold a bouquet of light pink and white flowers sprinkled with silver-green eucalyptus leaves. The classic white lace of the dress my mom picked out for me sparkles in the sunlight and my long white veil trails behind me. I fight back tears as the four-piece band plays one of our favorite songs by the Lumineers. Many times over the past few years when Aaron and I needed a spiritual lift, we'd put on their music and find ourselves jumping around our living room, doing our silly hipster dance and getting lost in each other and the songs.

I see the joy on Aaron's face as I approach. Standing next to him is Doug, my lawyer, who's officiating. He's been with us for some of our lowest moments as a couple, and it's only fitting for him to stand with us during our highest. "Denise and Aaron are shining examples of how to find love in tragedy, strength in sorrow, power in reconnection," he says.

We've tried our best to keep our sense of humor throughout our ordeal, so we asked him to marry us by serving him with a mock subpoena to "appear and produce" at our wedding. He got a laugh out of it, of course, and when the time comes, he shows his sense of humor as well: "By the powers vested in me by the state of California, I now sentence you to twenty-five to life!" As everyone laughs, he adds, "I mean, pronounce you husband and wife. You may kiss the bride!"

The heaviness of the past several years seems to lift as we cycle through tears and laughter throughout the day. Through the vows we wrote ourselves. Through our fathers' emotional toasts.

"We were interviewed by a Vallejo detective," says Aaron's father, Joe. "I told him you've been a great kid. You've been a leader and a peacemaker. [You] always seemed to do the right thing automatically.

"I didn't tell him, but I tell all of you now, that I have been, and always will be, so very proud of him," he says, his voice breaking as he fights off tears. He ends his speech by raising his glass to our attorneys, who fill two tables. Who knows where we'd be without them?

My father too mentions meeting "Vallejo's finest," as he refers to those detectives. "Do you know they didn't have one good thing to say about you?" he teases Aaron, drawing laughter from the guests, before taking a more serious tone. "He's actually my hero. He saved my daughter's life."

The strong, everlasting connections among all of us here create an aura of strength and love. Misty Carausu and her husband are there, overwhelmed by the steady flow of our family and friends thanking her for solving our case. It's incredible how these complete strangers quickly became such pivotal people in our lives, with whom we will forever share a special bond.

Everyone gathers around Aaron and me for our first dance, and even the members of the band cry as I squeeze him, brushing the tears from his cheeks as we sway to our song, "Riser." "I'm a riser / I'm a get up off the ground, don't run and hider. . . ." To an outsider, it may seem like an unusual song for a first dance but it's perfect for us.

We all went through so much to get to this moment. It feels like a happy ending, but what's even more special is that we know this is just the beginning. The beginning of a lifetime of beautiful moments to come.

WE TAKE A little "mini-moon" the following week in Sonoma wine country, where we had spent many of our first dates. In perfect timing, Dierks Bentley is on tour in Northern California, playing in Mountain View the Friday after our wedding. So our good friends Dan and Danielle surprise us with VIP tickets. It's a once-in-a-lifetime experience we could only have dreamed of. As we watch the VIP preshow performance in a tent of about fifty people, I hold up a sign reading, JUST MARRIED 9-29-2018. RISER WAS OUR FIRST DANCE. We're standing only about ten feet away from the small stage when Dierks reads the sign, gives us a little head nod, and pumps his fist.

Later, during the main concert, in front of thousands of people in the audience, Dierks says, "This next song has a special meaning to a lot of people. This couple over there just got married, and this was their song. . . ." He points to us holding up our sign and the crowd cheers as I nearly pass out from his recognition.

Aaron and I grab each other, hugging, dancing, and crying, getting lost in each other again as our song is played live. Those in the crowd may not know who we are or what we've been through and why this song means so much to us, but we feel their love surrounding us all the same.

57

DENISE

WE LOVE BEING newlyweds, though we still have to manage the ever-present stress that surrounds the state criminal case. As heartbroken as we were about Mr. Rogers, we know we have a lot of love to give and how much joy animals bring us, so we adopt two rescue cats whose mischievous antics keep us entertained.

Thanks to the settlement and my steady work schedule, Aaron finally has the financial freedom to pursue his dream. He teams up with a talented personal trainer to create a business working with Olympic and professional athletes, while continuing to provide care for patients recovering from severe injuries or illnesses as well.

In February 2019 we go to court for the preliminary hearing. Muller is once again representing himself and has the right to cross-examine us. Just a few days earlier, for Valentine's Day, Aaron surprised me with matching black bracelets engraved with the word RISER as a reminder of our resilience and our ability to overcome anything. We are both wearing them as we testify for hours under the watchful eye of Muller. He hired and fired two public defenders, and even successfully pushed a judge to recuse himself from the case by arguing he had a conflict of interest because he had been represented in the past by Dan Russo, Aaron's criminal defense attorney. The judge didn't put up any resistance, and a new one was assigned. The circus continues.

We aren't allowed to be present for each other's testimony, so we don't have that support to lean on as we go over each horrific detail of the kidnapping. In a courtroom full of reporters, strangers, and my family, the prosecutor asks me question after question about the rapes, including which part of him touched which part of me. I can't just give a blanket statement like "He forced himself inside of me . . . touched me orally . . ." No, that's not enough. I have to say that his penis entered my vagina, that his lips and tongue touched my inner thighs and vagina. I have to give each excruciating, intimate detail. As I'm doing so, my dad stands up and bolts out of the courtroom. This is exactly why a law enforcement officer should be able to give hearsay testimony in our place. This is humiliating and retraumatizing. Henry never told me I would have to be this graphic and it feels like a punishment. I understand having to be this precise with investigators and nurses, but here?

The stress of being interrogated by law enforcement, the fear that I'm not performing well enough, the sense that I'm not being believed, all come flooding back. I hear family members sniffle and cry as I recite these grotesque events through my own pained sobs. All the while, I don't know if Muller will choose to cross-examine me when I'm done, and I'm both angry and disturbed to be put in this position.

What's even harder to process is that Muller, the suspect in the criminal cases, has more rights than we do as the victims. The United States Constitution lays out specific protections and rights for suspects, which is absolutely necessary, but nothing for victims. Some state constitutions enacted amendments for victims' rights, but many aren't enforced. He's allowed access to evidence and information that we may never see, some of which may affect our personal safety and privacy. He can find out information about us, but we can't about him. If we want him charged, we have to testify, even be forced to answer questions *from* him! I'll be held in contempt if I don't answer a question, but it's his right not to take the stand. My character and my trauma will get picked apart by both the defense and the prosecution. As the victim, I'm the one that gets caught in the cross fire.

It's no wonder some choose not to testify. If victims don't feel safe or feel they won't be treated with respect and dignity, they are less likely to participate in court proceedings. As a result, criminals get away with their crimes, and our justice system and society as a whole are compromised. But people simply do not know or have any reason to learn about this injustice until it's too late, when you are revictimized by the system.

On this day, though, I'm at least spared from being questioned by my rapist. Muller decides not to, responding with a crisp "Certainly not, Your Honor," when the judge asks him, as if he cares so much about my well-being. We're told that later in the hearing, Muller tried to portray himself as a victim, complaining to the judge it was just him defending himself against these "millionaires" with private prosecutors, meaning Aaron and me and our criminal defense attorneys, who showed up at the hearing for no reason other than to support us. Nothing's changed. He's the same man who held me captive.

The purpose of the hearing is to determine if the case should go to trial, and for which charges. We expected it but we're still gratified when the judge rules that all charges are moving forward.

In the next year, Muller will accuse the Alameda County Sheriff's Office of planting evidence, including a bag of cocaine they found at the South Lake Tahoe house. He subpoenas both Dan Russo and Doug Rappaport but doesn't do it correctly, so Doug doesn't attend the hearing about it. Angry that Doug didn't bend to his will, Muller sues him, forcing Doug to spend several thousand dollars to get the case dismissed. Although it is a frivolous lawsuit, this first complaint in his career causes a spike in Doug's malpractice insurance, which Muller knows could happen. I don't know what Muller's game plan is, other than to sling mud and try to take everyone else down with him. I guess he has nothing to lose, and this may simply be keeping his mind busy behind bars.

IN MARCH 2019, I'm invited to join a roundtable discussion with five other kidnapping survivors hosted by Elizabeth Smart to share our experiences, including how we were able to move forward in our lives and the challenges our recovery entailed. I'm honored to be included. For so long, I've been traumatized by not being believed and having to prove my innocence. So to be considered a legitimate kidnapping victim with these inspirational women is surreal. It's incredibly validating to be in a group of women I don't have to explain things to, who just get it. I'm horrified to hear what they've had to overcome, what strangers have said to them, and how they too have been judged. But more than that, my spirit is uplifted and reenergized by our conversation.

I confess that I've been struggling with whether to have children; do I really want to bring a child into this world knowing firsthand the degree of evil that exists out there? And what's more difficult to admit, I've wondered whether I'm strong enough to be a mom, given how much I still struggle emotionally. If I'm broken, how can I possibly cultivate life? Would it be selfish and impossible to even try?

I ask the women for their advice and about their experiences as mothers, and my doubts and fear fade. What an incredible gift they gave me. They are the epitome of strength and resilience. If they can do it, so can I.

ONE MORNING IN July 2019, I wake up feeling unusually euphoric and elated. There is a deep shift inside me I can't explain. As the feeling grows, the thought comes: *Oh, my God, am I pregnant?*

A test confirms it! I've spent more than four years rebuilding my life, trying to mold myself back together. But not until this pregnancy do I truly feel whole again. Our baby's spirit living and growing within me restores my own.

I'm overwhelmed with happiness when we find out we're having a little girl. For the past several years, I've had to deeply reflect on my own life, my challenges as well as my accomplishments. Now we get to experience it all over again through her, to have the honor of protecting and encouraging her, of nursing her wounds and guiding her to become a strong, empowered woman. Although I know we have a lot to give as parents, she has already given me so much. I can't wait to meet her and see who she becomes. More than anything, I can't wait to see Aaron completely melt with her in his arms, the same way my dad does with me.

OLIVIA LOUISE QUINN is born March 25, 2020, five years to the day after I was released. It's a miraculous fresh start, a sense of life coming full circle and showing us that no matter what difficulties we may face, there is always a chance for renewal. We realize we are truly blessed and know that what could have been a devastating end was really just the start of something remarkable.

Epilogue

A FEW WEEKS AFTER Muller's arrest in July 2015, Dan Russo walked into a Vallejo courtroom for a hearing and the judge, a friend, made a comment from the bench about Dan's recent representation of Aaron.

The faces of the three defendants before him went pale. They were three young white guys with long, stringy hair, probably in their early twenties, charged with a string of burglaries and car thefts on Mare Island.

"That sounds like Muller's crew," Russo remarked to one of their attorneys. This time it was the attorney whose face lost its color.

Were they Muller's accomplices? All these years later, Russo can't say for sure. What he can say is what he believes to be true. Those defendants were somehow connected to Muller.

"It was just too much of a coincidence," he said. "These guys were only hitting homes on Mare Island. That was highly unusual. Burglars don't operate in just one neighborhood. That's unheard of in my experience representing hundreds of burglars over forty years."

Who was with Muller the morning of March 23, 2015, at Aaron's home on Mare Island remains one of the many unanswered questions about the case all these years later. Why was Jennifer Jones, Aaron's ex-fiancée, the target of the intruders? Who hired Muller's group to target her? Where are Muller's accomplices? Who wrote the emails to Henry Lee and Kenny Park? The FBI found audio recordings the kidnappers used and the videos of Denise's rapes on Muller's electronic devices but have said nothing about the emails. Neither has the Solano County prosecutor.

And the man who could answer all of these questions refuses to do so.

Instead, Muller continues to play his cat-and-mouse game, going back and forth between representing himself and using a public defender; appealing his federal conviction, then withdrawing it; slipping bombshell allegations into his court filings whenever he can. In one, he speculated that the former Fairfield cop Jennifer cheated on Aaron with (whom she is now married to and has a child with) staged the home invasion and kidnapping to "scare her away" from Aaron and back into his arms. But like so much in this case, it appears law enforcement has done nothing to find out the truth and it's unlikely they ever will.

Denise and Aaron have found a way to accept the fact that they may never get the answers they seek, just like so many other crime victims. They choose to draw strength from what they've gone through, to try to make some good emerge from their ordeal. Denise completed an eight-week online program to get certified as a victims' advocate, both to learn more about the issues they face and to somehow blend this work with her background as a healer in physical therapy to help survivors not just recover but thrive after their trauma. She hopes one day to share her experience with local and national law enforcement so they can better understand crime from a victim's perspective. And true to the altruistic spirit that runs through Aaron's family, his mom, Marianne, became a volunteer with her local rape crisis center. She's one of the people the center calls to go with a rape victim when they undergo a SART exam. She only wishes Denise had had access to that service herself.

In an effort to get some sort of closure, Denise recently started writing to sixty of the people who sent her hate-filled messages on Facebook. She's tentatively encouraged that a few actually responded, apologizing profusely and vowing not to rush to judgment in the future. She even reached out to thank the one Huntington Beach police officer who was kind to her after she was released and hopes one day to meet with the nurses who performed her SART exam, once Muller's state case comes to a conclusion, whether that be through a trial or through a guilty plea.

Denise and Aaron have also taken classes in Krav Maga, an Israeli form of self-defense, because they are acutely aware that at least two of their assailants are still at large.

THE VALLEJO POLICE Department remains deeply troubled. In June 2020, the California attorney general announced an agreement with the police to reform and revise its policies and practices. They have their hands full. The following month, the website OpenVallejo.org revealed that a small secretive group of officers within the department bent the points of their badges each time they killed someone in the line of duty, some of them even celebrating their kills with rituals like backyard barbecues. One of them was allegedly Detective Sean Kenney, who questioned Aaron's parents. Captain John Whitney, who filed a wrongful termination claim against his former employer, told the website he was forced out of his job after raising concerns about the badge bending and other police misconduct, some connected to Denise and Aaron's case. There will likely be more shocking revelations as Whitney's claim against Vallejo makes its way through the court system.

What happened that night in March 2015 changed the course of Denise's and Aaron's lives and forever changed who they are. They hope that by sharing their journey from victims to suspects to survivors they can shine a light on the flaws that plague our criminal justice system. They want others who have been sexually assaulted or falsely accused or persecuted by the police to know they are not alone. Their hope is to become catalysts for change in all of these areas.

Reliving this nightmare was not easy for them, but they are guided by the words of their favorite author, Dr. Brené Brown: "You can choose courage, or you can choose comfort, but you cannot choose both."

They chose courage.

AUTHOR'S NOTE

The first-person portions of this book are based on Aaron's and Denise's recollections and journals and, where applicable, were verified through official police and court records and recordings or fact-checking with others who were part of those conversations described in the book. Some transcripts, such as Aaron's interrogations by Detective Mat Mustard and FBI special agent Peter French, and Denise's by the Huntington Beach police, were condensed for clarity. For the third-person chapters, I conducted interviews with Aaron's and Denise's families and attorneys, as well as with Misty Carausu, and later fact-checked those chapters with them. Any information that is not from those interviews is sourced in the endnotes.

The name of Aaron's ex-fiancée has been changed to Jennifer Jones to protect her privacy. All other names are real. She declined to be interviewed for this book. Her husband, a former police officer in Fairfield, California, did not respond to a request for comment.

Matthew Muller, the only person charged so far in the kidnapping, has entered a not-guilty plea on the state charges of kidnapping, rape by force, robbery, burglary, and false imprisonment. Muller, who is a disbarred attorney and has been representing himself on and off, did not respond to a request for comment sent in August 2020 via letter and to an email address he uses for his court filings. On November 6, 2020, a Solano County judge ruled Muller not competent to stand trial based upon the court-appointed psychologist's evaluation and report. The trial is on hold while he undergoes treatment to restore his competency. His newly appointed attorney, Thomas Barrett, chief deputy of the Solano County Alternate Defender Office, declined to answer my questions, saying, "Given the current procedural posture, I cannot address any case specific questions that are the subject of a factual dispute."

Various members of the Vallejo Police Department who are referenced in the book did not respond to requests for comment, including Lieutenant Kenny Park, Detective Mat Mustard, former detectives Terry Poyser and Sean Kenney, former chief Andrew Bidou, and former captain James O'Connell. The FBI declined to comment on the actions of agents David Sesma, Peter French, and Jason Walter. Agent Sesma did not respond to questions sent directly to him. Neither did Assistant US Attorney Matt Segal or former *San Francisco Chronicle* reporter Henry Lee.

—*Nicki Egan*

ACKNOWLEDGMENTS

Since the events of March 2015, we've experienced firsthand what it feels like not to be the author of your own story. Before our eyes, we saw the most horrific thing we've lived through, and our very identities, altered, rewritten, and misrepresented. Talking through our trauma in therapy was a helpful first step in our recovery but writing it all down became an integral part of our healing, allowing it to be released from our minds and our bodies. Difficult emotions certainly resurfaced during this process, but more than anything, it's been empowering and cathartic. It allowed us to revisit and reexamine those emotions from a safer place, accept what happened, and literally close the book on that time in our lives. For years, we felt like we had to hold on to that trauma, afraid that if we didn't, the details would be lost, and the world would never see the truth. Now the truth is here, in its entirety, and we can finally let it go.

We are grateful to the whole team at Berkley for giving us this platform to tell our story, and especially to our editor, Tracy Bernstein, for seeing the importance of what we had to say, for being flexible and understanding throughout the process, and for her expertise.

Thank you to our agent, Sharlene Martin, for taking a chance on us and connecting us with our cowriter, Nicki Egan.

Nicki, thank you for always believing in us and advocating for our vision for the book, guiding us through the writing process and supporting our involvement every step of the way. This book wouldn't be what it is without your commitment, diligence, and skill. You became our confidante, ally, and friend.

We are eternally grateful to our friends and families for supporting us, for loving us unconditionally and for helping us get through the most difficult times in our lives. We can't thank you enough for your encouragement and willingness to share your own trauma. This book would not have been possible without you.

Dan and Danielle Buljan, we would have fallen apart without your friendship. You graciously opened your doors and gave us food, shelter, shoulders to cry on, warmth, and laughter. And baby Dom, your carefree, sweet spirit lifted ours when we needed it most. We love you all.

Ethan Quinn, you are our champion. We couldn't have gotten here without you. Our brothers—Joey, Devin, Matt, and Ethan—and their partners—Danielle, Vanessa, and Kathryn—have been our biggest cheerleaders. You were patient and willing to listen when we needed to talk through a new hurdle or simply to vent. The countless laughs we've shared have been restorative and healing.

Our parents helped us in countless ways, before the kidnapping and after. You have provided a solid foundation for us to thrive, in the best and worst of times, and we feel fortunate to come from such strong, united families. A special thank-you to our moms for keeping baby Olivia entertained as we worked on the final edits of our book.

Sweet baby Olivia, you have given us countless moments of overwhelming joy and laughter. You motivate us to push our limits, so maybe we can influence some positive change in this world for you.

They say, "Not all heroes wear capes." That's certainly true in our case. Our criminal defense attorneys—Doug Rappaport, Lauren Schweizer, Dan Russo, Amy Morton—and their entire legal teams were our saviors in our darkest moment. They risked their reputations by coming out so publicly in our defense and were relentless in their pursuit of the truth. We're grateful to our civil attorneys—Jim Wagstaffe, Ken Nabity, and Kevin

Clune—for taking on such a monumental case with an uncertain outcome. Thank you all for believing in us and fighting tirelessly for justice. A special thanks to Doug for suggesting the title of our book, *Victim F.*

Misty Carausu, you will always have a special place in our hearts and in our lives. When we thought all hope was lost and our lives as we knew them were shattered, you stepped in and saved us. If it weren't for your objectivity, tenacity, and determination, we don't know where we'd be. We are fortunate to have developed a friendship with you and your husband, Dacu, that will last a lifetime.

We appreciate local reporters Melanie Woodrow from ABC7 Bay Area, Steve Large from CBS13 Sacramento, Jodi Hernandez from NBC Bay Area, Evan Sernoffsky, formerly of the *San Francisco Chronicle*, Brittny Mejia from the *Los Angeles Times*, and many others for keeping the story alive throughout the years, asking the tough and necessary questions, and restoring our faith in the media.

Our heartfelt thanks go to our therapists—Dr. Kelly Land, Dr. Beatrice Ann Grant, Julia Pinsky, Nicole Heinrich, and David Resnikoff—for expertly and compassionately walking with us on our road to recovery.

We are grateful to the employers and coworkers who allowed us a safe space to rebuild our professions. We were also lucky enough to have patients who were warm and empathetic as we've continued to fight in the public eye and in the courts. We want to thank you for helping us heal and find purpose again.

To the many other victims and survivors out there: We have been fueled and inspired by all of your strength and bravery. This is our humble attempt to pay it forward.

Denise Huskins and Aaron Quinn

I am so grateful to you for choosing me to help you tell your story, Aaron and Denise. I'd followed your case as it unfolded but I didn't know all you had endured until we started working together. Not only are you both kind and caring; you are two of the strongest, most resilient people I've ever met. You somehow got back up each time you were knocked down, while maintaining grace and dignity under circumstances that could have easily broken you. I am in awe of your strength, your love for each other and your baby, your devotion to your families and theirs for you, and your passion for helping others. I have no doubt your honesty and bravery shine through in this book and will serve as an inspiration to others struggling with hardships in their own lives.

And thank you both for showing me around Vallejo and introducing me to your friends and family in August 2019. A special thanks to Aaron's parents, Joe and Marianne Quinn, who graciously welcomed me into their home on that trip. I'm also deeply grateful to them, Ethan, Matt, and Kathryn Quinn; Mike and Devin Huskins; Jane Remmele; Daniel Russo; Doug Rappaport; and Jeff Kane for sharing their pieces of this story with me and helping me fact-check. And a heartfelt thank-you to Misty Carausu for walking me through the extraordinary detective work that led to the capture of Matthew Muller. Misty, you are the epitome of what a police officer should be.

We were so lucky to have the brilliant Tracy Bernstein as our editor. Her calm, steady guidance and expertise helped shape this book into the powerful narrative it now is. Thank you, Tracy. We could not have asked for a better editor. Nor could we have asked for a better publisher. From Claire Leonard's thorough legal review to Craig Burke's wonderful publicity team, we knew we were in the hands of the best in the business.

I also want to thank agent Sharlene Martin for trusting me with this sensitive project and connecting me with Aaron and Denise. After thirty years in journalism, I find there are few stories that outrage me the way this one has and I'm truly grateful for the opportunity to help them tell it.

My parents, Bill Weisensee and the late Veronica Weisensee, raised me with love and laughs and taught me to dream big. I feel so lucky to have been raised by you both. Thank you, Mom and Dad.

Last, I want to thank my husband, Sean Egan, for always supporting me in all my endeavors. You are truly a role model for what a husband should be. I don't know how I got lucky enough to find you, but I will always be grateful I did. I love you and the life we've built together with our houseful of animals.

Nicki Weisensee Egan

NOTES

CHAPTER 8

The details of what Ethan, Joe, and Marianne Quinn were going through are from interviews with Ethan and Marianne Quinn in July 2019; written comments from Joe and Marianne Quinn in July 2019; and follow-up fact-checking with them. Other information about Ethan came from news articles, including these: Yarbrough, Beau. "Sen. Leland Yee Arrest: The 26 Defendants in Case Involving Firearms, Money Laundering and Other Charges." Mercurynews.com. March 16, 2014; Kasler, Dale. "Alfred Villalobos, Fixture in CalPERS Corruption Scandal, Apparently Commits Suicide." *The Sacramento Bee.* January 14, 2015; Ho, Vivian. "FBI Agent Says Mayor Lee Was Target of Bribery Probe." *San Francisco Chronicle.* April 11, 2017. The information about Detective Kenney comes from these articles: Glidden, John and Nate Gartrell. "Ex-Vallejo Officer Involved with Multiple Officer-Involved Shootings Starts Consulting Firm." *Vallejo* (CA) *Times-Herald.* March 29, 2019; Stock, Stephen and Robert Campos, Anthony Rutanashoodech, Luke Johnson, and Molly Forster. "NBC Bay Area Investigation Links Group of Vallejo Police Officers to Majority of Use of Force Incidents." NBCbayarea.com. January 6, 2020.

CHAPTER 10

The quotes and background information about Jeff Kane and Jane, Devin, and Mike Huskins are from interviews with them in July 2019 and follow-up fact-checking afterward.

Other quotes from Mike Huskins are from this story: Anthony, Laura. "Father of Vallejo Woman Possibly Kidnapped Finds Disappearance Puzzling." ABC7News .com. March 24, 2015.

CHAPTER 11

All of the details and quotes came from interviews with Ethan Quinn and Dan Russo in July 2019 and follow-up fact-checking afterward as well as from various news stories about Russo including: Burchyns, Tony. "Solano County Superior Court Judge Bowers Temporarily Reassigned to Civil Cases." *Vallejo* (CA) *Times-Herald*. April 14, 2011; Widiojo, Irma. "Hung Jury in Insanity Case of Vallejo Man." *Vallejo* (CA) *Times-Herald*. November 22, 2014.

CHAPTER 12

The quotes from Detective Mat Mustard about Aaron and Denise's case are from his declaration in the civil lawsuit Aaron and Denise filed against Vallejo (US District Court Case #2016-cv-00603, Denise Huskins and Aaron Quinn vs. City of Vallejo, Kenny Park, Mathew Mustard and Does 1-25). The quotes from Captain Andrew Bidou are from his deposition in that same civil lawsuit.

The background about Captain James O'Connell is from his deposition in that same civil suit.

The quote from Mustard about the accidental-overdose case he believed was a homicide, the coroner's comments about him trying to pressure her, and Ganz's law license suspension are from the decision in State Bar of California Case No. 14-0-021363- PEM, Andrew Michael Ganz vs. Michael Daniels.

The description of Mare Island is from https://discovermareisland.com/about.

The other background about Vallejo, the Vallejo police, Mustard, Bidou, and community reactions to the kidnapping are from local news stories, including these: "Crews Search Bay near Vallejo for Missing Woman." ABC7News.com. March 24, 2015; Burchyns, Tony. "Ex-Solano Pathologist Says Police, Prosecutor Pressured Her." *Vallejo (CA) Times-Herald.* March 12, 2014; California News Wire Services. "Northern California's Top 12 'Most Dangerous' Cities List: FBI Crime Stats." Pinole-Hercules (CA) Patch. December 2, 2011; Chang, Richard and Bill Lindelof. "Police Search for Apparent Kidnap Victim from Vallejo." *The Sacramento Bee.* March 24, 2015; Gueverra, Ericka Cruz. "How Did Things Get So Bad Between Vallejo and Its Police?" KQED.com. August 23, 2019; Hicken, Melanie. "Once Bankrupt, Vallejo Still Can't Afford Its Pricey Pensions." Money.CNN .com. March 10, 2014; Trapasso, Clare. "How an Obscure, Crime-Ridden Bay Area City Became America's Hottest Market." Realtor.com. August 17, 2016.

CHAPTER 19

The background on Doug Rappaport is from a July 2019 interview with him.

The information from Mike and Jane Huskins is from the July 2019 interviews with them and subsequent follow-up interviews and emails.

CHAPTER 21

You can watch raw footage of Park's press conference here: https://abc7news.com /news/raw-video-vallejo-pd-believes-womans-kidnap-report-was-hoax/573559/.

The press release is in the mediation brief for Aaron and Denise's lawsuit.

CHAPTER 22

The information about Doug's text and call with his wife is from the July 2019 interview with him and follow-up emails with him and his wife.

CHAPTER 23

The news stories referred to are: Bhattacharjee, Riya and Jason Kandel and Christine Cocca. "Vallejo Kidnapping for Ransom 'Orchestrated': Police." NBCbayarea

.com. March 26, 2015; and KXTV staff. "Vallejo PD: Kidnapping of Denise Huskins an 'Orchestrated Event.'" ABC10.com. March 26, 2015.

The quotes from Dan Russo's press conference are from these stories: DeBolt, David. "Vallejo Reels as Revelations Tumble in on Alleged Kidnapping Case." *Contra Costa Times*. March 27, 2015; Ellis, Ralph and Ed Payne. "Denise Huskins' Abduction: Lawyers Say Boyfriend Not Lying." CNN.com. March 26, 2015; Sernoffsky, Evan and Henry K. Lee and Kale Williams. "Kidnap? Hoax? Mystery Grows: Vallejo Woman's 'Horrific' Ordeal Was Real, Attorneys Say." *San Francisco Chronicle*. March 27, 2015.

CHAPTER 26
You can watch Doug Rappaport's press conference here: https://abc7news.com /missing-woman-denise-huskins-kidnapping-ransom/575529/

CHAPTER 27
This is the story Denise saw posted on a friend's Facebook page: Arata, Emily. "Real Life 'Gone Girl' Allegedly Staged Her Own Insane Fake Kidnapping." Elitedaily.com. March 26, 2015.

CHAPTER 30
The first email from the kidnappers is in the mediation brief in Aaron and Denise's lawsuit against Vallejo.

CHAPTER 31
The stories Denise is referring to are these: Barnard, Cornell. "Lawyer for Vallejo Woman Says Kidnappers Sent Apology Email." ABC7News.com. March 30, 2015; and Lee, Henry and Evan Sernoffsky. "Purported Vallejo Kidnappers Demand Apology from Police." SFGate.com. March 30, 2015.

CHAPTER 33
The plea bargain statistics are from this 2019 study: https://www.pewresearch .org/fact-tank/2019/06/11/only-2-of-federal-criminal-defendants-go-to-trial-and -most-who-do-are-found-guilty/ft_19-06-11_trialsandguiltypleas-pie-2/.

NOTES

CHAPTER 36

The details about Misty Carausu are from interviews with her in November 2019 and January 2020 and subsequent interviews and emails.

The details about the other crimes Muller was suspected of are from the August 14, 2015, affidavit for a search warrant for Muller's electronic devices; you can read that here: https://www.documentcloud.org/documents/2301656-august-14-search-of-electronic-devices.html.

The details about the Dublin home invasion are from the police report and various news articles, including: Sernoffsky, Evan. "Dublin Man Accounts Attack by Masked Man Suspect in Vallejo Kidnapping." SFGate.com. September 3, 2015. Bay Area News Group. "Vallejo Kidnapping Suspect: Victim Testifies in Dublin Home-Invasion Case." *East Bay Times*. September 2, 2015.

CHAPTER 40

The affidavit is in the mediation brief for Aaron and Denise's civil suit against Vallejo.

The comments from Captain Whitney are from this story: Large, Steve. "Vallejo Police, City Leaders Reticent to Offer Apologies in Denise Huskins Case." Sacramento.cbslocal.com. July 15, 2015.

Muller's attorney did this interview about Muller's mental health: Fernandez, Lisa. "Matthew Muller, Vallejo Kidnap Suspect, 'Bipolar' and 'Extremely Smart,' Friend and Lawyer Say." NBCbayarea.com. July 15, 2015.

The Muller interview Denise quotes from is this one: Goodrich, Juliette. "Suspect in Bizarre Vallejo Kidnapping Talks to KPIX5 in Jailhouse Interview." Sanfrancisco.cbslocal.com. July 17, 2015.

The article Aaron was reading to Denise is this one: Dooley, Sean and Lauren Effron. "So-Called 'Gone Girl' Mystery: Victim Thought She Was Going to Die, More Details Inside the Kidnapping Case." ABCNews.com. July 17, 2015.

The article about Muller's credentials is this one: Woodrow, Melanie. "Harvard Law Grad Charged in Bizarre Kidnapping Police Called Hoax." 6ABC.com. July 13, 2015.

The Nancy Grace and Henry Lee information is from these sources: HLN. "Kidnap Hoax: Is She the Real-Life 'Gone Girl'?"; SFist.com. "More Twists in Vallejo 'Kidnapping': Kidnappers Say It Was Just a 'Dry Run,' Nancy Grace Says 'Nope.'" April 1, 2015; https://www.youtube.com/watch?v=QTBzfiHsYO0. March 26, 2015; *Inside Edition*. "Alleged Kidnap Hoaxster Denise Huskins Is Missing Again." Insideedition .com. March 26, 2015; and the February 3, 2019, *Dateline* episode about the case.

The *20/20* episode about their case aired on July 17, 2015.

CHAPTER 41

The statistics Aaron refer to are in this story: Emslie, Alex. "Questions Surround Surge in Vallejo Police Shootings." KQED.org; May 20, 2014.

CHAPTER 42

You can read the FBI affidavit for the search warrant for Muller's electronic devices here: https://www.documentcloud.org/documents/2301656-august-14 -search-of-electronic-devices.html.

Stories that use the information in the affidavit as proof Muller acted alone include these: Poulson, Kevin. "'Gone Girl' Suspect Confesses to Reporter—As FBI Listens In." Wired.com. September 2, 2015; Barmann, Jay. "Accused Vallejo Kidnapper Matthew Muller Confessed in Jailhouse Interview, Said He Acted Alone." SFist.com. September 2, 2015.

CHAPTER 49

A local ABC TV station ran a story about Mustard getting officer of the year: Woodrow, Melanie. "Attorney: Kidnapping Victim's Family Outraged over Vallejo Officer's Prestigious Award." ABC7News.com. May 13, 2016. You can see the photo on the Vallejo Police Department's Facebook page here: https://www .facebook.com/VallejoPD/posts/the-vallejo-police-department-recognized-some -of-their-own-at-the-2016-awards-an/1191588247526997/ and in the city man-

ager's April 29, 2016 biweekly public newsletter here: https://www.cityofvallejo
.net/common/pages/DisplayFile.aspx?itemId=3632564.

The local NBC affiliate did a story that included what Doug said about Sesma's
conflict of interest: Mahbubani, Rhea. "'Not Ready for Relief': Vallejo Kidnapping Victim's Attorney Blasts Police Department, FBI for Bungling Case."
NBCbayarea.com. September 29, 2016.

The O'Connell quotes are from his declaration and deposition in Aaron and Denise's civil suit against Vallejo.

Denise and Aaron found the information about David Sesma's promotion here:
https://ahidta.org/content/task-forces.

CHAPTER 50

The rape case Denise refers to is this one: Armstrong, Ken and T. Christian Miller.
"An Unbelievable Story of Rape." Themarshallproject.org. March 12, 2009.

CHAPTER 55

The interviews Muller did include this one: Hernandez, Jodi. "'I'm Not Guilty':
Matthew Muller Gives Jailhouse Interview About Bizarre Kidnapping, Assault on
Vallejo Couple." NBCbayarea.com. September 20, 2018.

Doug's comments were in this article: Woodrow, Melanie. "Convicted Vallejo
Kidnapper Matthew Muller Will Likely Cross-Examine His Alleged Rape Victim." ABC30.com, September 18, 2018.

EPILOGUE

The California attorney general's announcement about the Vallejo Police Department is here: https://oag.ca.gov/news/press-releases/attorney-general-becerra
-announces-agreement-review-and-reform-vallejo-police.

Muller's speculations about Jennifer Jones' husband are in a motion Muller filed
on January 8, 2020, in US District Court for the Eastern District of California,
case 2:15-CR-205-TLN-EFB, his federal kidnapping case.